DECORATIVE ARTS
IN EUROPE 1790-1850

Léon de Groër

DECORATIVE ARTS IN EUROPE 1790-1850

Translation from the French by Aileen Dawson

French-language edition, *Les arts décoratifs de 1790 à 1850*
Copyright ©1985 by Office du Livre S.A., Fribourg, Switzerland

English translation:
Copyright ©1986 by Office du Livre S.A., Fribourg, Switzerland

English translation published in 1986 in the
United States of America by:
RIZZOLI INTERNATIONAL PUBLICATIONS, INC.
597 Fifth Avenue, New York, 10017

Library of Congress Cataloging-in-Publication Data

Groër, Léon de, 1914–
    Decorative arts in Europe, 1790–1850.

    Translation of: Les arts décoratifs de 1790 à 1850.
    Bibliography: p.
    Includes index.
    1. Decorative arts -- Europe -- History -- 18th century.
2. Decorative arts -- Europe -- History -- 19th century.
I. Title.
NK925.G7613   1986   745'.094   85-42864
ISBN 0-8478-0621-9

Printed and bound in Switzerland

Contents

Preface

Books of this kind are usually compiled by a group of authors each of whom contributes chapters concerning his own country or specialist subject, with the end result that comparisons between one country and another are seldom made. The importance of stylistic crosscurrents is frequently ignored. Inevitably, the reader finds it difficult to gain an overview of the subject.

The publishers of this book, therefore, have turned to a single author. His task, however, has been a far from easy one. He has had to cover a wide range of material within the constraints of a deadline and within a relatively restricted framework. He has attempted to maintain a balance between chapters and not to give undue attention to any one country. The most influential and productive countries have, of course, received far greater attention than their less important neighbors. The first group includes France, England, Austria, Germany, Italy and Russia, while the remaining European countries have perhaps been given less than their due. The author could perhaps be criticized for focussing too closely on French decorative art, yet its important role during the first half of the nineteenth century has too often been unjustly neglected.

With regard to the content of this book, it would have been possible to omit much of what has been written about porcelain and wallpaper, as these subjects have recently been fully explored in several excellent publications. Carpets and clocks, however, have not so far been sufficiently studied by specialists, but it is not within the scope of this work to include detailed information on them. The author would like to acknowledge the assistance of all those who have facilitated his work, in the first place of his colleagues: Daniel Alcouffe and Serge Grandjean, Département des objets d'art, Musée du Louvre, Paris; Jean-Marie Moulin, Musée national du château de Compiègne; Jean-Pierre and Colombe Samoyault, Musée national du château de Fontainebleau; Gérard Hubert and Bernard Chevallier, Musée national du château de Malmaison; Jacques Perot, Musée national du château de Pau; Madame de Gary, curator, Musée des arts décoratifs, Paris; Monsieur Claude Fournet, director, Musées de Nice; Madame Jeanne Guillevic, curator, Musée Paul Dupuy, Toulouse; Monsieur Jean Coural, administrator of the Mobilier national and Madame Coural; Monsieur Jean-Louis Rocher, chief curator of libraries in the city of Lyons; Señor Didier Ozanam, director of the Casa de Velasquez, Madrid; Messrs. Peter Thornton, Simon Jervis and Harold Barkley, Victoria and Albert Museum, London.

Baronne van Ypersele de Strihou of Brussels was especially helpful. In Germany, special thanks are due to Dr. Hans Ottomeyer of the Münchner Stadtmuseum and Dr. Lorenz Seelig of the Bayerische Verwaltung der staatlichen Schlösser, whose advice and help were particularly useful. Dr. M. Landenberger and Dr. K. Mertens of the Württembergisches Landesmuseum, Stuttgart; Professor Dr. V. Himmelein, director, Badisches Landesmuseum, Karlsruhe; Dr. Stubenvoll and Herr K. P. Schmid of the Verwaltung der staatlichen Schlösser, Bad Homburg; Dr. Chr. L. Kuster of the Altonaer Museum, Hamburg and Herr Pompe, director of the Palace of the Princes of Thurn and Taxis, Regensburg all gave unstinting assistance in the preparation of this book.

In the Soviet Union, the author was assisted by the staff of the State Hermitage Museum, Leningrad (Mr. B. B. Piotrovskii, director; Mr. V. A. Suslov, deputy director; Mrs. N. I. Biriukova and Mrs. T. V. Rappe), of the Russian Museum, Leningrad (Mrs. G. A. Ivanova), of the palaces of Pavlovsk, Pushkin and Petrodvorets (Mr. Goldovskii) and of the Pushkin Museum, Moscow (Mrs. I. A. Antonova, director; Mrs. E. B. Georgievskaia and Mrs. G. A. Esipova), as well as of the estates of Ostankino (M. Cherviakov) and Arkhangelskoe. Miss Roos and Miss S. Kopisto, of the Finnish Museums Documentation Service, kindly translated into English numerous captions of photographs of Swedish, Finnish and Russian furniture.

His Majesty the King of Belgium, His Highness the Margrave of Baden, His Highness the Prince of Thurn and Taxis, and Monsieur Olivier Le Fuel have kindly allowed the author to reproduce objects in their collections.

Monsieur Bernard Tassinari allowed access to his archives.

Messrs. Brocard and Jansen, Paris, and S. Franses, London, as well as several auctioneers in Paris and Versailles are thanked for their assistance: Messrs. Antoine Ader, Rémi Ader, Jean-Louis Picard, Jacques Tajan; Messrs. Philippe Couturier, Jean-Paul Couturier, Raymond de Nicolay; Messrs. Jacques Martin and Olivier Desbenoît. Sotheby Parke Bernet and Co., Christie Manson and Woods Ltd. and the Instituto geografico de Agostini, Novara kindly allowed the author access to their photographic archives. The author extends his grateful thanks to all those mentioned and to the following members of staff at Office du Livre; Madame I. de Kalbermatten, Mr. Franz Stadelmann, and M. A. Le Coultre, who are chiefly responsible for the design and publication of this work.

I Imitation of the Antique

The theorists and their ideas

Artists in Renaissance Italy were the first to seek inspiration in antiquity. Attempts to imitate classical models then spread throughout Europe.

Ever since the Renaissance the Antique has served as a constant point of reference, although in practice its hold could often be tenuous. In most people's minds the baroque and rococo movements are not associated with the cult of antiquity, yet some elements in these two styles ultimately derive from classical art. These include columns, arches, entablatures and pediments, which are all interpreted with great freedom.

What is true for architecture also applies to interior decoration. The "grotesques" in Rome which inspired Raphael and later Renaissance artists gradually became so debased that the decoration of eighteenth-century interiors can be considered entirely original. The same applies to the various elements of these interiors such as finely sculpted panels, low chimneys, large mirrors, gilt bronzes and furniture.

In comparison with Renaissance furniture, which was structurally similar to that of the late Middle Ages, the chairs and other pieces of furniture made during the Louis XV period were veritable masterpieces of comfort and stability. They were simply and logically constructed, as well as being elegant and completely original.

The question why this furniture enjoyed such brief popularity, when less than a century later, around 1830 or 1840, it was to regain favor permanently with the public, is a puzzling one.

To understand this phenomenon, it is important to remember that the baroque style flourished in Italy, Spain and the German-speaking lands. It suited the temperament of artists working in these countries. In France, a country little given to extremes, art during Louis XIV's reign was dominated by classicism. In the Regency period, relaxation of and reaction to the established order opened the door to the rococo movement. French rococo is far more sober than the same style as interpreted by craftsmen on the other side of the Alps and beyond the Rhine. In France the rococo movement particularly affected interior decoration. The movement was never acknowledged by the Academy of Architecture nor by the majority of critics.

Father Laugier, a Jesuit, and the highly acclaimed author of books on architecture,[1] when writing about contemporary style, deplored the fact that good taste, which had been universal during the reign of Louis XIV, was later snuffed out and depraved. He praised the Greeks and Romans, censured the barbarian era and the Middle Ages, whilst according some merit to Gothic architecture. Above all, as a true child of the eighteenth century, confident of the power of understanding and reason, he condemned anything in architecture which lacked rationality. As a column is a supporting element, it should neither be added arbitrarily, nor—an even greater crime—should it be reduced to a pilaster. A pediment is naturally placed between the rampant arches of a double-pitched roof. It should not therefore be placed on the front of a building. Seen from this vantage point, baroque art is clearly illogical and therefore contemptible.

Laugier was not alone in this opinion. Comte Caylus, Cochin, the Italian Francesco Milizia and innumerable other authorities professed similar views. There seemed no other way of purging this impure form of art than by returning to the canons of antiquity.

A few years earlier antiquity had become better known, if not better understood, than it had been previously. Following the discovery of Herculaneum and Pompeii, eighteenth-century scholars and connoisseurs became passionately fond of the study of excavations and ancient monuments. However, the buried towns of Campania only really became known at the end of the century. The king of Naples allowed visitors limited access to these sites and reserved the right to publish the results of the excavations. Those privileged to be admitted to the sites or to view the objects assembled at Portici were forbidden to make sketches or take notes. Goethe, accompanied by the painter Tischbein, was refused permission to draw. Winckelmann himself had been unable to see certain pieces. Even in 1790, when Percier went to Naples, he was allowed to bring back only drawings of churches or monuments from the Renaissance period. The first volumes of the official publication called *Antichitá di Ercolano* appeared in 1758 and 1759. They were devoted to paintings, which could be no more than approximately reproduced in black and white. The last volume, which concerned lamps and candelabra, was not published until 1792. The work was, moreover, never on public sale. It was presented by the king of Naples to important visitors, whilst artists and the general public had to be content with the unauthorized versions which numerous publishers hastened to bring out.

Rome, therefore, remained the best place to study classical antiquities during the eighteenth century. The leading Roman families had brought together over a long period of time important collections of classical works of art, which were complemented during the course of the century by objects from the excavations which were carried out in great number in Rome and the surrounding areas. Even the Papacy became caught up in the fashion for classical antiquity. Pius VI (1775–99) built the museum at the Vatican to house his collections. In contrast to those of Naples, the monuments and collections in Rome were accessible. The city became a meeting place for travelers, scholars and young artists sent by their governments to finish their training in Italy. It was in Rome, the most international milieu in Europe, that the neoclassical movement that characterizes the end of the eighteenth century was born.

Its chief theoretician was Johann Joachim Winckelmann, a German living in Rome. In 1763 Winckelmann had become delegate for conservation of antiquities in Rome. In the following year he published his great work which had taken him many years to write. Winckelmann was not only a historian. He formulated a general theory of art, and it is his ideas which interest us here, since neoclassical artists all fell under his influence. Two of his ideas in particular have come down to us, the first being his idea of beauty: "...one of the great mysteries of nature, whose influence we all see and feel; but a general, distinct idea of its essential must be classed among the truths yet undiscovered."[2]

But, adds Winckelmann, without being able to define beauty we can know its attributes, which are those of unity and simplicity:

> From unity proceeds another attribute of lofty beauty, the absence of individuality; that is, the forms of it are described neither by points nor lines other than those which shape beauty merely, and consequently produce a figure which is neither peculiar to any particular individual, nor yet expresses any one state of the mind or affection of the passions, because these blend with it strange lines, and mar the unity. According to this idea, beauty should be like the best kind of water, drawn from the spring itself; the less taste it has, the more healthful it is considered, because free from all foreign admixture.

This doctrine contributed powerfully to the insipid and inexpressive nature of most early nineteenth-century painting and sculpture. It did not have as pernicious an effect on architecture and the decorative arts, although the impersonal and stiff character of the caryatids on Empire furniture was the result of it. In architecture and sculpture Winckelmann's ideas on unity and simplicity in works of art blended with those of Laugier. He maintained that the best proportions are those which give the simplest mathematical relationships: one to two, for example, would be preferable to one to three; the proportion *par excellence* was one to one, the perfect square and the perfect cube.[3]

Laugier's work, like that of Winckelmann, was very widely known. Sir John Soane (1753–1837), undoubtedly the most gifted of all English architects of his generation, had many copies of Laugier's works in his library. It was from Laugier, rather than from classical monuments (represented by the temples in Sicily and Paestum) that late eighteenth-century architects derived their taste for the simplest geometric forms, such as the square, the cube, the round-headed arch, and the semicircular apse. The

tollhouses at the gates of Paris designed by Ledoux, the abbot's lodgings at Royaumont and the Admiralty buildings at St. Petersburg are all examples of round or cubic buildings. Ledoux and Boullé even drew up plans for houses in spherical form.

The bias toward simplicity is an important aspect of the architecture and decorative art of this period. This tendency was in harmony with the feelings of simple austerity which Rousseau's disciples attributed to the Ancients. In the eyes of contemporaries, antiquity, elegance and purity were almost synonymous terms.

In 1801 Landon spoke of shapes "regenerated at the pure stream of antiquity" and of "the feeling of elegance and simplicity which we admire in the works of the Ancients."[4] In the preface to their *Recueil,*[5] Percier and Fontaine stated: "it is a delusion to believe that there are shapes preferable to those which the Ancients have handed down to us."

All this was the general opinion, but the taste, temperament and ability of each artist must be taken into account when one considers the ideas of these artists and their translation into reality. It remains to be seen how closely the models provided by the Greeks and Romans were followed in practice.

We shall consider this question in almost every chapter of this book. First we may examine several characteristic objects, the first of which are to a greater or lesser extent copies of pieces from museum collections.   1–7

Percier and Fontaine

Percier and Fontaine have the reputation, which is not unjustified, of adhering to a rigorously classical approach. They themselves express their convictions in the phrase which we quoted earlier. Let us, however, examine one of their designs.

M. Olivier Le Fuel, who is a descendant of the Jacob family, owns a series of watercolors by Percier, including one which he has kindly allowed us to reproduce; it is a   8 bedroom with blue hangings. The chief feature is the bed which rests on a platform and is surmounted by a large baldachin or canopy forming an alcove. This way of showing off a bed by enclosing it within curtains goes back, in the West, to the late Middle Ages or perhaps even earlier. To our knowledge it has no precedent in antiquity. The large mirrors formed of a single piece of glass, like those visible at the back of the alcove, are a French invention of the eighteenth century. The commodes, one of which can be seen at the right and another at the left, go back only to the seventeenth century; before this chests were in use.

The bed derives from classical models, but it cannot be   9, 10 considered a reproduction of any particular bed. In order to conform to the practice of his own time, Percier successfully raised bedheads so as to create a boat-shaped bed or *lit en bateau*. This kind of bed remained fashionable until about 1840.

The *jardinières* which frame the bed are related to the tripod found in the Temple of Isis, but the model has been   1 modified to such an extent that it cannot be called a copy.

The most curious pieces of furniture are the armchairs on either side of the bed. This time the source is clearly two armchairs surrounded by cupids in a fresco preserved at the

Archeological Museum in Naples. For these late eighteenth-century chairs, stuffed with horsehair, Percier has kept the proportions of the classical chairs and even their drapery, although this serves no function and is in fact superfluous. It should be recalled that classical chairs were not upholstered but had cane or webbing seats on which cushions and sometimes movable drapery could be placed. The only licence which Percier allowed himself was to lighten the rather hideous feet of the chairs which were his models.

There would be little point in studying other details of this room, since this would lead only to the same conclusions. Percier, who showed great respect towards his classical models, wherever possible used designs which he had brought from Rome. This did not stop him from adapting classical models to the necessities of modern life. In the final analysis, the room he designed bears a closer relationship to interiors of the age of Louis XVI than it does to Roman ones. Its novelty appears above all in the decorative details, which are closer to the classical repertoire than had been the case previously.

Yet Percier is a true artist. He added his own contribution to the elements which he drew from tradition, both ancient and modern. Rather than being mere imitators of antiquity, Fontaine and Percier were creators of the Empire style.

Chairs in classical style

Most classical armchairs were by no means attractive. Those made of wood were spoiled by the heaviness of their feet. Those made of stone, like certain seats found in baths or theaters, were heavy by their very nature and the volutes or lion's paw feet which decorated them did not make them look any lighter. Few artists, therefore, imitated these chairs. Instead they took their inspiration from the Greek chair, which was more elegant and moreover had been adopted by the Romans themselves.

The history of the adoption of this chair by eighteenth-century decorators, and the gradual transformation of the models which derive from this Roman chair, allows us to follow the evolution of neoclassical art over a period of forty years.

The Greek chair *(klismos)* was considered by the Ancients as a comfortable seat. According to specialists[6] it was made of wood. No original has survived; however, it is well known to us thanks to paintings on vases, to chairs depicted in reliefs, and from the evidence of several statues of seated women, such as that of Agrippina the Younger in the Uffizi Gallery.

The form of this chair remained almost the same for several centuries; the slightly sloping back was surmounted by a thick, arched crosspiece which curved around the back of the sitter and on which he or she could rest one arm. The seat was caned or reeded and covered with a cushion. The curved legs were so slender that the solidity of the chair seems rather in question.

As yet no one has given a satisfactory explanation of this point. Architects and decorators in the eighteenth century merely reproduced the tapering legs of these chairs in their drawings. The chairmakers *(menuisiers)*, therefore, found themselves obliged to solve this practical problem. They did so either by attenuating the curve of the legs, making them blunt instead of pointed, or by replacing the arched front legs by straight ones. This solution, which had been foreshadowed by eighteenth-century English chairs, became the rule. Most chairs made in France during the Empire and Restoration periods have straight front legs and arched back legs.

Another aspect of the construction of the chair in classical times must have puzzled later designers. On vases and on reliefs chairs are generally seen in profile, so that the person seated on the chair hides part of the backboard. We now know that the back was attached to the chair by three uprights, a wide one in the center and two smaller ones at either side, springing from the back legs. However, this method of construction was not known at the end of the eighteenth century and so chair designers often kept only the lateral supports. This did not, however, prevent the chairs they produced from being extremely elegant. Some craftsmen had the ability to give chairbacks most attractive proportions and shapes. These chairs are almost always higher than classical ones.

In 1776 the Greek chair was correctly reproduced by Clérisseau in a decorative medallion in the large drawing room of the Paris town house belonging to Grimod de La Reynière.[7] Several years later the first architectural designs appeared which attempted to restore classical chairs to their rightful place. In 1785 Jean-Arnaud Raymond drew up plans for a new house for the picture dealer Lebrun, the husband of Madame Vigée-Lebrun. A section of the design for the gallery clearly shows classical chairs with wide backboards and arched legs.[8] In the following year the architect Le Queu provided chairs of the same form for the Montholon town house.[9]

An Italian example which is contemporary if not slightly earlier can be found in the gilded chairs from the Villa Borghese in Rome, rebuilt and redecorated by Antonio Asprucci between 1780 and 1787.

Between 1785 and 1788 an architect of Italian origin, Giuseppe Bonomi, decorated the Etruscan gallery of Lord Aylesford's manor at Packington, Warwickshire. Aylesford was himself an "antiquary" and amateur architect. The gilded chairs in this gallery are covered in black velvet, embroidered in red, to match the color of the walls. They reproduce fairly accurately the shape of a late Roman chair. They can be dated to 1788.[10]

The chairs for the pavilion at Haga in Sweden, which were built and decorated for King Gustavus III by Louis-Adrien Masreliez, are almost contemporary and rather similar to the ones we have mentioned. In addition, an English chair of uncertain date which we reproduce can also be related to the ones already discussed.

Apart from Asprucci's chair, which is the least "antique" of this group, these early chairs in Etruscan style are clumsy. The horseshoe-shaped backboard makes them look heavy. It was furniture designers and craftsmen working in Paris who made improvements. From 1790 Etruscan-style chairs became fashionable in Paris.

The design reproduced in Plate 16 is taken from a remarkable album in the Musée des arts décoratifs entitled *Mobilier de Madame Elisabeth,* 1790. Madame Elisabeth was the younger sister of Louis XVI for whom a fine house was built at that time at Montreuil near Versailles.

Unfortunately the origin of the album remains unknown. In the nineteenth century it belonged to the great collector Sir Richard Wallace. The designs are (or are said to be) by Dugourc, designer to the Royal household, Grognard, another decorator, and Meunier, who may have been a carpenter. Many are unsigned but none appears to be later than the date on the cover of the album. This point is important since it proves that the lighter Parisian interpretation of the classical chair existed from 1790.

18 Etruscan chairs appear in numerous paintings and drawings, from the following years,[11] which allows us to assign probable dates to those which survive. Most seem to have been made between 1791 and 1800. They all differ in some way from authentic classical chairs. For example, the seat may be round, the front legs straight, the backboard placed too high or else the corners may be curved or rounded. Naturally, the construction conforms to the traditions of the eighteenth century. A fairly large number 19–22 of chairs by Georges and Henri Jacob have survived; several 17 by Molitor also exist. A larger number are by unknown makers, since from 1791 carpenters and cabinetmakers in Paris were no longer obliged to stamp their work.[12]

Percier and Fontaine, in their *Recueil,*[13] show a chair in the classical style for a room belonging to "Citoyen V." 23 Krafft and Ransonnette[14] reproduced a similar chair without giving its source. At the beginning of the Empire period chairs of this type suddenly became very rare. The Jacob brothers (1796–1803) certainly made them, since six chairs in the Etruscan style bearing their stamp were delivered to Fontainebleau between November 14 and 24, 1804,[15] when Napoleon was hastily preparing the palace for the arrival of the Pope. These chairs are among the most 24 attractive and least orthodox of their time. At the same time eighteen other mahogany chairs by a different maker were delivered to Fontainebleau. They are not stamped but may also be considered to derive from the classical chair, although they are even less like the original. This type, 25 which is rare in France, was very popular, as we shall see, in certain other countries.

Classical style chairs enjoyed only brief popularity. They were fashionable for a mere fifteen years or so, although they had been in use for several centuries in Greece and in the Roman Empire. French decorators and cabinetmakers abandoned them between 1800 and 1805, but the form of 26 these chairs lived on in an adapted form as a more modest ordinary chair with a straw seat. Before studying this chair in countries other than France, we may consider the armchairs that were made to match chairs in classical style.

The Ancients made a clear distinction between the armchair (or throne), which was a seat of honor, and the chair, which was inclined rather than upright, comfortable, and intended particularly for women. It was only in the late Roman period (third and fourth centuries A.D.) that the two categories of chairs can be said to have merged.

In contrast, at the end of the eighteenth century sets of seat furniture included both chairs and armchairs. This obliged furniture makers to invent armchairs to match chairs in classical style. To judge from the number of examples which are only partially successful, even when made by as talented a furniture maker as Georges Jacob, this problem was more difficult to solve than it at first seemed.

In some cases, however, Jacob managed to create chairs with armrests that successfully matched the back. Jacob himself can be seen in a portrait dated 1792. He is shown in the midst of his family, sitting on an armchair in classical style of his own manufacture. Several chairs of this type must still exist.[16] The two armchairs illustrated cannot be 27, 28 much later than the one shown in the painting.

Another type of armchair that was fairly successfully based on an antique model is shown in a design by Percier, 29 which he apparently made in Rome after an unknown bronze classical chair. The source of the design was of little importance. Contemporaries were convinced that they had discovered the classical original of the armchair, which was given the name "curule." It was essentially a stool to which 30, 35 a back was added. However, furniture makers found it difficult to make a chair in wood which was based on a bronze original. The feet were rather fragile since the flaring or saber-shaped legs customary at the time were substituted for the original semicircular back legs.

The fashion for curule armchairs lasted no longer than the previous rage for chairs in classical style.

As we have seen, the chairs made for the gallery at Packington Hall, Warwickshire, were among the earliest made in imitation of Greek originals. They do not seem to have influenced other English furniture makers. Certain English chairs made around 1800 reveal some of the characteristics associated with the chair in the classical style, but these appear rather to have been influenced by French examples, knowledge of which was transmitted by the architect Henry Holland (1745–1806), by the furniture designer Thomas Sheraton, or by others.

Henry Holland had just rebuilt Carlton House for the Prince of Wales, a great francophile. Sheraton wrote of the Prince's dining room; "The chairs are of mahogany made in the style of the French, with broad top rails hanging over each back foot; the legs are turned, and the seats covered with red leather."[17]

In the engraving accompanying this description the front 31 legs of the chairs are well turned, but the back legs are of saber form. The splat is visible, rather than being covered with leather, and the chair itself seems to be of circular shape. These two characteristic features are undoubtedly French.

In an advertisement issued by his firm after the publication of his book (1793), Sheraton reproduced his chairs once more, this time giving them four saber-shaped legs. In the book itself there are only two examples of chair 32 backs which project. It is this shape, in a modified form, which was taken up by numerous English furniture makers for the backs of chairs in classical style. Such chairs bear 33, 34 little resemblance to the ones shown by Sheraton, but despite often complicated detailing they preserve the elegance and lightness of neoclassical chairs from the preceding period. English chair backs, unlike their French counterparts, retained this feature until after 1800. During the Regency English chairs even acquired a characteristic 36, 37 elegance. British furniture makers did not reproduce the form of their classical models, but nevertheless managed to create a harmonious blending of the back, splat, and saber-shaped legs. This method of matching the legs to the splat of the seat was imitated in France and all over Europe after 1815.

In England Thomas Hope was the most enthusiastic admirer of the classical style. He advocated a return to classical models in furniture design. Hope has not been mentioned until now since he has always been considered by the English as an original amateur and his influence was slight. During the year following the conclusion of peace with France by the Treaty of Amiens (March 1802–May 1803) Hope went first to Italy, then to Paris. He certainly returned with a good deal of information, since his work *Household Furniture and Interior Decoration executed from designs by Thomas Hope,* which appeared in 1807, reproduced, in many cases, antique furniture which had 133 hardly been modified, as well as designs by Percier and other designs which may be of French origin.[18] Those 135 designs which are apparently the work of Hope himself are somewhat idiosyncratic.

It would be tedious to follow in detail the evolution of the "antique" chair in different European countries. However, let us look briefly at Sweden. Isolated by the Napoleonic wars, furniture makers remained faithful during the whole of the Empire period to a type of chair which had originally 38–40 been designed during the reign of Louis XVI. The arms and legs are curved, and the back has a large crossbar extending to the seat by means of rails or a crosspiece. To a contemporary coming from the south of the Baltic, these chairs would have seemed old fashioned. However, they are now greatly appreciated for their solidity and elegant proportions.

After it had disappeared in France, and become rare in England and Italy, where it had often taken on a rounded form, the classical style chair reappeared almost everywhere during the Restoration period. However, it was now so greatly modified that it can hardly be said to owe a debt to antiquity. All that remains of the Greek chair is the slightly curved back and occasionally the general outline of the legs. Yet several examples are more orthodox and, rather 41–43 curiously, one of the latest examples is relatively close to the Greek or Roman originals. Everywhere greater knowledge 44 of archeology went hand in hand with the development of eclecticism. The same maker delivered to the Worshipful Company of Goldsmiths in 1834 both chairs in the classical style for the dining room of their building and some most unlikely chairs in "Louis XIV" style for a drawing room. 443 Both sets were designed by Philip Hardwick.

Before leaving the subject of the classical chair, a few words must be said about the model with which we concluded our discussion of French chairs. Contemporaries 25 probably considered it a legitimate variant of the classical chair, and it certainly enjoyed a surprising success over many years. It offers an interesting example of the way styles evolve. Almost classical to begin with, they became ever freer until they acquired characteristics that one can only call baroque. Such chairs may be found in Italy, Germany, Austria, Scandinavia and Russia. 45–50

We may end this sketch by pointing out that it was only during a brief period that artists sincerely attempted to reproduce models from antiquity. It is hard to set chronological limits to this period, since some artists were ahead of the bulk of their contemporaries while others lagged behind them. However, one can date the efflorescence of neoclassical style to the years 1790–1805. Even then imitation of the Ancients was rarely literal. After 1805 antiquity was interpreted, consciously or unconsciously, according to each artist's personal inspiration.

1 Bronze tripod from Pompeii. Museo Archeologico Nazionale, Naples.

2 Bronze and ormolu tripod. Musée Masséna (formerly in the Prince Essling Collection), Nice.
Although close to the Roman original reproduced opposite, this tripod is most usefully compared with the one used at the baptism of the king of Rome in 1811 (now in the Kunsthistorisches Museum, Vienna), from which it differs only in a few insignificant details. It has an ormolu flower motif in the middle of the socle and is less richly decorated. The Empress Marie-Louise's tripod, presented to her by the people of Milan, was made entirely of ormolu and lapis lazuli. It came from the workshop of Luigi and Francesco Manfredini, who were doubtless also responsible for the tripods in the Masséna Museum.

The classical tripod, which is more fluid in outline, remains superior to the copies made of it. The later tripods are marked by the defects common to many copies of earlier works of art—that is, they are rather stiff. Some details, such as the bearded heads

issuing from the upper part of the lion's paw feet, are over-elaborate.

3–5 Three classical bronze candelabra. Musée du Louvre, Paris. These monumental objects, which are more than three feet in height, were in every day use in antiquity. The upper part forms a small lampstand. Two other models have hooks all round from which oil lamps were hung.

6 Ormolu candelabrum. Neues Schloss, Baden-Baden.
This candelabrum, reproduced by gracious permission of the Margrave of Baden, must have been made in Paris or Milan. Although more splendid than, and of superior craftsmanship to, the classical originals, it is a faithful, almost servile copy. Even the hooks from which oil lamps were hung are reproduced, although they have no function here.

7 Detail of candelabrum in Plate 6.

1

2

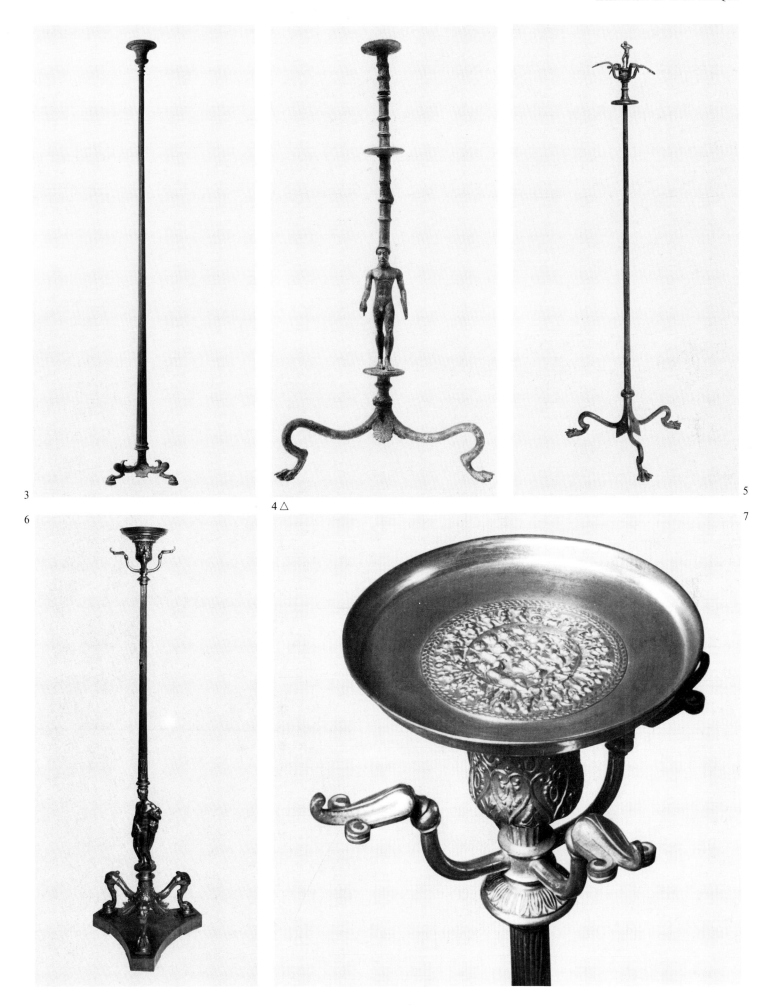

3

4 △

5

6

7

8 △

9 10

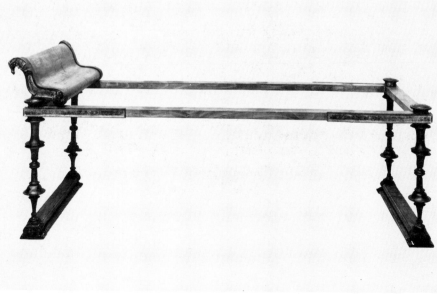

11

8 Design for a bedroom. Watercolor by Charles Percier. Olivier Le Fuel Collection, Paris.
The walls are hung with blue fabric to match the upholstery of the furniture. The baldachin of the bed is bordered with pink material, which is also used beneath the frieze around the room. On this frieze figures and flowers are painted in natural colors on a pale blue ground. The furniture is in mahogany with gilt bronze mounts.

9 Classical bronze bed. Musée du Louvre, Paris.
This Roman bed from the classical era, which is in part restored, was intended for use in a dining room. The bedhead is of a commonly found form. Wooden beds had much larger legs which might taper in parts.

10 Low relief sculpture from a funerary monument originating from Hierapolis, Phrygia. 2nd century A.D. Badisches Landesmuseum, Karlsruhe.
Despite the crudity of the stone carving, the details of the furniture can be made out. The bed is like the boat-shaped ones popular in the Empire period, but has rather long turned legs which are emphatically curved (one can be seen at the extreme right). The armchair in which the figure at the left is seated is probably of wicker.

11 Two thrones between two cherubs. Fresco from Pompeii. Museo Archeologico Nazionale, Naples.
The throne on the left has turned legs, while those on the right-hand throne are rectangular in section. Both sets of legs have been given a distinctive shape, either on the lathe or by chiseling.

12 Classical chair of red marble. Musée du Louvre, Paris.

12

13 Greek stele, 5th century B.C. Musée du Louvre, Paris.
This chair is covered by drapery. On other examples it can be seen that the rounded wooden member forming the splat is joined onto each of the legs.

14 Gilt wooden chair. Villa Borghese, Rome.
Italo Faldi, who has catalogued the sculpture in the Borghese Gallery, has discovered the dates when various decorative vases made to designs by the architect Asprucci entered the Borghese collections, as records of payments were preserved in the Borghese archives which are deposited in the Vatican. From the same source it should be possible to discover the exact date of fabrication of these chairs, which cannot be later than 1785 or 1786.

The chairs in the Villa Borghese were copied elsewhere in Italy, as well as in Germany (there are examples based on them in the city museum at Regensburg, in the Museum für Kunst und Gewerbe, Hamburg and in the Museum at Celle, Lower Saxony) and in Russia, at Pavlovsk.

15 Chair of painted wood in the classical style. Victoria and Albert Museum, London.
The painting on this chair was inspired by "Etruscan" black-and-red figured vases. The makers of the earliest chairs in the antique style almost always decorated them with a frieze of figures borrowed from painted vases or from classical bas-reliefs. These scenes were painted or stuck onto the seat rail.

13

14

15

18

16

17

16 Design for a chair. Watercolor drawing. Musée des arts décoratifs, Paris. Album entitled *Mobilier de Madame Elisabeth,* 1790.
The legs of this chair are so pointed that they would have to have been modified by the chairmaker. The chairback has been

decorated with a frieze of small figures painted in white on a blue ground.

17 Mahogany chair inlaid with copper. Stamped by B. Molitor. Exported to Switzerland, 1973.

18 Count Gustav-Moritz Armfelt seated in front of a bust of Caesar and another of Gustavus III, Armfelt's former master.
Portrait painted in Florence, 1793, by Louis Gauffier (1761–1801). Replica in the National Museum of Finland.
The painter Louis Gauffier, who won the Prix de Rome in 1784, remained in Italy during the revolutionary period and died at Florence. His picture illustrates the way styles evolved in Italy, where, as in France, classical influences were very strong. Both the furniture as well as the hangings at the back of the room are strictly classical.

19, 20 Carved mahogany chair, stamped G. Jacob. Mobilier national, Paris.
The chair, like many made by G. Jacob, is of circular form. A classical frieze printed on silk is stuck onto the seat rail. The leather upholstery is original. Six of these chairs were acquired by the Mobilier national at a Paris auction held on March 15, 1944.

18

19

20

20

21 22

23

24

21 Mahogany chair, stamped G. Jacob. Musée Paul Dupuy, Toulouse.
The seat is circular. There was probably once an ornamental panel in the center of the back.

22 Mahogany chair. Musée national du château de Pau.
This attractive chair is unstamped but may well have been made by G. Jacob. The cane seat was apparently designed to be covered with a cushion, as had been the fashion on classical chairs.

23 Classical-style chair. Engraving published by Krafft and Ransonnette in *Plans, coupes et élévations des plus belles maisons et des hôtels construits à Paris et dans les environs*, 1802.

24 Mahogany chair with ebony and pewter inlays on seat rail. Stamped by Jacob Frères. The Emperor Napoleon's library, Musée national du château de Fontainebleau.
These chairs, delivered in 1804, were described in Jacob-Desmalter's memorandum as follows: "Six mahogany chairs, plank back with double scroll ornament; inlaid with ebony and pewter; green leather seat printed in silver... 72 francs." The Jacob firm must have kept these chairs for stock as, in principle, use of the stamp "Jacob Frères" ceased on the death of the elder of the two brothers, which took place on October 23, 1803.
  Other more or less comparable chairs were formerly at Malmaison. They can be seen in one of the watercolors commissioned from the painter Lœillot by Eugène de Beauharnais's widow, who wanted a souvenir of the main rooms of the château. One chair of this second type is still in the Mobilier national. The back has a second transverse member which is decorated with a central openwork and inlaid motif similar to that found on the upper seat rail, which is itself ornamented with motifs differing slightly from those on the chair illustrated here.
  Malmaison was refurbished in 1800 by Fontaine and Percier. These chairs may originally have been designed by Percier.

25

26

27

25 Mahogany chair. Musée national du château de Fontainebleau.
The rounded back terminating in two scrolls is not really new. It can be seen on chairs by Georges Jacob in Louis XVI style now in the Metropolitan Museum, New York. It reappears on comfortable chairs made for Napoleon, such as the one in the library in the château at Compiègne, but the shape remained rare in France until the Restoration and was always used very discreetly.

26 Rush-seated cherrywood chair. Restoration period, Lyons region. Private Collection, France.
Ordinary chairs like this one were generally made by specialist craftsmen, called *chaisiers,* who rarely changed their models. The *philosophe* Maine de Biran (François Gontier) is shown in a chair like this one in a portrait painted by Duvivier in Year VI (1797 or 1798). Another can be seen in a portrait of Ingres and his wife painted in Rome in 1818 by Alaux. This shows that almost the same type was also being made in Italy. The attractive light "Chiavari" chair, as it was called, which was made in Italy, derives from these works of craftsmanship.

27 Carved mahogany armchair, stamped G. Jacob. Mobilier national, Paris.
The classical frieze on paper stuck to the seat rail is well preserved. Several other armchairs of this model survive. Carefully built and finely proportioned, they must have been part of the furnishings of the Tuileries when it was occupied by Napoleon Bonaparte as First Consul.

28 Mahogany and lemonwood armchairs, stamped G. Jacob. Sold on April 7, 1976, Palais Galliera, Messrs. Laurin, Guilloux, Buffetaud and Tailleur.

29 Curule armchair. Design by Percier. Olivier Le Fuel Collection, Paris.

30 Curule armchair, mahogany. Olivier Le Fuel Collection, Paris.

28

29

30

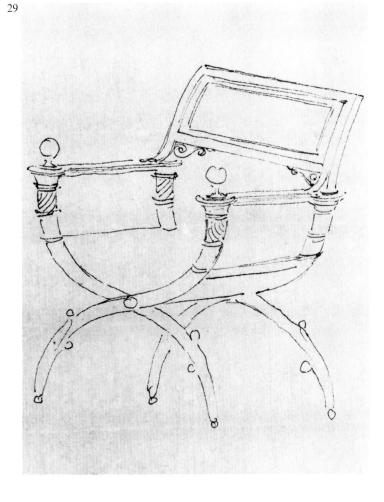

31 △

32   33

34

24

35   36

31   *A Dining Parlour in imitation of the Prince of Wales's.* Engraving published by Thomas Sheraton in *The Cabinet-Maker and Upholsterer's Drawing-Book,* Plate 60.

32   Back of a painted chair. Engraving published by Thomas Sheraton in *The Cabinet-Maker and Upholsterer's Drawing-Book,* Plate 25. The engraving is dated 1793.

33   Carved mahogany armchair decorated with brass studs. About 1800. Victoria and Albert Museum, London.
The four legs are saber-shaped; the back is lower than French chairbacks.

34   Painted wooden armchair, partly gilt and with painted decorative motifs. About 1800. Victoria and Albert Museum, London.
The upper part of the slightly curved front legs is in perfect harmony with the top rail, which curves forward. Most English Regency chairs share this characteristic.

35   Curule armchair, gilt wood, stamped G. Jacob. Exported to the United States, 1970.

36   Satinwood chair. Stourhead, Wiltshire, England.
Thomas Chippendale's son, also called Thomas, took over the family business in 1779. He went bankrupt in 1804 for reasons which had nothing to do with the quality of his furniture. Not long before he went out of business he made tables and chairs for Sir Richard Colt Hoare at Stourhead. This furniture is perhaps some of the best to be produced in England at the time.
These chairs are well balanced, solid and simple. Twelve of them were delivered in 1802 and were put in the Picture Gallery. The seat rail which overlaps the back, showing that the chair is in the "Greek style," the shape of the back legs, and the front legs surmounted by a column which forms part of the armrest, are all features reminiscent of French chairs of the same period or slightly earlier. The cross of St. Andrew on the back is one of the earliest examples of this motif, which reappeared during the Empire period in France and was especially popular during the Restoration era.

37

37 Molded mahogany chair. England, about 1810. Musée des arts décoratifs, Paris.
The front of the chair is similar to that in Plate 36. The back and legs form a pleasing continuous line which was to be copied in France and all over Europe after 1815.

38 Swedish Empire-style chair of painted wood. Originally painted gray. Private Collection, Finland.

39 Swedish painted wooden chair. Stamped by Efraim Ståhl, chairmaker in Stockholm, active between 1794 and 1820. Ostrobothnian Museum, Oulu, Finland.

40 Swedish Empire-style chair, of painted wood. Private Collection, Finland.

41 Gilt wooden chair. About 1820. Hermitage Museum, Leningrad.

42 Design for a chair. Chair No. 152 in Joseph Danhauser II's catalogue. Vienna, 1830–38.
This chair, which is simpler than Whitaker's chair, is nevertheless ornamented with unexpected excrescences on and below the seat rail.

43 Engraving from Whitaker's *Designs of Cabinet and Upholstery Furniture in the most modern style*, 1825.
After 1815, the taste for ornamentation became more marked both in architecture and interior decoration. Without completely abandoning his classical model, the designer has felt it necessary to add a kind of acroter and other superfluous decoration.

38   39

40

41

42

43

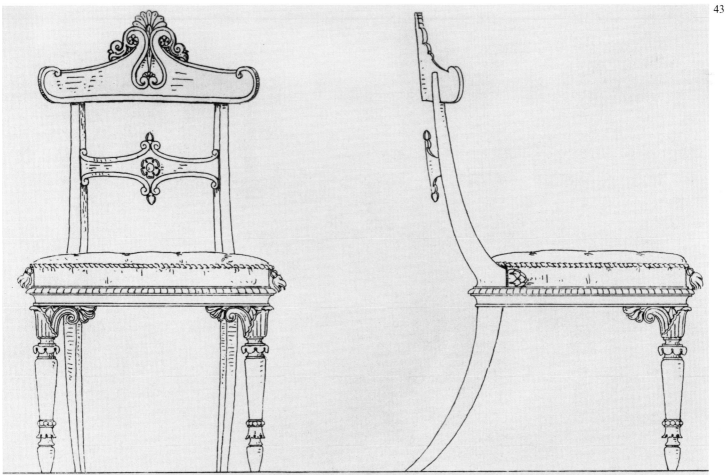

44

45

46

47

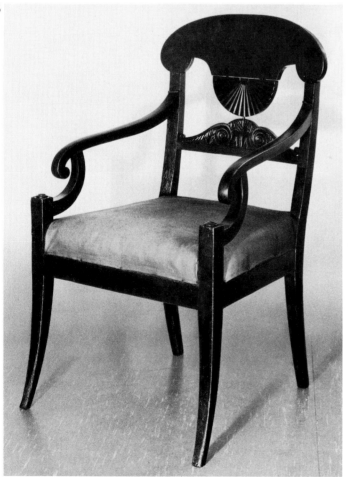

48

49

50

44 Mahogany dining chair made in 1834 for the Worshipful Company of Goldsmiths, London, to a design executed by Philip Hardwick. London, Victoria and Albert Museum.

45 Swedish chair, mahogany. National Museum of Finland, Helsinki.

46 Armchair of birch, stained dark brown. National Museum of Finland, Helsinki.
Several Swedish chairs made in the 1820s have similar armrests and backs.

47 Chair of wood, stained black. Schloss Ehrenburg, Coburg. Ordered from the Viennese chairmaker Friedrich Hasselbrink, this chair was delivered to Coburg in 1816.

48 Gilded wooden chair. Russian Museum, Leningrad.
The Russian Museum was formerly the palace of the Grand Duke Michael, Tsar Alexander I's brother. It was built between 1819 and 1820 by the architect Carlo Rossi, who also designed the furniture for the palace. This chair was in the White Drawing Room which still has its original furniture. Rossi, an excellent architect, was less gifted at designing furniture: his pieces are overloaded with ornament, as is most richly decorated furniture of the period.

49 Gilded wooden chair. Hermitage Museum, Leningrad. Probably designed by Carlo Rossi.

50 Chair veneered with burr poplar. Armfelt Museum, Helsinki. This chair, which came from Åminne (Joensuu), must have been bought in St. Petersburg in 1819.

II   Interior Decoration and Furnishings

The elements of interior decoration

Many furnishings, such as tapestries, seat covers and curtains, deteriorate quickly. Fashions as well as occupants change, and it is rare for an interior to look the same for longer than twenty years. However, many French provincial country houses that were only occasionally occupied still had their original furnishings until recently. Unfortunately the cost of upkeep of these houses, thefts, fires, and the division of estates on the owner's death, is reducing very quickly the number of country houses in which their original furnishings survive. Soon only a few royal castles and country houses where the tapestries and furniture are periodically restored will be able to show us homogeneous interiors furnished in the original fashion. We therefore frequently have to rely on such sources of information as archives, designers' and architects' drawings, or even paintings—which fortunately survive in quantity from the nineteenth century.

The taste for comfort and the love of one's personal surroundings were certainly more strongly felt in the nineteenth century than earlier, and were doubtless more marked in the last century than in our own. Now, frequent travel, and the abundance and diversity of the distractions open to us, have reduced the time which we spend in our own homes. In former times a rich man, or one who had made money, dreamed of building and furnishing a beautiful house according to the latest fashion. In the seventeenth century and during the greater part of the eighteenth century this objective was dictated above all by considerations of prestige. The taste for comfortable and convenient rooms dates only from the end of the eighteenth century and became more widespread in the nineteenth.

Perhaps more than at any other time, architects during this period were concerned with the most trivial details of interior decoration. However, their designs frequently omitted furniture and tables, which were not even given space. Let us look at some of these drawings, beginning with 8 a bedroom designed by Percier, whose furniture has been described in the preceding chapter. The layout in Percier's drawing is symmetrical and faultless. Any modifications would apparently disrupt the whole scheme, and yet such modifications would have to be made for practical reasons, since Percier provides neither lighting nor bedside tables.

Every interior in the *Recueil de décorations* follows the same principle. The impression given is of an exhibition hall rather than an actual living space. In the case of the room designed for Citoyen V. there is no way of even hanging an engraving on the wall or of including a commode or dressing table. The citizen had to be content with an imposing marble console table in the form of a classical table on which were a statue and two stone vases. As for Monsieur O. (the banker Ouvrard), he was obliged, according to the scheme drawn up by Percier, to sleep between two antique therms symbolizing Silence and Night, together with large marble vases and a frieze showing funeral processions and sacrificial scenes. Above the bed there is a less austere subject: Diana's chariot is being driven by Love towards the sleeping Endymion. Monsieur G. (Gaudin, Finance Minister) was the only client of Fontaine and Percier who succeeded in getting a bookcase and pictures in his bedroom. The pictures are attached to the base of a hanging which goes almost all the way round the room. They are very close to one another. This arrangement was by no means original. Nor were Fontaine and Percier the only architects to envisage the furnishing of a room as an ensemble to which nothing could be added and from which nothing could be taken away. All the architects of that time shared the same concept, at least as far as the main rooms were concerned. The examples given illustrate the luxury and cost of some of these decorative schemes. Even when on St. Helena, Napoleon still had bitter memories of 51–54 the expenses incurred by Josephine for the furnishing of their first house in the rue Chantereine. He strongly reproached Prince Eugène, his stepson, for allowing himself to be overcharged by the architects responsible for redecorating his Paris residence. It was a *petite maison* which had cost more to furnish than to buy. Today this house, the Hôtel de Beauharnais, is the most complete as well as the most luxurious example of a Parisian town house of the Empire period.

Despite his taste for economy, Napoleon himself was extravagant, but his expenditure was intended to stimulate national industries. The revival and development of silk weaving in Lyons is due entirely to his personal initiative. On his orders the main rooms of Napoleon's palaces were lined with silk, and this fashion spread to foreign countries. Charles IV of Spain, who from 1800 employed Jean-Démosthène Dugourc, formerly a designer for the Royal 55 Household in Louis XVI's time, the king of Bavaria, and other important figures ordered silk hangings from Lyons. In 1827 the dowager empress of Russia ordered from France textiles intended for the decoration of her new quarters in the Winter Palace. This silk was as costly as the furnishings designed by Percier. Only a few leading dignitaries could imitate royalty on this scale, and even in the secondary rooms in palaces there are less expensive textiles, such as the so-called "economical" damasks, silk noil and sateens, and even sometimes printed cottons and wallpaper.

Textiles and wallpaper will be described in detail in the last chapter of this book, but a few words may be said here about a fashion which goes back to the time of Louis XVI and which became far more widespread during the Empire period and the following years.

The bedroom at the Bagatelle which was decorated in 1777 by Bélanger for the Comte d'Artois (the future Charles X) is designed to resemble a tent. The bed curtains are fixed to uprights resembling lances, while the firedogs are in the form of mortars. Rooms which resemble the interior of a tent, their walls and ceiling covered in textiles, became even more common after the Revolution. The vestibule and the Council Chamber at Malmaison, which were furnished by Fontaine and Percier in 1800, are hung with blue and white striped twill like a real campaign tent. The military origin of this type of decor was later forgotten.

Small intimate rooms such as boudoirs or dressing rooms were hung with draped fabric, its pleats converging towards 56 the center of the ceiling. In larger rooms the walls were usually covered with pleated fabric which was hung from loops as in antiquity. The fashion for rooms decorated to resemble tents lasted to the early 1830s. Examples are a 76 Viennese boudoir which is shown in a watercolor by Johann Stephan Decker, the Comte de Mornay's room and Queen Hortense's salon and dining room at Arenenberg.

Pleated drapery in classical style was also simulated. It was painted in *trompe l'œil,* as in the small salon published in a sectional drawing by Fontaine and Percier. Textiles were also replaced by wallpaper. Quite a number of wallpapers issued between 1810 and 1830 had designs imitating draped textiles.

Italian-style decoration

For a long time the Italians had specialized in stucco[1] and decorative tempera and fresco painting. Although stucco was frequently used from the eighteenth century onwards, Italian architects, helped by artists and craftsmen of their own nationality, were the most skilled at using and combining these techniques. They played an important role in Russia at the beginning of the nineteenth century. We have chosen four examples of Italian decoration carried out in Russia by Vincenzo Brenna (1740–1819), Giacomo Quarenghi (1744–1817) and Carlo Rossi (1775–1849). The 58, 59 first two of the rooms chosen are at Pavlovsk, near Leningrad. This palace was burnt down during the last war but has been completely restored since 1945. The interiors appear today in all their freshness and are undoubtedly authentic, since the restorers made use not only of photographs but also of the architects' original designs and of sketches by painters. Only the textiles and their tassels and fringes seem somewhat less than splendid in this very tastefully reconstituted ensemble.

Brenna, who was Paul I's favorite architect, decorated most of the rooms at Pavlovsk between 1789 and 1800. His style bears some relationship to that of architects active during the first wave of the classical style, such as Piranesi and Charles de Wailly. Brenna borrows their rather theatrical forms, somewhat freely based on antique sources. However, Brenna's imagination was tempered by his delicate touch in the treatment of details.

Quarenghi, who was, with Cameron, the principal architect of Catherine II, spent only a little time at Pavlovsk after Brenna's departure for Italy. Slightly younger than Brenna, Quarenghi was much more classical and "correct" in his approach, in the sense that he invented nothing that he had not seen in Palladian architecture or in the monuments of Rome. Yet Quarenghi was neither servile nor pedantic. He worked simply and naturally in a style which he had assimilated perfectly. The layout of his buildings is always logical and the proportions well thought out.

Carlo Rossi was born in St. Petersburg in 1775, the son of an adulterous union between an Italian dancer and an unknown father. When little more than a child he came under the protection of Brenna, who was responsible for his education. In 1796 Rossi was Brenna's official assistant. In 1802 he left for Italy with him, returning only in 1806 after having completed his architectural education in Florence. It is apparent that Italy had an important role in the education of Russia's greatest nineteenth-century architect. In general Rossi's works rise above any comparison, but he is closest to contemporary Italian architects, especially as regards his interiors. Thus the painted frieze around each of the wall panels in the small salon in the Elagin Palace is a 62 motif which reappears in numerous Italian houses. This palace, which was rebuilt and redecorated between 1818 and 1822 for the Dowager Empress Maria, mother of the Emperor Alexander I, attracted the latter's attention to Rossi. Not long afterwards Rossi was entrusted with important building projects, including the Mikhailovskii Palace, erected for one of the emperor's brothers. The White 60 Room in this palace, dating from between 1822 and 1825, is one of the most beautiful rooms built at the beginning of the nineteenth century. The proportions are perfect and the rich decoration is cleverly placed so that some surfaces are left entirely plain to provide a contrast. The entire interior, down to the columns, is decorated in polished stucco, which is partly gilded. The furniture, which was actually designed by Rossi and was from the outset intended for this room, 48, 63 is too rich and too luxurious. It seems clumsy and emphasizes the regrettable lack of curtains.

In Italy all houses of a certain standing have painted ceilings. Walls entirely covered with frescoes are frequently found there. Often, as in the unpretentious example which we illustrate, painted decoration extends over a certain part of the wall. Therefore, in former times, there were very many painter-decorators in Italy. Even today there is still 64 an appreciable number of these artists. They have always been in demand and have worked in every European country. Naturally, there are also excellent painter-decorators in France. They use oils, working in a detailed and careful fashion, whereas the Italians, who are used to fresco painting, are more spontaneous and lively.

Several craftsmen specializing in stucco should be mentioned. The works of the charming Carlo Bevilacqua can be seen in Venice. Stefano Tofanelli painted some witty grotesques in the Villa Mansi at Segromigno near Lucca.

Two artists with wide ranging talents were Giuseppe Borsato, who was an architect as well as a painter-decorator, and the famous Felice Giani, an excellent fresco painter, illustrator and artist, who worked in France as well as Italy. Then there were Salvatore Giusti, who decorated the ballroom in the palace at Capodimonte, and two Italians working in Russia: Giovanni Scotti, who repainted most of the ceilings in Pavlovsk after the fire of 1803, and Barnaba Medici, who often worked with Carlo Rossi.

These last two artists were responsible for the decoration of the Elagin Palace, which is characterized by one of the most common decorative motifs of this period: young women floating weightlessly either in the middle of wall panels[2], doors[3] or even on a ceiling as at Govone in Piedmont. Here these young women symbolize the Hours, and in an attempt to lend them greater stability the painter has provided them with a spear to stand on. Elsewhere they are shown standing on a terrace, as in Bevilacqua's decoration of the Villa Pisani at Stra, on a cloud, as in the Malachite Room of the Winter Palace in St. Petersburg. All these variations cannot hide their origins. These figures are all based on the dancers on a black ground depicted in the frescoes from Pompeii in the Naples Museum. It is a curious fact that these dancers were reproduced many times whilst other paintings from Pompeii did not enjoy the same success. The relentlessly logical outlook of our ancestors prevented them from appreciating fantastic architecture and landscapes, and Percier and Dugourc dared only to borrow a few small columns and birds from the more fantastic frescoes. Arabesques alone, which had been known since the sixteenth century, seemed a safe subject.[4]

Neoclassicism and eclecticism

There are hardly any noticeable differences in style between the rooms that we have already looked at, from the earliest (Pls. 51, 52) to the more recent (Pls. 61, 67). Stylistic differences do exist, but they are subtle and even contemporaries could not always distinguish them. For example, Empire furniture was still fashionable under Louis-Philippe. Queen Marie-Amélie, whose portrait by Hersent is at Versailles, chose to be painted in an Empire-style armchair by Jacob. Louis-Philippe gave his daughter Louise-Marie Empire furniture when she married the king of Belgium in 1832.

The Malachite Room in the Winter Palace, St. Petersburg, built by the architect Alexander Briullov (1798–1877) is an example of the continuity of the neoclassical style. It remained consistent right up to its disappearance, which was imminent at the time when the Malachite Room was built in 1840. Architects of the day considered it a point of honor to be able to work in several styles. Briullov built a large dining room in Doric style, a small one in Pompeiian style, a Gothic salon and a bathroom in Moorish style, all in the Winter Palace.

At the same time in France Eugène Lami was working on a project to furnish the Duke of Nemours's appartment at the Tuileries in Louis XV style, while the Inspector of Royal Furniture (Mobilier royal) who was in charge of the château at Pau ordered or bought furniture which he believed to be in Renaissance style.

Neoclassical decoration did not disappear all of a sudden but was gradually modified by the unscrupulous addition of furniture and objects in all manner of styles, which led to the comfort-loving disorder that characterized the well-to-do in the second half of the nineteenth century. The first signs of this degeneration may be seen well before 1850. Its spread can be followed, for example, by studying the way pictures were arranged in apartments.

Large houses had long since had picture galleries. These were still to be found at the beginning of the nineteenth century, but as the taste for painting spread, everyone wanted to have pictures. Gradually they invaded all the available space, and in so doing ran the risk of attenuating, if not ruining, the fine order that had once reigned in architect-decorated apartments. At the beginning, no doubt, it was just a matter of adapting this order to novel circumstances with as little fuss as possible. For instance, Queen Hortense, when exiled to Augsburg, filled her drawing room with all the great paintings she was so fond of. In Naples there was a palace[5] of which the decorative scheme, borrowed from Percier, reproduced the false draperies, held up by false piques, such as could be seen in Citizen C...'s Parisian home; and although this scheme did not need anything to complement it, in Naples it was overladen with twenty or so little pictures or miniature portraits, hung very close together without regard for the disposition of the wall hangings. The original scheme was complete in itself and the equilibrium of the decor was even further destroyed in the Naples house by a secretaire piled with bibelots placed against the wall.

The library at Petworth House, as painted by Turner in 1828, had walls covered with pictures wherever there are no bookcases. The pictures were hung in the darkest corners, and even on the piers of the huge arch which separates two parts of the room.

It is hard to escape the impression that we are concerned here not with a question of necessity, but with one of taste —that is, a taste for well-filled space. There is a great deal of furniture in this room which is so disposed as to leave only a few passageways.

The next stage was marked by a taste for "artistic disorder." This is a misnomer, since artists were by no means the originators of this style, which could be better seen in the apartments belonging to collectors such as Alexandre du Sommerard, who gathered together a miscellany of old objects. Tired of constant rigorous symmetry, people tried to alleviate it by taking liberties, as one can see by studying a watercolor completed by Delacroix in 1832. It shows the Comte de Mornay's room as it appeared after the return of Mornay and Delacroix from a trip to North Africa. The asymmetrical positioning of the pictures and the rather haphazard placing of the whatnot (étagère) between the chest of drawers (commode) and the bookcase are hardly noticeable against the blue and white striped wall hanging and do little to disturb the classical arrangement of the room. A blackened urn, which could be antique, a large blue vase and some books, are placed as if by chance on various pieces of furniture, while a saddle and some oriental armor brought back from the expedition have been arranged as trophies. A leopardskin stretched out on the carpet foreshadows a fashion which was to last until the end of the century. It is difficult to know whether to compliment Delacroix or the Comte de Mornay on the happy contrast of colors which makes this room so attractive.

The artist A. Kalb has depicted Nicholas I's study at the time of his death in 1855 in a drawing which he himself engraved (see Plate on p. 71). This study is a small and intimate room on the third and topmost floor of the Winter Palace. The emperor was in the habit of retiring to this room to work alone, away from unwelcome visitors. It seems likely that he spent many hours here. He died in this room on the folding bed which can be seen in the foreground. We do not know whether the bed was kept in the room to allow the emperor to sleep there after working, as Napoleon did, but this is of little importance, since the presence or absence of the bed does not alter the character of the room. It is spartan, sentimental and bourgeois. The simple and somewhat improvised appearance was evidently intentional, and might even be called affected. Both the man and the times in which he lived were permeated by sentimentality and bourgeois values. Like all his contemporaries, Nicholas I surrounded himself with portraits of his family. His son and heir, the future Alexander II, was in the place of honor to the right of the window. The other portraits are extremely small, and are almost miniatures. They are grouped together in exactly the same way as photographs soon would be, and were within range of the person seated at the desk. The emperor was also surrounded by pictures of landscapes or battles. These were hung at random without any regard for esthetic arrangement. Of the three chairs shown, two are vaguely Gothic, of a type which was fashionable around 1800. The other chairs are of more recent date and do not match each other. They have nothing in common with each other except that they are all covered with leather. Finally, the emperor paid no attention to the architecture of the room; this long narrow vaulted room would have made a fine monk's cell. However, the walls are covered with a vulgar flower-patterned paper and the window has been draped with an ugly festooned curtain. All this is typical of the mid-nineteenth century. Men were capable of reading and thinking but no longer of looking around them. It is hard to see how the emperor could contemplate without a shiver the large bronze bust perched on the pendulum clock which is squashed between two pictures.

Arrangement of furniture

We have already referred twice to the arrangement of furniture within a room. During the eighteenth century it was placed along the walls so as to leave the center of the room completely free. However, this layout was doubtless not always practicable. It is evident from inventories that in many cases the number of seats was too great to allow them all to be arranged against the wall. Yet this system remained the rule and in drawings or watercolors seats are often shown in serried ranks along the walls. In dining rooms, for example, the table is shown in the middle of the room while the chairs are ranged around the periphery. In drawing rooms one occasionally even sees two parallel ranks of chairs running along a wall.

It goes without saying that these arrangements

represented the position of the furniture when it had been tidied away. During the day tables and light chairs were moved according to need, while larger chairs were always left in the same place. The first stimulus towards change in room organization may have come about through a desire to find a comfortable corner by the fire. Instead of disposing sofas and daybeds along the wall on either side of the chimney, as was done in the gallery built by Sir John Leicester or in the Duchess of Berry's room in the Tuileries,[6] they were placed at right angles to the wall so as to allow those seated to see the fire and enjoy its heat. This type of arrangement, which was to become the norm, can be found in England in rooms dating from the early years of the nineteenth century. It is also found in France where Empire *pommiers* (couches) are often arranged in this way.

Guéridons and round tables dating from the beginning of the nineteenth century were larger and heavier than their predecessors. Because of their form they were generally placed in the center of a room or at least at some distance from the walls. As it was difficult to move them from this position, it was natural for chairs which could not be arranged along the walls to be placed around these tables. Now the center of the room was no longer empty. It could even become crowded, as popular taste began to favor the accumulation within rooms of the most varied pieces of furniture, plants and bibelots.

However, we must remember that such changes took place slowly. The evolution of taste towards what some have called decadence took place only gradually. Around 1850 rooms which were already overcrowded can be found as well as those which still remained relatively unencumbered.

Colors

It is still possible to buy textiles in Empire style, although manufacturers usually limit the range of colors to red, yellow and green, so distorting our image of Empire furnishings. White, blue and even violet, mauve and various shades of brown, red and buff were also in fashion.

The following range of main colors appears in damasks ordered or purchased by the officials in charge of Imperial furnishings: two whites, twelve blues, twelve reds, ten yellows, twenty-four greens, two browns, and two violets. The range of color represented would be different if one took account of other categories of textiles such as velvets, gros de Tours and satins, and it would then include more whites.

We have seen the luxury and refinement shown in the choice of colors for furnishings dating from the beginning of the century. Let us examine several slightly later examples. In Empress Josephine's music room at the Tuileries (1805) there was a moiré hanging in pale yellow with *gris-de-lin* stars which had a wide border brocaded in silver on a ground of *gris-de-lin*. The mahogany chairs were covered with the same moiré.[7]

Queen Caroline of Bavaria's drawing room in the Residenz in Munich (built by Charles-Pierre Puille and Andreas Gärtner between 1799 and 1810) had doors and wood paneling painted in white with carved and gilded moldings and decoration. The furniture was of gilded wood

34

and the seats were covered with blue and gold silk. Over white curtains was another set of curtains in blue and gold. The chimney was of black marble. To complete the furnishings there were eight large bronze candelabras in the form of figures supporting torches and two bronze statues placed in niches. Over the doors were figures painted to simulate bronze on a white ground.

In the emperor's large room *(grand cabinet)* at the Tuileries (dating from 1807–09) the hanging was in a color described as *tabac d'Espagne* (pale brown) with a wide blue and gold border. The door curtains and the seat covers were in the same fabric and the window curtains in *gros de Tours* were gold with the same border. The hanging was replaced in 1809 by Gobelins tapestries which were almost the only tapestries woven in the Empire period, and two years later the gold curtains were replaced by white damask ones. In the Council Chamber in the Royal Palace at Turin (built by Pelagio Palagi, 1835–38) the doors, paneling and furniture were covered with green velvet edged with a Greek key motif in gold. At the château at Pau, which was refurnished about 1840–45, the administration of the royal furniture depository *(Garde-Meuble)* suggested for the first time furnishings in Renaissance style. This style was in fact so little known that the furniture ordered was actually in 445, 447 Louis XIII or even Louis XIV style rather than that of the Renaissance. Antique furniture purchased from dealers or at auctions completed the ensemble. Most of these pieces are either fakes or have been substantially altered. Today Pau merits our attention as a complete and well preserved example of Louis-Philippe style. The consistent use of textiles in Empire style and of old tapestries taken from the collections preserved by the *Garde-Meuble* was justified on grounds of economy. The inventory valuations of these tapestries are surprisingly low. This can be explained by the fact that the tapestries were treated with a certain lack of respect and were cut down when necessary.

In the large dining room, which was known as the dining room with a hundred places *(des cents couverts)*, the beams of the ceiling were left exposed, the doors and paneling were of waxed oak with gilded moldings and the walls were covered with tapestries. The curtains were of green velvet and the chairs were covered with green leather.

The large drawing room had a coffered ceiling in oak and the plaster was painted to imitate wood. Its moldings and reliefs were gilded. The doors and the paneling were of waxed oak with gilded moldings. The walls were covered with tapestries and the seat furniture was of carved oak covered with crimson damask which matched the damask curtains. The king's bedroom had the same tapestries and fabrics as the great drawing room.

In the queen's bedroom the ceiling and wood paneling were of waxed oak. The bed and the seat furniture were of carved and turned oak, whilst the curtains at the windows and around the bed were of white lampas with blue and gray. The highly detailed descriptions in the inventories reveal that a wide variety of colors and color combinations were used. The taste for red (or rather reds, since the words scarlet, orange-red, crimson, Etruscan red, purple-red and purple are also used for different shades) which prevailed during the nineteenth century becomes noticeable after 1830 and above all after 1850. There is a marked difference between the taste of the Louis XVI period and that of the closing years of the eighteenth century or of the first years of the nineteenth. It concerns the intensity of the colors used rather than their range. During the Directory and above all during the Empire periods architects favored bright colors and contrasts.

Decline of neoclassicism, "romantic disorder"

This all too brief review of rooms dating from the first half of the nineteenth century has perhaps not sufficiently emphasized the gradual decadence of the classical style. Decadence is perhaps the wrong word, since many charming objects date from this era; however, a certain decline was manifest since evolution of the style led to its eventual disappearance.

Restrained decoration and rigorous proportions were quickly succeeded by richness of effect, which was sometimes produced merely by abundant decoration. The neoclassical ideal gave way to nostalgia for previous eras, which coexisted strangely with the conviction that progress should affect the arts as much as the sciences.

Around 1840 decorative styles became extremely eclectic and rooms became more and more cluttered. Many contemporaries deplored this tendency, whilst others, such as Balzac, felt at ease among a romantic assemblage of bric-a-brac:

Love would not know where to alight amid work-tables of Chinese carving, where the eye can find thousands of droll little figures wrought in the ivory—the outcome of the toil of two families of Chinese artists; vases of burnt topaz mounted on filigree stands; mosaics that invite to theft; Dutch pictures, such as Schinner now paints again; angels imagined as Steinbock conceives of them (but does not always work them out himself); statuettes executed by geniuses pursued by creditors (the true interpretation of the Arab myths); sublime first sketches by our greatest artists; fronts of carved chests let into the wainscot, and alternating with the inventions of Indian embroidery; gold-coloured curtains draped over the doors from an architrave of black oak wrought with the swarming figures of a hunting scene; chairs and tables worthy of Madame de Pompadour; a Persian carpet, and so forth. And finally, as a crowning touch, all this splendour, seen under a softened light filtering in through lace curtains, looks all the more beautiful. On a marble slab, among some antiques, a lady's whip, with a handle carved by Mademoiselle de Fauveau, shows that the Countess is fond of riding.

Such is a boudoir in 1837...[8]

These criticisms did not prevail, for a love of bric-a-brac survived until the end of the century.

51 Elevation showing one side of a drawing room in a house on the rue du Mont-Blanc, Paris, executed by the architect B....
Plate 88 of *Plans, coupes et élévations des plus belles maisons et des hôtels construits à Paris et dans les environs,* published by Krafft and Ransonnette in 1802.

The description is as follows:

A Mahogany paneling
B Wood panels in yellow wood with inlaid bronze fillets.
C Mahogany door.
D Silver fillets on panels.
E Door panels of yellow wood, gilt bronze ornaments.
F Bronze ornaments on a white ground.

G Cornice and door frames in white stucco with bronzed ornaments.
H White bas-reliefs on pale blue ground.
I Gray-blue stucco ground.
K Colored arabesques on a light blue ground, white surrounds.
L Mahogany window surrounds.
M Dark lilac curtains with gold fringe.
N Yellow marble chimney, gilt bronze ornament.
O Mahogany frame of pier glass, gilt bronze ornament.
P Mirror.
Q Frieze, bronzed ornaments on a white ground.

This drawing room may have been in M. Récamier's house: see Plate 52.

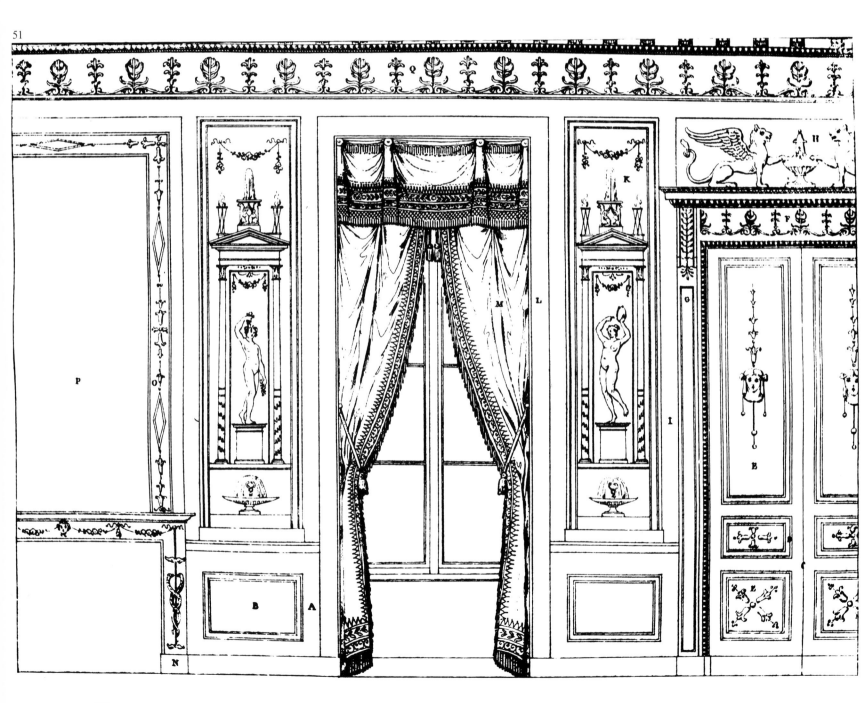

51

52 One of the walls in Madame Récamier's room. Engraving published by Krafft and Ransonette, Plate 91.

In 1798 Monsieur Récamier bought Necker's old Paris town house in the rue de la Chaussée-d'Antin, subsequently rue du Mont-Blanc. The architect Berthault, a pupil and collaborator of Percier and Fontaine, was given the task of refurbishing the Récamiers' new home and of designing the furniture, which was made by the Jacob brothers.

The key given by Krafft was as follows:

A Stylobate of oriental alabaster.
B Mahogany pilaster.
C Arabesques, the capitals gold on a white ground.
D Violet ground.
E Mahogany surrounds.
G Greek fillets and ornaments in silver.

H Yellow wood panels, figures and crowns in silver.
M Violet silk curtain.
M* Violet silk curtain, printed in black with ornamental motifs.
N Buff-colored silk pelmet, printed in black with ornamental motifs.
O Mahogany pedestal with gold ornament.
P White marble figure.
Q Mahogany mirror frame with gold fillets.
R Mirror.
S Mahogany furniture.
T Bronze figure.
U Gold ornament.
V Yellow wood panels with silver figures.
I Marble bas-reliefs.
K&K Frieze and architrave of violet granite with colored ornaments.
L Granite arch with colored ornaments.

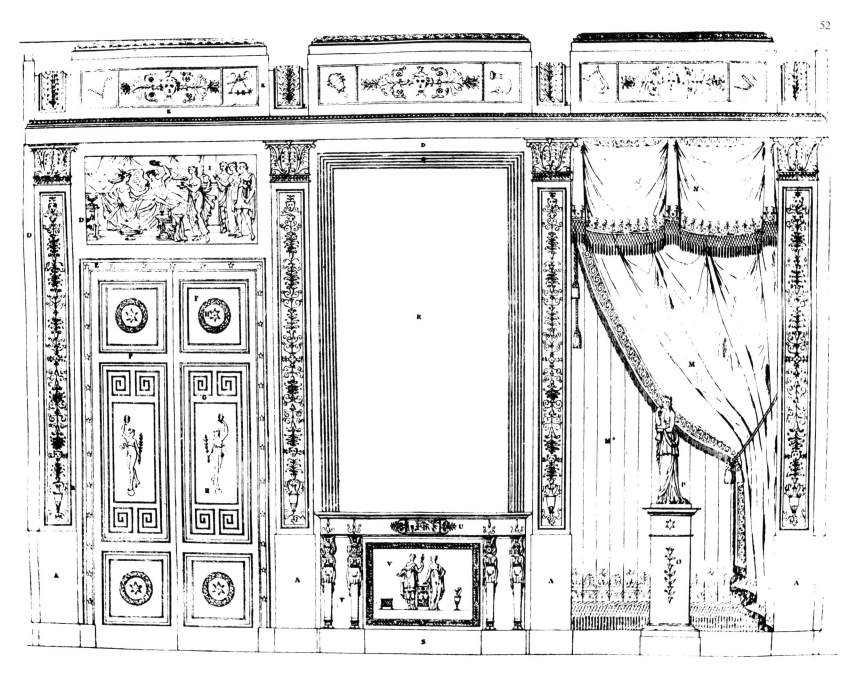

52

53

54

53, 54 Wall decoration of two rooms in the château at Soisy-sous-Etiolles (Essonne), France.
Watercolor drawings in the Musée des arts décoratifs, Paris (D. David-Weill gift).
One of the walls is part of the drawing room, the three others are from one of the bedrooms. The decoration was completed in 1804.

55 Queen Marie-Louise's drawing room in the Casita del Labrador at Aranjuez, Spain.
This pavilion, built and furnished by King Charles IV at Aranjuez under the direction of the architect Isidro Gonzales Velásquez, is a precious surviving example of early nineteenth-century Spanish decorative schemes. Times has altered and softened the colors of the wall hangings, which are of Lyons silk with a design by Jean-Démosthène Dugourc. However, the effects of time are hardly noticeable as the other colors in the room are so lively and fresh. The chandelier, which is of slightly later date, must have been installed by Ferdinand VII (1813–33) and was probably ordered from Paris.

56 Queen Hortense in her boudoir, in the rue Cerutti, 1811. Watercolor by A. Garneray. Olivier Le Fuel Collection, Paris.
Between 1810 and 1814 Queen Hortense, who was separated from her husband, lived in the rue Cerutti, Paris. The fireplace and the furniture either side of the sofa are in Louis XVI style. The *jardinière* beside the window is now at Malmaison (Pl. 119). A large alabaster lantern is suspended from the ceiling. The walls are apparently completely covered with mirrors, partly obscured by the curtains and wall hangings.

Par Percier et Fontaine.

Face latérale d'un petit Salon exécuté à Paris chez le C.C.

57

59 Empress Maria Feodorovna's boudoir at Pavlovsk. ▷
The somewhat unusual porticolike chimney surround was devised by the architect Brenna in order to set off two red porphyry columns brought back from Rome by the heir apparent, the Grand Duke Paul, later Tsar Paul I. The white marble pilasters decorated with arabesques also came from Rome. The vaulted ceiling, repainted by Scotti after the fire of 1803, is decorated with other arabesques and landscapes within cartouches. Brenna's decorative scheme dates from 1792. He is responsible for the subtle harmony of the colors in this room: the whiteness of the stucco and marble is relieved by gilding and several touches of color in the arabesques, landscapes, the red porphyry columns and the vases on the mantlepiece. Parquet flooring such as that in the foreground of our illustration was introduced into Russia by German craftsmen, and can be seen in numerous palaces and country houses.

57 One side of a small Paris drawing room built by Citoyen C.
Engraving from Percier and Fontaine's *Recueil de décorations intérieures,* p. 7.
This decorative scheme was executed in 1799 for François-Bernard de Chauvelin, former French ambassador in London. His house was in the rue Chantereine, close to General Bonaparte's residence.

58 Pilaster Drawing Room at Pavlovsk.
Quarenghi's decorative scheme includes white and yellow stucco, the latter imitating Sienese marble, and bas-reliefs in bronze-colored stucco. The ceiling painted in monochrome gray with touches of bronze is the work of Scotti. We do not know whether the green and white curtains were specified by the architect or not; they harmonize well with the rest of the room. Gambs was responsible for most of the mahogany furniture.

58

59

60

61

◁ 60 The White Drawing Room in the Mikhailovskii Palace (Russian Museum), Leningrad.

◁ 61 Ballroom, Capodimonte Palace, Naples.
▽ Capodimonte Palace, which remained unfinished until Ferdinand II's reign, was completed between 1835 and 1838 under the direction of the architects Giordano and Niccolini. The high, spacious ballroom was decorated by the painter Salvatore Giusti. Most of the furniture dates from the Empire period and the room itself looks older in style than it really is. Only the large chandeliers are typical of the period.

62 Corner of a small Drawing Room in the Elagin Palace, Leningrad.
Decoration by Carlo Rossi and Barnaba Medici. The chimneys (or false chimneys) found in all palaces or great houses in Russia dating from the beginning of the nineteenth century bear witness to Italian and French influence. The usual method of heating was by large wood-burning stoves like those used in Germany and Scandinavia.

63 Group of chairs from the White Drawing Room in the Mikhailovskii Palace (Russian Museum), Leningrad.
The gilt wooden chairs and the table were designed by Carlo Rossi.

64 Drawing room in Ischia. Oil painting (24.5 cm × 31.5 cm) dated 1829.
In the nineteenth century high-ranking Russian families traveled extensively. Several, such as the Wittgenstein and the Trubetskoi families, spent the winter in Italy, and some made albums consisting of views of houses or places where they had lived. This small painting, which was recently on the Paris market, must have been part of a collection of this kind. Some details in this drawing room are typically Italian, such as the ceiling and walls decorated with paintings and the terrazzo floor, made of a composition of chalk and small pieces of marble. Other details confirm the date of the painting. These include the shape of the sofa, the small table and the Argand lamp placed on it, the Carcel lamp and the traveling clock on the other table and its dark colored table carpet with a white design. Table carpets were in fashion only for about twelve years.

62

63

64

65

66

65   The Dancing Hours. Fresco on the ceiling of the drawing room of the country house at Govone, Italy.
The refurbishing of the country house at Govone in Piedmont was begun in 1815 for the duke of Genoa who became King Charles-Felix in 1821 and was completed during his reign.

66   Dancer or bacchante. Fresco from Pompeii. Museo Archeologico Nazionale, Naples.

67   Malachite Room, Winter Palace, St. Petersburg.
Alexander Briullov, the architect who decorated this room in 1840, had passed more than seven years abroad. Between 1821 and 1829 he lived successively in Munich, Rome, Naples, Sicily, Paris and London. He must have known the Malachite Room at the Grand Trianon, as he has copied its color scheme of white, green, red (for the chairs) and gold. The gilded doors and entablatures, which are rather heavy, as well as the overdoors and the mantelpieces are all based on Italian models. However, the architect has combined these elements drawn from differing sources into a coherent, luxurious and original whole. Despite the large candelabra in the foreground, which have an almost medieval appearance, the architecture of the Malachite Room is still classical in style. One detail would have shocked architects of an earlier generation: the columns and pilasters are applied only to the wall and make no pretence of supporting the ceiling.

67

45

68

69

70

68   Sir John Leicester's Picture Gallery.
Sir John Leicester, a famous collector of contemporary English painting, moved to a house in Hill Street, London, in 1806. He immediately built a picture gallery which he opened to the public in 1819, publishing a catalogue of his collection. This view of the gallery is the frontispiece to the catalogue. It is interesting from many points of view, and shows his furniture which seems very modern. In particular, the chandeliers and lampstands, the latter in Louis XIV style, the carpet with its regular pattern which completely covers the floor, the sofas with their rounded ends, and the armchair in the left foreground with its tortuous outline, are all typical of the period. The heavy draped curtains at the entry to the alcove are also typical. Hidden under dust sheets on either side of the alcove are two X-shaped stools.

69   Queen Hortense's drawing room at Augsburg. Wash and sepia drawing. Bibliothèque Thiers, Paris.
"…At eight o'clock in the evening, surrounded by my children, I received the persons whose names were written on my list. Some played the piano, others played billiards. A large table allowed every member of the party to pursue his or her chosen occupation. The ladies worked or engaged in conversation. At ten o'clock tea was taken and very often animated discussions which would have lasted well into the night had to finish at midnight or one o'clock because of the poor health of the mistress of the house."

This passage from Queen Hortense's memoirs refers to her life in Paris between 1810 and 1814 but, to judge from this drawing, her existence was no different in Augsburg, except that members of the family were now more numerous than visitors.

Hortense was exiled in 1815 because of her faithful attachment to Napoleon during the Hundred Days. Her brother, Prince Eugène, who married a Bavarian princess, brought her to Bavaria and settled her in Augsburg where the king of Bavaria had decided she should live. She did not stay there long and bought a small castle at Arenenberg in Switzerland, on the shore of Lake Constance, as soon as she could.

This drawing of her salon is therefore easily dated. It must have been executed in 1817 or shortly afterwards. There are two Carcel lamps in columnar form on the table, which is covered with a velvet carpet edged with a fringe. Suspended from the ceiling is a huge lamp which is almost modern in outline. It is fixed to the ceiling by a counterweight system. The walls are covered with pictures, some of which are too large for the room. These paintings and most of the furniture came from the queen's previous residences, or else from Malmaison. Many of them are still at Arenenberg.

70   Design for the Duke of Nemours's Small Drawing Room in the Tuileries Palace, Paris. Watercolor by Eugène Lami, 1842. Musée des arts décoratifs (D. David-Weill gift), Paris.

71

71   Tsar Nicholas I's Study in the Winter Palace, St. Peters-burg. Lithograph by A. Kalb.

72, 73   Scenes of life at Brathay Hall, Westmorland. Drawings by John Harden. The second is dated 1804.
John Harden, a talented amateur painter, married the daughter of an Edinburgh banker in 1803. In the following year the couple settled at Brathay Hall in Westmorland. In his drawings Harden provided simple images of life in a country house in the north of England with a spontaneity and verisimilitude often absent from work of this kind.

Harden's drawings are a precious record of family life in cultivated middle-class circles. In the morning reading and letter writing took place, in the evening there was reading and sewing by the fire. The drawings also show contemporary furniture and the way it was employed. Stools, which seem to have been used much more than is the case today, can be seen in most of Harden's drawings. This was because of contemporary taste for classical antiquity, as this type of seat was commonly used by the Ancients. Small tables were placed around the room as needed, but the sofa, which is covered with a dust sheet, always stayed in the same spot by the fire.[9]

74   Audience Chamber, Schloss Ehrenburg, Coburg.
The Duke of Saxe-Coburg was able, with the reparations paid out by France, to rebuild or refurbish several of his residences. The fine classical architecture of this audience chamber does not really harmonize with the eighteenth-century French tapestry (one of the Gobelins factory's versions of the *Nouvelles Indes* series) or the Viennese Biedermeier furniture. The sofa and the two armchairs on either side of it must date from 1816 or 1817. The table and chairs seem to be of slightly later date.

△ 72

73   74

75   The Red Library, Petworth, Sussex, home of Lord Egremont.
Watercolor by J.M.W. Turner, 1828. British Museum, London.

76   Comte de Mornay's Room. Watercolor by Eugène Delacroix,
1832. Musée du Louvre, Paris.

III Neoclassical Furniture

Most types of furniture that we use today go back beyond the beginning of the nineteenth century. The only new pieces devised in the nineteenth century seem to be a few tables and a variety of large upholstered chairs. But although the types remain the same, there were changes in the shapes and even at times in the use to which these pieces were put. In order to follow the evolution of furniture in the nineteenth century we shall examine each category of piece separately.

Tables

Dining tables

From the eighteenth century onward in England dining tables were made of solid mahogany. Their legs were straight, tapering at the base, and were rectangular in section. Circular tables were also made. These were supported by a central pedestal which in turn rested on three or four feet shod with casters. A modification was introduced to dining tables when they were given two supports in this form, resulting in a most practical table, since the position of the legs left guests plenty of room. It was both light and elegant in appearance. Moreover it could easily be divided in two, as each part remained stable on its respective support. In addition one or more leaves could be
77 added at the center, allowing the table to be lengthened as necessary while maintaining its equilibrium and stability.

Most English dining tables from the Regency period (1810–25) were made in this way, but the earliest examples date from the 1790s. Sheraton designed a table of this type
31 for the Prince of Wales's dining room.

The ends of these tables could be rounded or squared off. At a later date they were squared off with rounded corners.

As communications between France and England were virtually nonexistent from 1792 until the end of the Empire period, this type of table was not copied by French craftsmen. A different kind of table evolved in France, which was, however, closely related to English tables made at the end of the eighteenth century. An example by Jacob-
78 Desmalter now at Fontainebleau is reproduced here. Circular tables such as this, with turned legs and flaps which could be folded away, were eminently suited to small or medium-sized dining rooms. A vast number of these tables were made in France. They were already being made (with fluted legs) at the end of Louis XVI's reign and continued

to be manufactured throughout most of the nineteenth century. The shape of the legs gradually became simpler and heavier in outline. Large fluted legs again became fashionable, but the method of construction and the general appearance remained the same.

In France, as in England, there was a need for tables which could be extended, reduced in size or even folded. Most houses did not yet have a room specifically intended as a dining room. Even in Imperial residences dining rooms also served as ballrooms or had other uses. Tables had to be collapsible and easily stored. Those of small or medium size could, as we have seen, be stored against a wall with one or both leaves folded—an arrangement which can be seen in a painting by Drolling exhibited at the Salon of 1816. A man is shown eating breakfast in a modest middle-class dining room. The table beside him is partly folded and pushed back against the wall. This was apparently the usual position of the table when it was not in use, so that the rest of the room, which appears to be less than four meters long, was left unencumbered.[1]

Just before or perhaps during the Revolution, large oval pieces were made which were perhaps the finest of all French dining tables. They could have up to ten legs, some of which could be folded beneath the table if necessary; the top also folded in two. When folded, the table was pushed against the wall so that it looked like a semicircular console table. In the empress's dining room at Compiègne there is a table of this type. It is rather heavy in appearance as it rests on large legs of square section, each terminating in a lion's paw.

The table in the other dining room, which was used by the emperor, is one of the most remarkable ever produced by Jacob-Desmalter, who also made the one we have just 79 mentioned. It is a long table with rounded ends which is formed of six separate parts. Each of these rests on two folding legs shod with castors similar to those used by several eighteenth-century cabinetmakers, including Cana-bas. Although the legs took up more space than the central leg of an English table, they could be completely folded away and the table itself could be stored in a corridor. It was ingenious, simple and attractive and it is surprising that it has never been copied. The lyre-back chairs in this dining room, which are of the same form as those in the music 459 room at the Tuileries, and the severely proportioned console tables form, together with the dining table, one of the finest ensembles of Empire furniture. Although manufactured in 1811, the pieces retain something of the extreme austerity of form characteristic of the finest neoclassical furniture of the revolutionary period.

The tables we have discussed up to now have all been of mahogany or veneered in mahogany. This was exceptional in France, and on the rest of the Continent too. Even Napoleon's and Josephine's house in the rue de la Victoire[2], which was elegantly furnished at great expense, there was a walnut dining table:

> For Citizen Buonaparte, rue de la Victoire ... a solid walnut dining table, circular with a folding leaf at each side, measuring 5 feet 6 inches in diameter, wax polished; valued with its metal fittings (3) at 120 *livres*.[3]
> (18 frimaire an VI – December 8, 1797)

Even though mahogany was an extremely expensive wood in France, this cannot have been the determining factor, which perhaps had more to do with local customs in that country. All over Europe, except in Britain, there was a long-established habit of covering the table with a cloth, and often with a table carpet as well, between meals. There seemed little point, therefore, in having a mahogany table if it were always covered.

Although mahogany was mainly used, along with walnut and cherry, numerous deal tables were made as well. These were usually mounted in oak for solidity. The large table at the château at Pau called the "table with one hundred places" is an example of this type. It is so large that successive curators of the château have never been able to afford to provide and care for a table carpet in keeping with the decor of the room.

Neither carpenters nor cabinetmakers—nor their clientele—were particularly interested in dining-room tables. Significantly, Hepplewhite and Sheraton did not illustrate a single example. Furniture makers showed far more interest in making smaller decorative tables which were almost always left uncovered. These included *guéridons* (or candlestands), tea tables, console or side tables, games tables and various other types of small table.

Guéridons

Originally the word *guéridon* was used for a tray with rounded ends either on a single foot or on a more complicated support which was surmounted by a candelabrum or other light fitting. *Guéridons* of this kind were still being made at the end of the eighteenth century. At Ostankino, near Moscow, there are *guéridons* based on antique tripods 80 and Hepplewhite's Drawing Book contains designs for candlestands. However, in France the word *guéridon* had by this time taken on a wider meaning. Today it is used to describe a circular or polygonal table about one meter in diameter. During the Empire period circular tables of this size with a marble top were called tea tables or dining tables, 81, 82 while smaller ones or those without marble tops were known as *guéridons*. Terminology was constantly changing. In 1811 Jacob-Desmalter delivered to the Hamlet at the Trianon "two tea tables of *guéridon* form." To simplify 89 matters, we shall use only the word *guéridon*.

The *guéridon,* taking the term in its widest sense, is one of the most characteristic furniture types of the first half of the nineteenth century. No drawing room was without at least one. As time went on these tables became larger and

after 1830 are more correctly called circular tables on 83, 84 account of their considerable dimensions. The so-called "family" tables at the Trianon, which were delivered in 1837, are 1.62 meters in diameter. Queen Hortense maintains in her memoirs that she was the first to introduce into the drawing room "a circular table at which one could do needlework or otherwise occupy oneself in the evenings as they do in the country." If this is true, her idea was quickly copied. During Louis-Philippe's reign families usually sat together in the evenings around a large table. The king himself set an example by having a family drawing room in each of his residences where there were round tables with numerous drawers. The young princesses, their mother and their aunt kept their needlework and books in these drawers.

From the beginning of the nineteenth century in England library and drawing room tables were made with several drawers fitted below the table top. The upper part of the table was now of flattened drum form. The single baluster-shaped leg now increased in size and became polygonal. The triangular support characteristic of Empire-period *guéridons* was replaced by separate legs of X shape, reminiscent of the legs of certain eighteenth-century tables. 64

This extremely brief summary may not cover every specific instance, since there was a great variety of forms. Several *guéridons* chosen from different European countries 85–98 will be described in detail. It is often, but not invariably, possible to recognize the country of origin at first glance. During the First Empire only outlying countries such as England and Austria kept their own special shapes for candlestands. In the following period, that is from 1815 to 1830 or 1835, all countries showed a tendency towards isolationism and began to exhibit the nationalistic tendencies which were to mark the century as a whole. Between 1830 and 1850 international communication became far easier, and books and styles were diffused more rapidly. This process, which brought countries closer, probably took place unnoticed by the majority of the population.

The usual place for a *guéridon* or circular table was in the center of a room. It is sometimes seen in a different position, such as in front of a sofa, where it soon became almost a fixture. One of those at the table could then sit on the sofa, while the others were on chairs. The shape of the table was altered so as to make better use of the sofa, either by changing the form of the top, which became oval or elongated, or by replacing the table itself with one of an entirely different shape. The latter solution was adopted in 99 England from the early years of the century. The English sofa table is rectangular and frequently has folding flaps at either end. The legs, shod with castors and often joined by a crosspiece, are arranged in pairs parallel to the shorter sides of the rectangle. There are usually two drawers side by 100, 101 side below the top. Tables of this kind were very popular in Britain and also enjoyed great success on the Continent where they were copied after 1815. In or about 1816 the Viennese cabinetmaker Friedrich Hasselbrink delivered a table of this type to the Duke of Saxe-Coburg.[4] Unlike the low tables which we use in front of sofas, early nineteenth-century sofa tables measured 72 to 75 centimeters in height. They could therefore be moved and were versatile, many of them being put to use as writing tables.

Consoles

We frequently forget that the French word *console* was originally *table en console*. In England and Germany the original sense was preserved in the terms pier table, side table, or in German *Konsoltisch*. From the beginning of the nineteenth century side tables in fact had four feet, one side being designed to rest against a wall. Their usefulness was 102 limited, except in dining rooms where they could be used as dessert tables.[5] Vases, sculpture, clocks or candelabra could also be placed on these tables, although they were equally at home on commodes.

Yet in the early nineteenth century the side table retained the popularity it had won in the previous century. It found a place wherever there was a free space —between windows, opposite a chimney, in galleries and halls, and of course in dining rooms.

Whether made in the Italian, English or French style, 103 these side tables are attractive. By the final years of the eighteenth century most were free of the rich carved decoration that had distinguished their predecessors. They could now be appreciated for their shape, proportions, or marble top—or occasionally even for their discreetly painted decoration. Their sobriety was to their advantage rather than their detriment, and gave them a severe elegance which was then associated with the Antique, but was in fact characteristic of the late eighteenth century. Many side tables 104–108 made during the First Empire continued to enshrine the idea of sobriety and simplicity, whilst other tables were distinguished by their richness and elaborate decorative effects.

After 1815 side tables seem to have been less frequently used, perhaps because of their impracticality. They were replaced by commodes (or chests of drawers), sideboards, movable tables or elegant whatnots *(étagères)*. Console tables made after the First Empire took on a form which corresponded better with their name. The previous caryatid or columnar supports were replaced by consoles on which the tray rested. It was only when the baroque style began to enjoy renewed popularity that the console table experienced a revival.

Small tables

It would be difficult to list each category of small table. Their number increased from the eighteenth century onwards, but fluctuated along with the names and functions allocated to these pieces. The most common were games tables and work tables, made in many different shapes and 109–113 sizes. Writing tables, together with small tables for general 114 use, were also popular. One example is the Pembroke table first made in England in the eighteenth century and found later on the Continent. It was known in France as a *table à volets*.

At the beginning of the nineteenth century, drawing rooms or salons played a leading role in society life, which was as vigorous as ever. Upper class women entertained almost every evening. Their relatives, friends or acquaint-

ances usually attended several salons, going from one to the next without any advance warning, except for the announcement of their arrival by the footman or some other servant. Queen Hortense's drawing room in Augsburg (see Pl. 69) gives us a finely drawn picture of one of these evening parties where guests conversed, played music, did needlework, and read or played cards before tea was served. As they were indispensable items of drawing room furniture, it is worth mentioning the small tables, especially the games tables which could often be converted to other uses. Bills and inventories provide information about them. For example at the Grand Trianon during the First Empire a large number of different tables were used in the various drawing rooms:

Mirror Drawing Room:
1 tea table
1 occasional table *(table vide-poches)*   110
1 work table
1 reading table
1 drawing table
1 tric-trac table
1 piquet table
Chapel Drawing Room:
1 circular marquetry table (1.43 m in diameter)
1 quadrille table
2 reversis tables[6]
The Emperor's Family Drawing Room:
1 tea table (1.26 m in diameter)
2 piquet tables
2 bouillote tables
2 tric-trac tables.

Three rather rare games tables by Biennais survive in the 115–118 château at Pau, which we have chosen to reproduce here.

Jardinières

Jardinières or plant stands were also known in France as *tables à fleurs*. We shall therefore class them as tables. Indoor flowers and plants were common in the nineteenth century, especially after the Restoration in France (1814). Some rooms almost resemble conservatories with their skillful grouping of plants near the windows. From the First Empire onwards plant stands were in frequent use. Percier and Fontaine, succeeded by La Mésangère, designed some highly idiosyncratic models in the form of *guéridons* with two or more stages incorporating birdcages and even goldfish ponds. At least two of these structures have survived. One is at Naples in Capodimonte Palace, the other at Arkhangelskoe near Moscow, where it remains in its original position in the center of a small drawing room which is itself at the end of a series of interconnecting rooms. These two strange plant stands date from around 1820. We have chosen not to illustrate one of these curiosities, but rather two fine Empire plant stands. The 119 first belonged to Queen Hortense; originally in the bedroom of her house in the rue Cerutti, it is now at Malmaison. The 120 other, which is very similar, is in the castle at Homburg (Hesse), West Germany.

77

78

54

77 Mahogany dining room table. Rectangular top placed on three central legs shod with castors. England, early nineteenth century. Sold at Christie's, London, June 25, 1981.

78 Mahogany drawing room table. Musée national du château de Fontainebleau.
Stamped by Jacob-Desmalter, this circular table with turned legs and flaps is a very common model in France.

79 Table in the Emperor's Dining Room. Musée national du château de Compiègne.
This large mahogany table, which can be dismantled, is stamped by Jacob-Desmalter. It was delivered in 1811.

80 Candlestand. Engraving in Hepplewhite's *Cabinet-Maker and Upholsterer's Guide,* Plate 110, dated July 2, 1787.

81 Mahogany *guéridon*. White marble top, edged with mahogany. Gilt bronze ornaments. By Jacob-Desmalter, 1809. The Empress Josephine's study, Musée national du château de Fontainebleau.
If the date of this table were not known, it would be tempting to think it was older than it really is. The lightness of its construction and the fluted legs are reminiscent of Directory furniture.

82 *Guéridon*. Cherrywood and black-stained wood. Private Collection, Bremen.
The use of black-stained wood in contrast with slightly orange-toned cherry is common in Germany. Except for this detail it would be difficult to recognize this as a German piece, since it is so similar to contemporary French *guéridons*. The triangular socle on castors reminds one of several *guéridons* by Jacob.

83 Mahogany table with light wood inlays. Royal Palace, Brussels.
This table, still called the "family table," belonged to Louise-Marie, the eldest daughter of King Louis-Philippe of France. She became queen of Belgium in 1832. It was probably made by Alexandre Bellangé and exhibited at the Products of Industry Exhibition held in Paris in 1834. The exhibition report states that one of the large drawing room tables by this cabinetmaker was purchased on the king's orders and presented to the queen of Belgium.

81

82

83

56

84   Detail of table in Plate 83.

85

86

85   *Guéridon*. Thuya wood, patinated bronze and gilt bronze. Top mounted with a Sèvres blue-ground biscuit porcelain plaque under glass. Musée du Louvre, Paris.
This *guéridon* was formerly at the Palace of Saint-Cloud, refurnished at the beginning of the nineteenth century for the First Consul. A second *guéridon* of the same type is in the Royal Palace, Brussels.

86   *Guéridon*. Thuya wood, patinated bronze and gilt bronze. Victoria and Albert Museum, London.
This table also comes from the Palace of Saint-Cloud. It is very close to two other contemporary *guéridons,* one of which is now at Malmaison, the other at the Grand Trianon. The latter was the work of Jacob-Desmalter after a drawing by Percier, which has survived. It is likely that Percier also designed this *guéridon*— the most attractive of the three, due to the high quality of the bronze winged lions.

87   Thuya wood and gilt bronze *guéridon* mounted with Sèvres ▷ porcelain plaques. Musée national du château de Fontainebleau. The few *guéridons* manufactured at the Sèvres factory during the Empire period are amongst the most luxurious and well-made pieces produced in porcelain.
   This "Seasons Table" has simple lines and perfect proportions. It is one of the most attractive of these *guéridon* tables, although it shares their common defect: the rather overelaborate appearance of the top, which is decorated with several small scenes and too many diverse ornamental motifs.

74581

88   Design for the *guéridon* in Plate 90. Illustration from Hope's *Household Furniture and Interior Decoration*, 1807.

89   Gilt wood *guéridon*, partly painted white; white marble top. Musée national du château de Versailles, Grand Trianon.
This table, which was delivered in 1811, was placed in the master drawing room in the hamlet at Trianon. It is described as follows in Jacob-Desmalter's invoice: "A tea table of *guéridon* form, 30 inches in diameter, carved triangular pedestal, arched triform foot below, finished, gilded and painted, white marble top." The *guéridon* made in 1809 (see Plate 81) already had a socle of the same form.

90   Mahogany *guéridon* inlaid with ebony and silver. Victoria and Albert Museum, London.
Executed after drawings by Thomas Hope published in his *Household Furniture and Interior Decoration*, 1807, this table is shown in a watercolor of Hope's residence at Deepdene, Surrey, in the album *Illustrations of the Deepdene* (1825–26) now in the Minet Library, Brixton. The ebony and silver inlays recall the

ebony and pewter inlays found on furniture by the Jacob brothers (1796–1803) and by Levasseur (see Plate 108).

91   Ebony *guéridon*, inlaid with copper. Gilt bronze ornaments; Italian marble mosaic top. Victoria and Albert Museum, London. The table is attributed to George Bullock, one of the leading cabinetmakers of his time, who died in 1818. Technically perfect, this table is already heavier in appearance than contemporary French and German pieces.

92   Circular table with central leg, of coromandel wood and gilt bronze. The top is decorated with an engraving after Thomas Stothard under glass. England, about 1820. Victoria and Albert Museum, London.
We often feel that the United States is ahead of Europe by several years in both good and bad ways. The same was true of England in relation to the rest of Europe at the beginning of the nineteenth century. It was in England that the elegance and lightness characteristic of the late eighteenth century first gave way to the overloaded and bastardized styles typical of the greater part of the nineteenth century. This table is an early example of this tendency.

92

93

94

93 Table from the White Room in the Mikhailovskii Palace. Gilt wood, white marble top, about 1822. Russian Museum, Leningrad.
Like all the tables in the Mikhailovskii Palace, this was designed by Carlo Rossi. The rather slipshod workmanship accentuates the impression of overelaboration found in this architect's designs, most of which survive.

94 Lemonwood *guéridon* with silver ornaments. Residenz, Würzburg.
Designed by the French architect Nicolas Salins de Montfort, and beautifully made by a Frankfurt cabinetmaker named Johann Valentin Raab, this luxurious table is most attractive. It can be dated between 1807 and 1809.

95 Mahogany and gilt bronze *guéridon*. Palace of the Princes of Thurn and Taxis, Regensburg.
The fluted edge of the table and its base seem to show English influence, but this is not confirmed by the general form of the table or its decorative details. The table was probably made in Bavaria about 1820.

96 Carved walnut table with walnut veneer. Top decorated with a porcelain plaque. Victoria and Albert Museum, London.
This table, which was exhibited at the 1851 Universal Exhibition, is the work of the Bath cabinetmaker Henry Eyles. It is completely baroque in spirit but is linked to the classical tradition by its decorative motifs. The swirling form of the top is indicative of the piece's late date.

95

96

98

97

99

97, 98 Two black lacquer *guéridons* decorated with Chinese scenes. Musée national du château de Versailles, Louis-Philippe's Great Drawing Room in the Trianon.

Jean-François Goudel, who supplied these *guéridon* tables in 1839, called himself an "artist in Chinese, Indian, English and French lacquer." The fashion in France for black lacquer furniture during the Second Empire began much earlier. Many "Napoleon III" pieces in fact date from Louis-Philippe's reign. The Great Drawing Room, created in 1838 in place of two smaller drawing rooms, was furnished in a mixture of styles typical of the period. The hangings are of yellow cannetillé, figured in blue with an Empire-style design. There are two large sofas in the new style covered in the same fabric. The Empire chairs and armchairs have yellow and blue cannetillé covers with a different design. There are two console tables, two large tables and two *guéridons* in black lacquer.

Despite their oriental decoration, these tables are typically Louis-Philippe in style. Note especially the form of the legs and the rather complicated shape of the turned support.

99 Oval table of mahogany veneer, gilt wood and gilt bronze. Armfelt Museum, Helsinki.

This table, which is probably Swedish, was formerly in the manor of Joensuu (Åminne in Swedish) at Haliko.

100 Rosewood sofa table decorated with pale wood fillets, shod with castors. England, Regency period. Sold at Christie's, London, June 28, 1979.

100

101

101 Mahogany sofa table; top decorated with Chinese subjects in reserve. H. 71 cm, W. 196 cm. Victoria and Albert Museum, London.
Of English origin, tables of this shape, with or without flaps at either end, were imitated on the Continent after 1815. This example is interesting as it can be dated from the pen-and-ink drawing which covers the top and is signed *Henzell Gouch, 1815*.

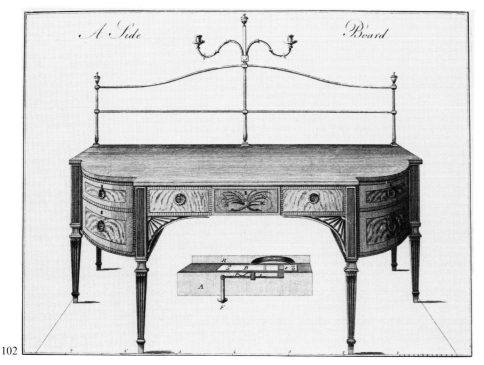

102

103

104

102 Sideboard. Plate 26 in Thomas Sheraton's *The Cabinet-Maker and Upholsterer's Drawing-Book,* engraving dated October 29, 1792.

103 Painted top of a gilt wooden console table stamped G.I.V.R. Victoria and Albert Museum, London.
This console table came from Carlton House, the Prince of Wales's residence which was decorated by the architect Henry Holland at the end of the eighteenth century. Painted furniture was far more common in England than in France at the beginning of the nineteenth century. The central motif on the table top reproduces a well-known fresco by Guido Reni called "Aurora."

104 Mahogany console table, delivered on July 25, 1805 for the Interior Drawing Room (now called the Salon des Glaces) in the Grand Trianon. Musée national du château de Versailles, Grand Trianon.
This table was described by Jacob-Desmalter as follows: "A mahogany console table measuring 4 feet 3 inches, the front legs [formed as] pilasters surmounted by Egyptian heads of gilt bronze; apron decorated with rosettes and palmettes and the base of the pilasters with gilt bronze moldings; lower part mounted with mirror fitted into the veneer; blue-gray marble top...."

105 Mahogany and gilt bronze console ▷ table; Belgian black marble top. Musée national du château de Pau.
Black marble was one of the most commonly used tops for furniture of medium quality in the Empire period. The Egyptian caryatid heads are of black-stained wood, partly gilt.

106

108

107

109

106 Black-stained wood console table; capitals and other ornamental motifs of carved gilded wood. Schloss Ehrenburg, Coburg.
This piece is as sober and well made as a French Empire-period console table by a good cabinetmaker, and is distinguished from its French counterparts only by the use of black-stained wood, the lack of a marble top and the use of wood rather than gilt bronze for the ornamental motifs. It was delivered by the Viennese cabinetmaker Friedrich Hasselbrink in 1816 along with ninety-five other pieces, including chairs.

107 Detail of a mahogany console table inlaid with ebony. Victoria and Albert Museum, London.
Most French furniture inlaid with ebony, pewter and copper dates from the late eighteenth and early nineteenth centuries. The fashion for this kind of decoration also flourished in England, too, as can be seen from the caryatids and inlays on this table.

108 Mahogany table inlaid with pewter and ebony, mounted with Sèvres porcelain plaques and gilt bronze. Bayerisches Nationalmuseum, Munich.
Although this piece is built like a console table, it is not one, since it was designed for the center of a room. This is evident from the fact that each side is decorated. The porcelain comport fixed to the socle is inscribed "Given by His Majesty the Emperor and King [Napoleon] to His Royal Highness the Prince of Bavaria on the occasion of the marriage of the Princess Stéphanie Napoléon to the Prince of Baden."
The wedding took place in 1806. The prince of Bavaria can only be the heir apparent, later King Ludwig I, after whose death in

1868 the table became part of the Museum collections.
The table is not stamped. It is usually attributed to the Jacobs, who made numerous pieces of furniture inlaid with ebony and pewter. M. J. Bourne showed recently that it must in fact have been made by Pierre-Etienne Levasseur (see *Connoisseur*, No. 778, 1976, pp. 296–99). Levasseur was responsible for a secretaire and chest of drawers made for Godoy, the Spanish prime minister. The marquetry decoration and other elements found on these pieces recur on the table illustrated.

109 French work table. Pl. LIV, dated November 5, 1792, from Thomas Sheraton's *Drawing Book*.
The engraving is entitled "A Lady's Work Table," but the author states in the text that it is of French workmanship. The table is similar to the small tables called *tricoteuses* made at the end of Louis XVI's reign. There was a *tricoteuse* in Marie-Antoinette's boudoir at Fontainebleau.

110 Mahogany occasional table *(table vide-poche)* crosspiece in baluster form, legs and tops of legs in gilt bronze. Musée national du château de Versailles, Grand Trianon.
Delivered on August 21, 1810 by Jacob-Desmalter for the Games Room (*Salon des glaces*) in the Empress Marie-Louise's apartments. The X-shaped legs, bold outlines and sober decoration of this table are typical of small tables from this workshop.

111 Swedish worktable. Porvoo Museum, Finland.
J. P. Berg of Stockholm, whose label is stuck onto this table, was active as a cabinetmaker between 1803 and 1816. The delicacy of the legs, which are turned at the end, is an unusual feature.

110 111

112 J. P. Berg's label on the table in Plate 111.

113 Mahogany worktable. Victoria and Albert Museum, London.
This table, which is said to be American and to date from about 1850, could well be a French piece made during Louis-Philippe's reign. Spiral turning or bobbin turning, as in the barley sugar legs and stretcher on this table, were highly fashionable at this time. Both these parts of the table are based on seventeenth-century furniture but the legs are neo-classical in style.

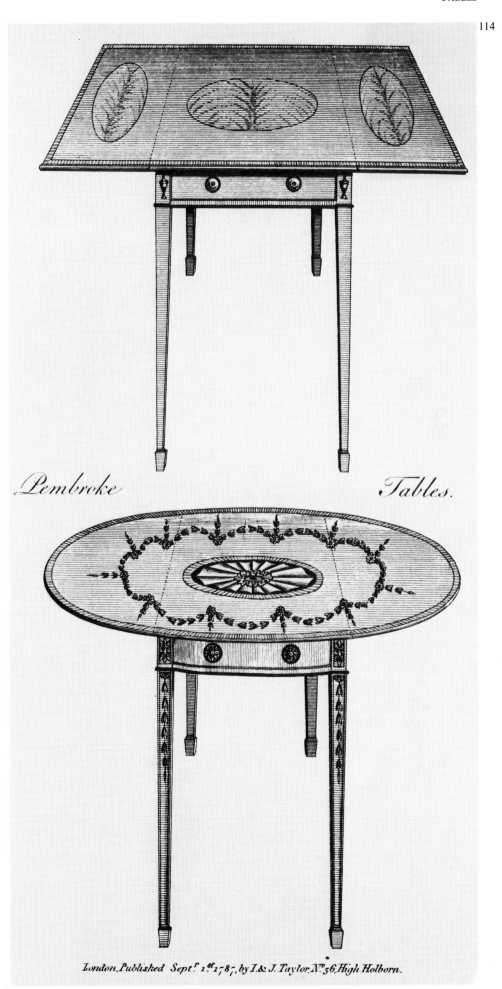

Pembroke *Tables.*

London, Published Sept.ʳ 1.ˢᵗ 1787, by I & J. Taylor, N.º 56. High Holborn.

114 Pembroke tables. Pl. 62 in Hepplewhite's *Cabinet-Maker and Upholsterer's Guide,* engraving dated September 1, 1787.

115 Mahogany quadrille table, decorated with copper fillets. Musée national du château de Pau.

Jacob-Desmalter's surviving invoices for this table show that he delivered a series of games tables to the Grand Trianon between 1805 and 1809. None of them is stamped, but they are the same model as various games tables known to be by Jacob. The piece illustrated, simple and well-proportioned, is certainly worthy of the great cabinetmaker.

116–118 Three figured mahogany games tables ornamented with gilt bronze. Musée national du château de Pau.

More luxurious than the tables made by the Jacob brothers, these three pieces were the work of Martin-Guillaume Biennais. They are not stamped but one of them is marked *Au singe violet* ("At the sign of the Violet Monkey") on the lock, this being the name of Biennais's shop. He was not only one of the two leading Empire-period goldsmiths but also the maker, or at least the supplier, of small pieces of furniture. The chequers table (Pl. 116) and the backgammon table (Pl. 117) have removable tops and can be converted into writing tables. The circular *bouillotte* table, with its green baize top, folds out to become a dining room table.

115

116

117

118

119 *Jardinière* which once belonged to Queen Hortense. Mahogany and gilt bronze. Musée national de la Malmaison.
This *jardinière* can be seen in Garneray's watercolor of Queen Hortense in her boudoir (see Plate 56).

120 *Jardinière* of light wood and gilt bronze. Schloss Homburg, Hesse.

119   120

Beds and Other Bedroom Furniture

Beds

The author of the book published under the name of Hepplewhite explains in a few words the importance of beds in terms of prestige for his contemporaries: "Beds are an article of much importance, as well on account of the great expense attending them, as the variety of shapes, and the high degree of elegance which may be shewn in them."[7]

It goes without saying that the expense did not relate to the cost of the wood for the bed, nor to the cost of the carpenter's work, but rather to the textiles which covered and surrounded it.

Even after the middle of the nineteenth century it was customary to sleep under bed curtains. The arrangement goes back as far as the Middle Ages. From the fourteenth or fifteenth century, that is from the time when artists began to depict interiors accurately, beds shown in paintings bear an extremely close resemblance to those used by our parents or grandparents. White sheets are folded over the blanket leaving a deep border showing; there is a big bolster under large pillows, and, naturally, there are curtains around the bed.

The use of curtains was certainly not confined to the upper classes. Nuns in convents, students in colleges and the sick in hospitals all slept in beds surrounded by curtains, since this was the only way to keep warm and obtain a measure of privacy in poorly heated and draughty dormitories.

For the most part beds had four pillars of circular section, which were sometimes decorated. They supported a "ceiling" of the same dimensions as the bed itself. The rich had beds covered with fine fabrics while the poorer classes had to be content with more modest textiles, but both nearly always had curtains around their beds. A visit to the loft of a French peasant's house dating from the last century usually reveals at least one baldachin from a bed dating from the reign of Louis-Philippe. Even officers' camp beds 121 had bed curtains and Hepplewhite gives two examples of these. Napoleon's own iron camp bed, which he installed in his office in 1811, is still at Fontainebleau. Surmounted by a small baldachin, it is enclosed by green silk curtains.

From the beginning of the eighteenth century beds surmounted by a baldachin began to replace four-posters, except in Britain and to some extent in Italy. Apart from camp beds, Hepplewhite's book, which appeared in editions 122, 123 of 1788, 1789 and 1794, shows only four-posters. Sheraton,[8] who was more conscious of foreign influences, illustrated a French bed (Pl. XLV) which is actually a model known in France as a *"lit à la polonaise"* and has a baldachin suspended from iron supports. Two other beds in Sheraton's work are based on French beds in Louis XVI 124 style (the sofa bed, Pl. 31 in the 1791 edition and the alcove bed, Pl. 40 in the 1792 edition). Sheraton also gives four examples of beds with columns or pillars, and like Hepplewhite devotes a whole plate to illustrating pillars for beds.

In 1826 four-posters were still in favor in Britain. George Smith[9] also gives examples of designs for bed pillars, which are heavier in appearance than the ones shown by Sheraton.

He writes "and in point of comfort the old English four-post bedstead, with its curtains and drapery, will always be found to claim a preference before any other, although it does not follow from hence, that it is necessary to close the curtains so effectually as to exclude the free ingress and egress of fresh air."[10] Smith's phrasing shows that in Britain, as on the Continent, it was now habit and perhaps also concern for dignity rather than necessity which dictated the use of beds surrounded by curtains. Such beds had a certain ceremonial value at a time when the bedroom was considered the most splendid room in many great houses. Despite George Smith, beds in the Continental style, without the normal four posts, were in use in England. Boat-shaped beds were imported from France and were copied. At Apsley House the Duke of Wellington slept in a small and rather unassuming bed of the type popular in France during the First Empire. Perhaps Wellington's bed is not the best example, since he surrounded himself with more foreign things than most of his compatriots, but it is not difficult to find other evidence to prove the point, such as the bed designed by John Buonarotti Papworth in 1829 for Frederick Cass, or the one which the Marquis of Salisbury prepared in 1846 for the arrival of Queen Victoria at Hatfield.[11]

Both Continental and British beds had curtains. In the first half of the nineteenth century a bed was the result of cooperation between architect (or designer), upholsterer and carpenter. This should always be remembered and any attempt to separate the various elements, such as the wooden parts (which were known in France as *couchettes* even when made of costly woods), the baldachin, the curtains and the bedding itself, should be avoided.

Most early nineteenth-century French beds were qualified by the phrase *à l'antique,* although their relationship to classical models is tenuous. These beds are more closely related to their eighteenth-century counterparts.

Today we have no hesitation in placing large beds in the center of very small rooms, leaving only a narrow passageway either side of the bed. Our forebears preferred to put their beds in an alcove or along a wall, so as to leave as much space as possible in the room. In the reign of Louis XVI beds were already being positioned in this way. The two ends were made to match and had identical headboards which were decorated with columns or baluster-shaped supports. This type of bed remained popular from the Revolutionary period until the middle of the nineteenth century. Only the shape of the bedhead changed from the canopied type, popular in the Louis XVI period, to ones 125–127 with pediment supports; still later scrolled bedheads were adapted.

A type of bed known in France as *en travers,* popular in the Directory period and at the beginning of the First Empire deserves mention. Its uprights were rectangular in section and were surmounted by classical antique heads or vases. Their lack of ornamentation and uncluttered design place them among the finest of all Empire-style beds. They must have been designed before 1800, since in April or May of that year one of these beds, the work of a craftsman named Cantenot-Moritz, had been made ready for Napoleon's visit to Dôle where he was to inspect workshops and forges. A provincial cabinetmaker was bound to copy Parisian styles of furniture and it seems likely that the first examples of beds decorated with classical heads were devised in the capital three or four years previously. Krafft reproduces one of these beds[12] and gives the name of its maker, Bellangé. The specimen now at Malmaison originally came from the Tuileries. It is distinguished by the high quality of the carving of the heads and, as it bears the stamp of Jacob-Desmalter, used between 1804 and 1814, may be one of the last to have been made.

After 1805 beds of this type became rather rare. They gave way to beds with straight headboards and more particularly to boat-shaped beds which were to remain in fashion for many years and were made all over Europe. We shall not attempt to describe in detail all the different varieties of boat-shaped beds, but shall choose a few examples, where possible those whose curtains and baldachins have survived. As we have already stressed, it is important to see the beds made at this time in their proper setting. This is too rarely the case, either on account of lack of space or is the result of a certain distaste now felt for the theatricality of the furnishings which made the bed somewhat reminiscent of a throne. The pleasure of retiring for the night in a country house to a curtained bed with a wool mattress is one which most of us have never known. Babies are the exception, since cradles with curtains not unlike miniature versions of early nineteenth-century beds are still on sale today.

Our ancestors' beds were much higher. A pile of mattresses usually rested on a webbing base fixed to the bed frame. After the invention in Germany of the sprung mattress, which began to be widely used around 1840, there was no further need for more than one mattress. The consequent lowering of the level of both sheets and blankets sometimes spoilt the appearance of older beds which had been designed with height in mind.

At the beginning of the nineteenth century nearly all beds were double, although they could be placed in various positions in relation to the walls of the bedroom. Narrower beds were used only by children or single persons.

Twin beds were not unknown. Sheraton illustrates a rather curious bed which he calls "A Summer bed in two compartments." It is in fact two twin beds placed side by side under a dais or platform, with a narrow space in between. A rather insubstantial arched member joins the feet together.

La Mésangère also illustrates designs for twin beds. One from a volume which appeared in 1802 was copied by Osmont, an upholsterer, and was then published in an Italian work. Twin beds became more common after 1840, especially in Britain. Long before this date, however, twin beds were often pushed together to make a large double bed, a practice which was common in Sweden and the German-speaking countries. The Swedish example illustrated here must date from before the beginning of the nineteenth century.

A pair of twin beds in mahogany placed side by side parallel to the wall under a baldachin was part of the new furnishings installed in 1817–18 in Queen Caroline of Bavaria's bedroom at the palace of Nymphenburg, Munich. A similar pair, differently positioned, can be seen in Regensburg in the palace of the princes of Thurn and Taxis. A third pair is shown in a watercolor by S. Decker depicting the Archduchess Sophie's bedroom at Laxenburg.[13] This pair was made in Vienna, where the other two pairs may well also have originated. It is interesting to note that the Germans are still in the habit of placing two mattresses next to each other to make one large bed.

Bedside tables

During the eighteenth century bedside tables were functional in appearance. They usually stood on four waisted legs and had a door or curtain concealing a compartment. This model appears in Hepplewhite's work under the unmistakable heading "pot cupboard."

In the nineteenth century bedside tables took on a more pretentious air. They were often designed in the form of altars or classical pedestals, which could be either cylindrical or rectangular. Jacob-Desmalter delivered a bedside table for Napoleon I's bedroom in the Trianon on July 10, 1810. It is representative of the kind of table known as a *somno*.[14] Although this example is in Empire style, the rounded corners of the socle and the marble top share stylistic affinities with bedside tables of the Restoration period. These later tables nearly all have rounded corners and the marble is often molded. The example illustrated is perhaps not typical of the later period, but it is attractive. It serves to show the links between the furniture of the Empire period and similar pieces made twenty years later: the only distinguishing feature is the molding of both the marble top and the socle, which date the table to the Restoration era.

Dressing tables, washstands and cheval glasses

Men's dressing tables differed considerably from those designed for ladies. However, once again terms tended to be used loosely. For example Hepplewhite illustrates a type of small table which he calls a ladies' dressing table but would have been called a *toilette d'homme* in Paris. These tables had several drawers to hold toilet articles. The table top could be opened up on either side and contained a mirror which was raised and supported rather like a music stand. Similar tables had been made in France since the time of Louis XV, and when closed could be used in other ways.

Toilet tables changed shape in the Empire and Restoration periods. Their mirrors were no longer folded in, but were attached to two columns or pillars and could be tilted. Often of considerable size, these mirrors were the main feature of the piece. Two examples are illustrated here. Despite their similarities, one is Italian and the other French. They are in fact washstands, although others of similar form which have a marble top were intended as hairdressing tables.

Ladies' dressing tables with mirrors were sometimes covered in lace or pleated material which went down to the floor. This fashion lasted for at least a hundred years if not longer. A table of this sort can be seen in John Zoffany's portrait of Queen Charlotte of England and her children dated 1764[15] and in a watercolor of 1863 by J. B. Fortuné de Fournier depicting Empress Eugénie's dressing room at Saint-Cloud.[16] Other examples are shown in a fine watercolor in Dugourc's album of 1790,[17] in a fashion plate published by Ackermann in 1822[18] and in a watercolor by

F. X. Nachtmann thought to represent the bedroom of Elizabeth of Bavaria, Queen of Prussia, in Munich around 1840.[19] The Empress Eugénie's dressing table at Pau is also 155 covered with pleated lace which reaches to the floor. The mirror in this instance is not on the table but is fixed to the wall above the table. It is of Venetian manufacture and was supplied in 1857. It is not shown in the illustration.

Although bathrooms were rarely installed at the beginning of the nineteenth century, washstands were in universal use. They were kept either in the bedroom itself or in the adjoining dressing room. Many are of little esthetic interest, but the most elegant of them are works of art in their own right. The "Athenian" washstand belonging to 157 Napoleon is illustrated opposite.

Finally we illustrate a cheval glass *(psyché)*, a piece of furniture which adorned boudoirs of the First Empire and 156 Restoration periods. With the invention around 1835 of wardrobes with mirror doors, cheval glasses became ever rarer as the century wore on, since they were more cumbersome.

121 Camp bed. Plate 102 from Hepplewhite's *Cabinet-Maker and Upholsterer's Guide* dated October 1, 1787.

122 Four-poster. Plate 98 from Hepplewhite's *Cabinet-Maker and Upholsterer's Guide* dated July 2, 1787. The author specifies that the bed was made with dove-gray satin curtains lined with green silk.

123 Bed pillars. Plate 105 from Hepplewhite's *Cabinet-Maker and Upholsterer's Guide* dated July 23, 1787.

124 Sofa bed. Plate 31 in Sheraton's *Cabinet-Maker and Upholsterer's Drawing-Book* dated September 30, 1791. The baldachin and the bed itself are both very reminiscent of Louis XVI beds and daybeds with three sides.

121

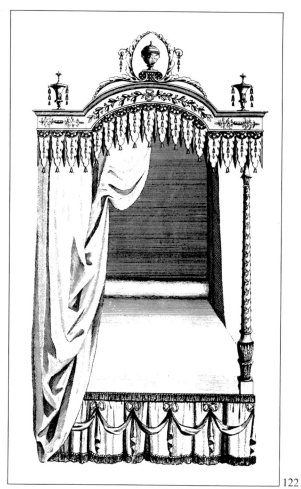

122

123

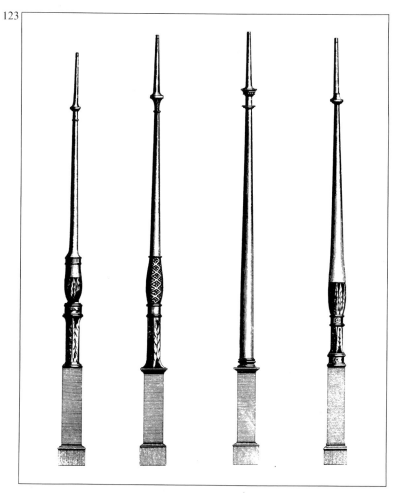

124

125 Painted wooden bed with matching ends. Private Collection. Like many Parisian beds made during Louis XVI's reign, this one is similar to Directory beds in several details, such as the pediments on the bedheads, the lozenge-shaped ornaments and the horizontal striations on the baluster supports.

126 Mahogany bed with gilt bronze mounts. Strasbourg Museum, Palais de Rohan.
This bed, with its matching ends with two decorative balusters at either end and surmounted by a scroll, is the most common model

made during the Empire and early Restoration periods in France. This bed is part of the furnishing of two bedrooms given in 1823 by the Comte d'Artois, later King Charles X of France, to one of his granddaughters on the occasion of her marriage to Comte de Faucigny-Lucinge.

127 Mahogany bed with gilt bronze mounts. Musée des arts décoratifs, Paris.
This bed is of the same type and from the same period as the one illustrated in Plate 126.

125

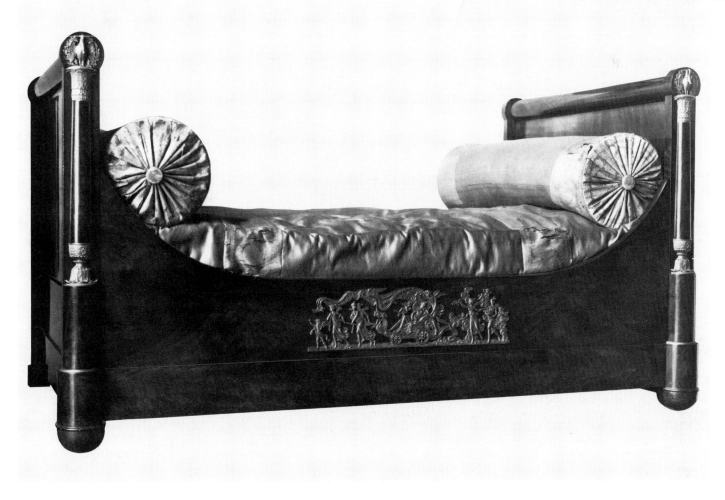

128 Bed in Napoleon's bedroom. Musée national de la Malmaison.
When he was First Consul, Napoleon often stayed at Malmaison. This bed, which bears a Tuileries Palace inventory number and is stamped by Jacob-Desmalter, cannot be the one he used at that period. It is merely an example of a fine bed made at the beginning of the Empire period. The yellow ground braid with its black ornamental design was rewoven from a sample from the Empire period that has survived in the Maison Brocard collection.

129 View of part of Napoleon's ▷ bedroom. Musée national du château de Versailles, Grand Trianon.
The furnishing of this room was entrusted to the upholsterer Darrac in 1809. He used a moiré "with a citrus-wood ground figured with a star motif in lilac silk." The borders were of silver brocade on a lilac ground. This fabric had been delivered to the Imperial furniture depository in 1805 by Pernon of Lyons and had already been used in the Empress Josephine's Music Room at the Tuileries Palace. It was rewoven in 1966 on the old looms after samples preserved in the Mobilier national.
The bed with its matching ends and the painted wood chairs were made for this room by Jacob-Desmalter. Darrac's invoice shows that the two bolsters, which are always found on beds with double bedheads made in the Empire period, were in this instance purely decorative.

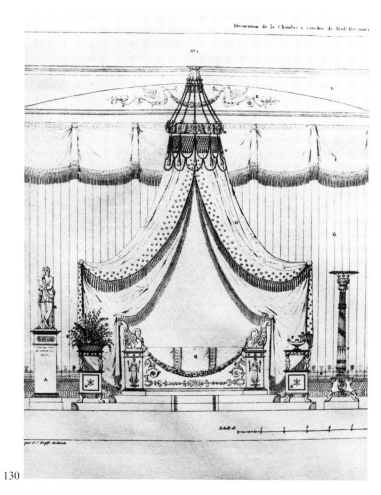

130

130 Madame Récamier's bed. Engraving published by Krafft and Ransonnette (see also Plate 52).

This bed, which is still in existence, is of mahogany and is decorated with gilt bronze swans and other ornamental motifs. At the back is a mirror and the bed is placed beneath a violet silk hanging. The bed curtains are of white muslin with gold stars and gold fringe.

131 Bed made in Paris for Madame Moreau. Plate 19 in Percier and Fontaine's *Recueil de décorations intérieurs*.

The bed was ordered in 1801 by Madame Moreau, wife of General Moreau (H. Ottomeyer, *op. cit.,* pp. 212–15). The bed was confiscated with the rest of Moreau's furniture after his arrest, and is now at Fontainebleau. It is of mahogany, ornamented with gilt bronze mounts and inlaid with cameo heads on a blue enamel ground.

132 "Fantastical bed" *(Lit de fantaisie).* Colored engraving published by La Mésangère, 1804.

The base and the bed, which seem to be based on Madame Moreau's bed, are of mahogany with gilt bronze mounts. There is a tentlike drapery above the bed, supported by pale green painted poles. The white satin curtains are ornamented with a green embroidered crown. The braid and fringe are pink, matching the cushions and bedcover which is itself covered with transparent lace. La Mésangère's Empire-style designs are fanciful and pleasing.

131

132

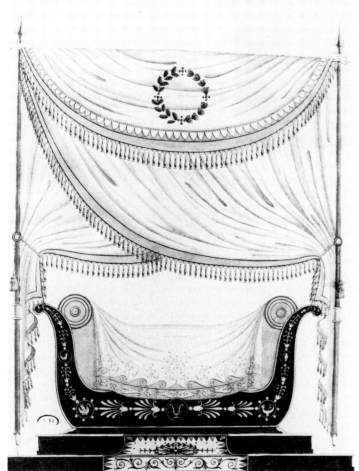

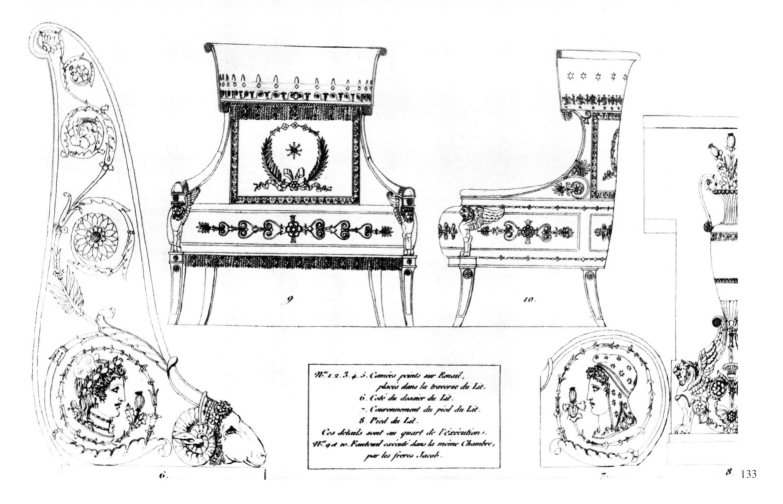

133 Side view of the backboard of Citoyen V's bed (left, no. 6). Detail of Plate 15 of Percier and Fontaine's *Recueil de décorations intérieurs* (3rd fascicule, before 1802).
The authors state that this bed was executed by Alexandre Régnier.

134 Empire-style bed of mahogany with gilt bronze decoration. Royal Palace, Brussels.

Some Empire-style boat-shaped beds can be directly related either to Madame Récamier's bed (Pl. 130) or to Percier and Fontaine's designs. The curved and carved side of this one replicates Madame Récamier's bed. The gilt bronze decoration on the ends is similar to that on Citoyen V's bed, except that the female head has been replaced by a lion mask. The modern bedding is too flat and destroys the original appearance of the piece, which was almost certainly made in Paris.

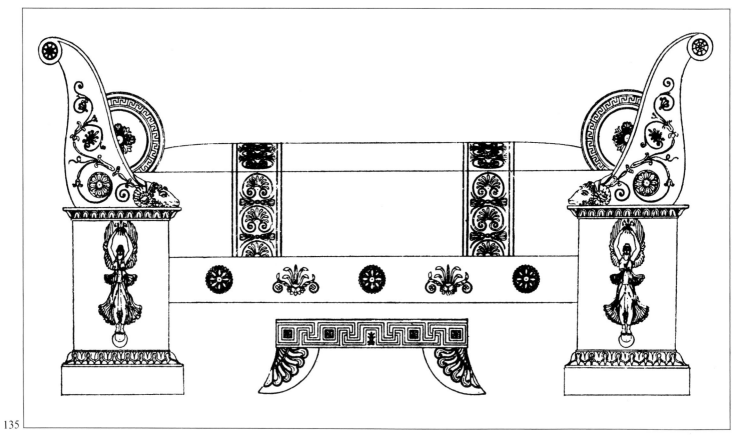

135

136

137

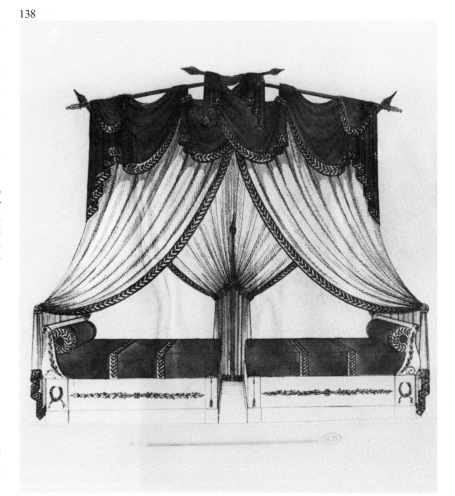

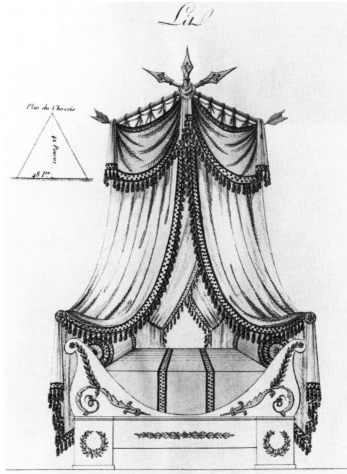

138

135   Mahogany and gilt bronze bed. Engraving published in
*Household Furniture and Interior Decoration executed from Designs
by Thomas Hope,* 1807.
The ram's head and the scrolls on the bedhead which occur in
Percier's work (see Plate 133) are repeated in Hope's bed. The bed
base is positioned halfway between the floor and the top of the
bed, as on the bed at Fontainebleau (see Plate 136) which is almost
the same shape. The female figures in gilt bronze derive from
Madame Récamier's bed.

136   Detail of a mahogany bed in the château of Fontainebleau.

137   Empress Josephine's bed at Malmaison.
Even after her divorce, Josephine seems to have taken care to
preserve her status as empress. Her room was refurbished after
1810. Her bed, by Jacob-Desmalter, was of carved and gilded
wood, as was the upper part. The red curtains were bordered with
gold braid. A large mirror was fixed to the wall behind the bed,
a not unusual feature in this period. Josephine also had an
ordinary bedroom in which she usually slept.

138–140   Three models of beds by the tapestry weaver Osmont.
Musée des arts décoratifs, Paris.
Like Empress Josephine's bed, those designed by Osmont have
white curtains which contrast with the lively colors of the pelmets,
braid and bedcovers. These very frequently have bands of braid
running across them.

139   140

141

141 Mahogany bed, decorated with gilt, chased bronzes. Strasbourg Museum, Palais Rohan.
This bed *en gondole* belongs to the same suite as the one in Plate 126, and therefore dates from 1823. Its unusual aspect derives from the balusters on the corners, which give it a more upright appearance than usual.

142 Mahogany bed. Colored engraving published by La Mésangère, 1827.
The bed is made entirely of mahogany: gilt bronze mounts were no longer in fashion. The curtains and bedcover are white. Discreet gilding is found only on the crowns around the upper part of the baldachin and on the paterae securing the curtains; some of the fringe is also gold.

143 Iron bed for an alcove. Musée des art décoratifs, Paris (album of designs by G. M. Egger, upholsterer in Paris, 1779–1830).
Iron beds were in use from the end of the eighteenth century. At the beginning of the nineteenth century they were often quite luxurious and were of polished iron ornamented with gilt bronze mounts. The designer of this bed probably intended it to imitate a Chinese or Turkish bed.

144 The King of Rome's cradle. Silver gilt and mother-of-pearl *(burgau)*, orange-red velvet upholstery. Kunsthistorisches Museum, Vienna.
On the birth of the king of Rome in 1811 the prefect of the Seine and of the City of Paris presented to the Empress Marie-Louise an extraordinary set of silver gilt furniture. Designed by Prud'hon and executed by Odiot and Thomire, it comprised a toilet table with an oval mirror, a washstand in the form of a tripod altar, a cheval glass, an armchair, a stool and a cradle. Only the cradle, which was part of the former Austrian Imperial Collections, survives. The other pieces, which Marie-Louise took with her to Parma, were melted down at her command in 1832 to provide succor for cholera victims.
The cradle makes us regret the disappearance of the other parts of the suite of furniture. Its simple lines are evident despite the richness of the work, which is of the highest craftsmanship. The sculptural elements are superbly executed. Only the skimpy curtains which now form part of the cradle are not in keeping with the rest of the piece. Prud'hon had envisaged a simple white veil covering the whole of one side of the cradle.

142

143

145   146

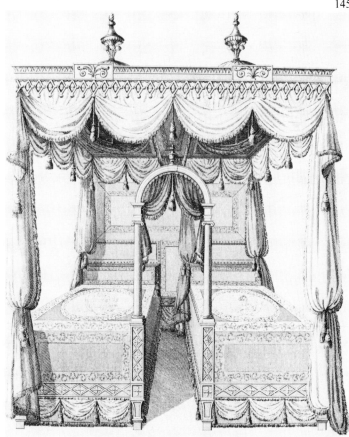

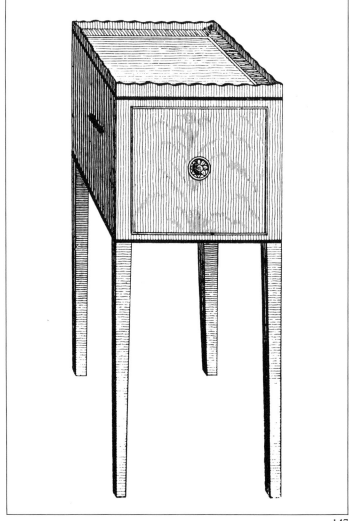

147   148

145 A summer bed in two compartments. Plate 41 dated June 20, 1792 in Sheraton's *Cabinet-Maker and Upholsterer's Drawing Book*.

146 A Swedish double bed. Louis XVI period. Private Collection, Finland.

147 Pot cupboard. Plate 89 dated September 1, 1787 in Hepplewhite's *Cabinet-Maker and Upholsterer's Guide*.

148 Bedside table from the emperor's bedroom at the Grand Trianon, of mahogany with gilt bronze mounts and slate blue marble top.
Delivered by Jacob-Desmalter on July 10, 1810. Behind the table can be seen part of the wall hanging, including the large border of silver brocade on a lilac ground.

149 Bedside table in pyramid form with designs in wood, black-stained wood, gilt bronze, white marble. Musée des arts décoratifs, Paris.

150 Mahogany toilet table with five drawers, stamped Gillows Lancaster. Sold at Christie's, London, November 29, 1979.
This table was part of a suite delivered by Gillows to Richard Oliver Gascoigne of Parlington Hall, Aberford between 1810 and 1813. The table was intended for one of the bedrooms. It was an elegant model in current production by Gillows, one of the best English furniture makers. An identical table from the same house is at Lotherton Hall, property of Leeds City Council, and two others were sold at Christie's, London, on June 28, 1979 (Lot 32).

149

150

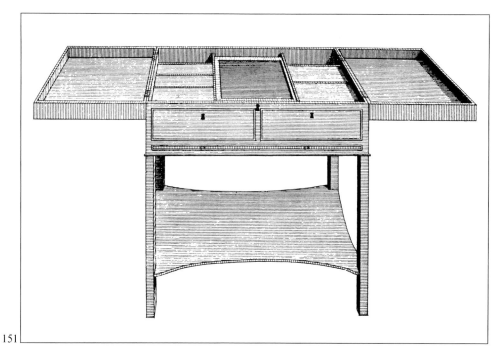

151

151 Lady's toilet table. Plate 72 dated October 1, 1787 from Hepplewhite's *Cabinet-Maker and Upholsterer's Guide*.

152 Mahogany toilet table with gilt bronze mounts. Villa Reale della Petraia, near Florence.
Florentine, period of Elisa Bacciochi, grand duchess of Tuscany (1809–14).

153 Ash toilet table with gilt bronze mounts. Musée national du château de Versailles, Grand Trianon.
The table was purchased in December 1809 from A. T. Baudouin, a furniture dealer, for the empress's bedroom.

152

154

155

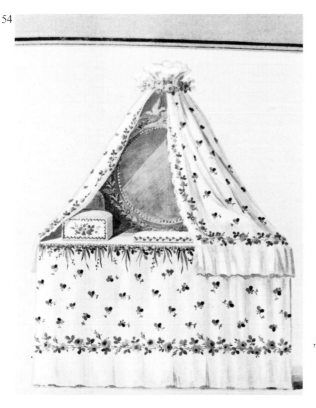

156

154 Lady's toilet table. Watercolor drawing from Dugourc's album, 1790. Paris, Musée des arts décoratifs. The fabric covering is white and is embroidered with naturalistic pansies and other flowers.

155 Empress Eugénie's toilet set from the château at Pau. The Sèvres porcelain dates from 1853–54.

156 The duchess of Berry's cheval glass and music box. Elm, ash marquetry, gilt bronze mounts. Musée des arts décoratifs, Paris.
The mirror was delivered in 1824 by Félix Rémond, cabinetmaker in the royal furniture depository and supplier to the duchess of Berry. It is still in Empire style.

157 Emperor Napoleon's tripod table. Musée du ▷ Louvre, Paris.
Tripod tables (called *athéniennes*) were inspired by classical tripods from Herculaneum and Pompeii and were first used in France at the end of the eighteenth century. Perfume burners, *jardinières,* and washstands were all known as *athéniennes* when they had three legs.
Napoleon's table is a luxurious washstand fitted with ewer and basin. The tripod support is of yew with chased gilt bronze mounts. It was made for the First Consul by the royal goldsmith, Biennais, who also made small pieces of furniture.
The inventories of the Tuileries Palace show that the table was in the emperor's bedroom in 1808–09. Marchand, Napoleon's valet who went with him when the emperor was exiled, arranged for the table to be taken to the Elysée Palace in 1815, and later to St. Helena together with the emperor's personal effects. The inscription engraved on the basin records that Napoleon used it until the very end of his life.
The tripod table is shown standing on a Savonnerie carpet formerly in Napoleon's Grand Cabinet at the Tuileries Palace.

Wardrobes, Bookcases, Desks, etc.

Wardrobes

Along with the cabinet with many drawers, which is of Italian origin, large wardrobes with elaborate carved and gilt decoration may be considered the piece of furniture that is most typical of the seventeenth century.

By the end of the eighteenth century these large wardrobes were still being made in Liège, in Normandy and in other provincial regions of France. But they were much rarer in Paris and other capital cities, where they had generally been replaced by cupboards.

In England, although there had been various advances and developments in furniture making, numerous ward-
158 robes continued to be made. Some were of considerable size. Sheraton illustrates an example of a "closet." Another type has drawers below like a French commode and doors above which conceal more drawers. Many of these cupboards can
159 still be seen in Britain. They are carefully constructed in high quality mahogany, whereas contemporary French wardrobes are usually rather simple affairs in walnut or cherry and are generally provincial in character.
160 It was not until the Gothic and Renaissance revivals shortly before the middle of the nineteenth century that the wardrobe regained its place of honor. It was then usually made of carved oak.

Bookcases

Bookcases and bookshelves have always existed side by side. Bookcases have the advantage, so long as they are not too large, of being movable, but bookshelves are usually less expensive to build. In practice shelves become necessary when the amount of books to be housed demand a room of their own. In Britain from the eighteenth century onwards every house of any size had a library. It was usually one of the finest rooms in the house and was often in daily use as a living room. The library at Woburn was built by Henry Holland for the Duke of Bedford at the very end of the eighteenth century. Sir Richard Colt Hoare's library at
75 Stourhead was furnished around 1805 by Chippendale the Younger, and the Petworth library appears in a watercolor by Turner of 1828. A great number of English watercolors and illustrations of interiors in other techniques from the first half of the nineteenth century show libraries. Reading was clearly an important part of British life at this time.

It is difficult to decide whether it was less popular in
161 France. There were certainly libraries in France, or at least book collections belonging to men such as Gouthière, the maker of gilt bronzes, and the picture dealer Lebrun, who was active shortly before the Revolution. Napoleon had a large library at each of his residences. Queen Hortense had two fine bookcases by Weisweiler and took her books with her to Augsburg and Arenenberg when she was exiled. Chateaubriand had a library, as did Madame Récamier, who had herself painted at Abbaye-aux-Bois against a background of books. Guizot's library at Val-Richer rivaled that of the Duke of Broglie at his château at Broglie. Yet

most late eighteenth-century Paris town houses rarely had a library, although they had several drawing rooms. Books were probably kept in the owner's private *cabinet*. Early nineteenth-century French bookcases are less frequently found in the trade than their English counterparts.   162, 163

Secretaire-bookcases

The secretaire-and-bookcase was very popular in Britain. It is also found in Germany and the Low Countries, where it was probably copied from English models. The title is self-explanatory. Because of its function it is higher than the French secretaire-bookcase *(secrétaire-bibliothèque)*, al- 164 though smaller secretaires were made in England. The 165 French model can be found in Holland, Belgium, Germany, 166 Austria, Italy and Russia. After the commode or chest of 167, 168 drawers it is probably the most common piece of furniture at this period. The flap is usually provided with a leather writing surface on the interior, except in Germany and Austria where it is of plain polished wood. Sometimes it is so high up that it is difficult to see how it could be used for writing. In fact most of the secretaire-cupboards were only occasionally used as writing tables. They are more of a bureau than a chest of drawers but are no more practical than the old desks with their many small drawers.

The French *semainier* with its seven drawers had the same 169, 170 proportions as the secretaire. The English tallboy was somewhat higher. Both were used as cupboards.   171

Bureaus

Despite their drawbacks, secretaires maintained their popularity throughout the first half of the nineteenth century. The bureau, however, retained much the same form during this period and was generally considered a rather utilitarian piece of furniture. Flat writing tables and cylinder-top desks had achieved great refinement in the eighteenth century, although the commoner types of desks still continued to be used. All these were still in production 173 at the beginning of the nineteenth century. Cylinder-top desks of mediocre quality were still made in almost the same way, but other types tended to be overloaded with scrolls or ornament in the form of chimeras or lion's paws. Jacob 174 was responsible for making some quite simple desks of reasonable quality, but most of them are not as fine as the eighteenth-century pieces. It is likely that the English library 172 table provided the model for the true nineteenth-century French desk, which has a flat top, supported by two pillars each formed of several drawers one above another.[20] Most 175 of these desks are functional in character, but although lacking the charm of their eighteenth-century predecessors they at least are in keeping with their surroundings.

The lady's desk, called a *bonheur-du-jour* in France, is a small desk provided with a writing-slide which can be opened out or pulled forwards. The *bonheur-du-jour* was especially popular in Louis XVI's reign and continued to be made during the Empire and Restoration periods. The later 176, 177, 31 versions were larger, and therefore probably more useful, but they lacked the elegance of eighteenth-century desks.

Chests of drawers

There was a chest of drawers in every nineteenth-century bedroom. They were also found in other rooms and no other piece of furniture enjoyed such popularity. The chest of drawers first appeared in the seventeenth century. Its form was simplified at the end of the eighteenth, when it took on a rectangular shape and was supported by rather low feet in accordance with contemporary architects' taste for geometric shapes.

178–181 The Swedish examples we illustrate could just as easily be German or Russian. The furniture maker David Roentgen was responsible for devising the copper or gilt bronze "antique nail" motifs which decorate the rounded corners of the commodes illustrated. Other elements such as the marble tops, handles and keyhole mounts could equally well be of 182 French manufacture. However, contemporary English chests of drawers preserve their own special character. They are simple and clean in outline, although a few remaining 183 sinuosities reminiscent of Louis XV furniture prevent them from being too severe.

Export of French furniture

It has long seemed likely that certain French cabinetmakers carried on making and exporting luxury furniture during the Revolution. Foreign orders must have been as important to them as orders from the Court. There was a noticeable drop in orders from French clients. The chance discovery of a fragment of a French newspaper of 1792 during the restoration of a small table by Weisweiler exhibited at Arkhangelskoe, near Moscow, confirms that a certain number of high quality pieces of French furniture in Russia were made during the early years of the French Revolution. These may well include a large *bonheur-du-jour* by Weisweiler and a console table by Thomire, both at 184 Pavlovsk, as well as a chest of drawers by Beneman and 185 another commode and secretaire. The last two pieces are richly decorated and ornamented with Sèvres porcelain plaques. A Russian publication states that the last two pieces are by Beneman, although another source claims that neither is stamped.

All these pieces, which were made in the transition period between the style of Louis XVI and the Directory, are doubly interesting because they are of a type little in evidence in France. The chests of drawers and the secretaire in the Hermitage can be compared to a secretaire of Parisian 186 workmanship now in the Victoria and Albert Museum. Of high quality, the latter is attributed, on rather unconvincing grounds, to Molitor. Its form and decorative details relate it to the secretaire and to the chest of drawers with porcelain plaques in the Hermitage Museum. Yet some of its bronzes, such as the two *chapiteaux*, the lower frieze, the handles and the keyhole mounts, are close to those on the other 184 Hermitage chest of drawers which bears Beneman's stamp. In view of the similarity of their construction it is tempting to attribute all these pieces to Beneman. The same rather characteristic bronzes can also be found on a commode in the Pitti Palace, Florence, which is thought to be of Italian workmanship. Although made several years later than the pieces we have been discussing, it is clearly related to the Beneman chest of drawers, even though it is in the Empire style.

The Jacob brothers

There is no trace of the elegance typical of eighteenth-century furniture in the two pieces of furniture by the Jacob brothers which we shall now consider. The first, a cabinet 187 or *meuble d'appui,* evokes the splendor of the First Empire. The second, a perfectly proportioned *commode à vantaux,* represents the delicate severity and spare elegance of 188 Percier's designs. The *meuble d'appui* is the richer and more remarkable piece. It is perhaps the only one of its type which has survived intact with its Imperial emblems. It belonged to the descendants of Edmond de Talleyrand-Périgord, Duke of Dino. He was the nephew and closest heir of Napoleon's minister, and the husband of the Duchess of Dino, whose role in her uncle by marriage's final years is well known.

It seems likely that Talleyrand was the first owner of this sumptuous example of the cabinetmaker's art. The *meuble d'appui* seems to be almost too richly decorated even for a dignitary of the French Empire. All the details suggest that it was destined for a place of honor in one of the Imperial palaces. Several features strengthen this hypothesis: the thick marble top, the amboyna wood veneer (reserved for the most expensive pieces), the caryatids which are actually fully formed bronze figures, and the abundance and quality of the gilt bronze mounts (which include a Napoleonic eagle repeated three times). Since no documents relating to this cabinet have yet been discovered, an explanation seems called for. It may perhaps be found in a Napoleonic decree specifying that high-ranking officials should furnish their official quarters at their own expense. Napoleon actually bought back from Duroc's widow the furniture which her late husband had had at the Tuileries Palace where he was Grand Marshal. Duroc had had to spend more than 200,000 francs furnishing the palace, where he entertained foreign ambassadors in Napoleon's absence.[21] It seems that Talleyrand had to furnish his quarters at the Foreign Ministry at his own expense in the same way. When he resigned in 1807 he was obliged to take his furniture with him.

Two further points should be mentioned. The first is that although the piece is stamped by the Jacob brothers and was therefore made before 1803, it nevertheless bears Imperial emblems which date at the earliest from 1804. They may have been added later, or, more likely, have been made and attached to the piece in 1804 shortly after it left the cabinetmaker's workshop.

It is certain that in 1814–15 this piece did not belong to the Office of Works responsible for the Imperial furnishing *(Mobilier impérial),* if it ever had, since all Napoleonic emblems were removed from furniture in the depository at the Restoration. It is curious that Talleyrand, who was King Louis XVIII's Foreign Minister, did not find it necessary to make similar adaptations to the cabinet so that it conformed to contemporary taste.

The history of the commode mentioned earlier is less complicated. It was purchased from Jacob in 1804 and placed in Madame Mère's (i.e. Napoleon's mother's) bedroom at Fontainebleau. Although made at the same time and in the same workshop as the cabinet we have just discussed, it is quite different in character. Closer to the kind of furniture usually designed by Percier, it has excellent proportions and fine decoration which is on the surface only. It is one of the most attractive commodes made during the Empire period.

The piece of furniture known as a *commode à vantaux* has drawers inside in the "English style." Many Restoration commodes are of this type. When the doors are closed, the commode is indistinguishable from a sideboard or a *meuble d'appui*, a term which is applied to any piece of furniture the same height as a commode, whatever its purpose.

Furniture decoration under the Empire and Restoration

189 Commodes and secretaires were generally made to match at this time. The most typical Empire examples have pilasters at either end, each surmounted by an Egyptian head. There were, however, other types. In each of Napoleon's palaces there was a series of more modest commodes and secretaires: these are all in much the same style. They are made of fine mahogany and have a black marble top, their only ornament being gilt bronze handles in the form of a lion's head with a ring depending from the jaws.

190–192 Shortly afterwards, around 1808, slightly different commodes and secretaires began to be made. Like many Louis XVI pieces they were flanked by column-shaped uprights. Furniture of this kind continued to be made after the Restoration, so that it is often difficult to determine the 193, 194 date of manufacture of such pieces, especially when they have gilt bronze mounts.

Most European countries were influenced by the French Empire style. Great Britain was no exception. The style may have been transmitted through Thomas Hope, or, more probably, through other channels.[22] However, the influence was not a happy one. Although the secretaire and buffet illustrated here are well designed, there are numerous pieces 195, 196 of Regency and George IV furniture in Great Britain which are heavy and ugly. The introduction of motifs such as heads, lion's claws or paws, swans, Egyptian caryatids and so on, which were of French derivation, seems rarely to have been successful.

All the motifs just mentioned were still in current use in France at the beginning of the Restoration period. The change of regime did not affect the fine arts. It is true that the painter David, who was already past middle age, had to seek refuge in Brussels, but this was because he was a regicide, having voted for the death of the king in 1793. All the others carried on as before. Gérard and Ingres continued their careers as portrait painters. Fontaine, who had been Napoleon's official architect, now worked for Louis XVIII in the same capacity. Saint-Ange, a designer accredited to the department responsible for the royal furniture *(Garde-Meuble)* made no changes to the style of his carpets.

It is true that new artistic ideas no longer originated at the court, since the king was not an important client. Cabinetmakers now worked for private buyers who were more numerous than before, as the Restoration brought peace after a long period of war and hence soon led to prosperity. Artistic ideas remained the same and taste evolved only slowly, moving in the direction of greater freedom as it liberated itself from martial symbols cast in gilt bronze. Around 1825 bronzes disappeared altogether. They were generally replaced by motifs which were still classical in style, such as rosettes and palmettes, executed in marquetry. Wood inlays were now becoming extremely fashionable, after being in eclipse for thirty years. Their decline had not been total, however, since one of the specialities of the Jacob brothers (1796–1803) was furniture with ebony and pewter inlays. Even in 1806 Napoleon presented a console table with rich marquetry by Levasseur 108 to the crown prince of Bavaria.

Ingres, who was without doubt the most scrupulous and exact of painters, completed a painting of Madame Rivière[23] in the preceding year. She is shown leaning against the back of a piece of furniture made of light wood with darker colored marquetry. Were this painting not securely dated, one would think that the couch or daybed dated from the Restoration period. This is such an easy error to make, that it is quite possible that today some Empire furniture in light wood is wrongly thought to have been made ten years or so later.

The fashion for light colored veneers dates from well before 1814. It is usually said to have had its origin in the scarcity of mahogany because of the Continental Blockade, but it was probably as much the result of a change in taste. Mahogany, after all, had been used almost exclusively for twenty years. Numerous pieces in light woods were ordered or purchased for the Imperial palaces during the last years of Napoleon's rule. To our knowledge none of these has marquetry in darker wood, but this became common at the beginning of the Restoration period. For example a small *guéridon* by the cabinetmaker Félix Rémond is made of lemonwood and purple wood, and is decorated with fleurs-de-lys and a portrait of Henri IV dated 1814.[24] In England 197 most furniture by George Bullock, who died in 1818, is inlaid with marquetry. The fashion for furniture of Brazilian rosewood or mahogany with marquetry in lemonwood or boxwood seems to arise slightly later, but both dark and pale woods appear to have been used for veneering. This technique reached its apogee at this time. As the shape of commodes and secretaires remained simple and uncluttered over a long period, it is not difficult to argue that pieces dating from between 1815 and 1840 are in no way inferior to their predecessors made under the Empire.

The two examples illustrated, a commode by Fischer and a low bookcase made for the Duke of Orléans, are un- 198, 199 doubtedly of high quality. Yet the art of furniture making was bound to be affected in the long run by the progressive deterioration of design which characterizes nineteenth-century architecture as well as the decorative arts. The decline became more marked as each decade passed and often went hand in hand with that other failing of the century: excessive ornamentation. This means that alongside fine quality furniture made between 1820 and 1830 there are numerous pieces of lesser artistic merit. The disappearance of the neoclassical style around 1830–40 seems to mark the turning point, both as regards furniture and other spheres of artistic activity. It is, however, difficult to make sweeping generalizations in such matters. A piece of furniture in Renaissance style, such as the one by P.-A. 200 Bellangé illustrated on page 113, has much in common with the last two pieces in classical style which we discussed.

158   Cupboard. Plate 8 in Sheraton's *Cabinet-Maker and Upholsterer's Drawing-Book*. Engraving dated April 14, 1793.

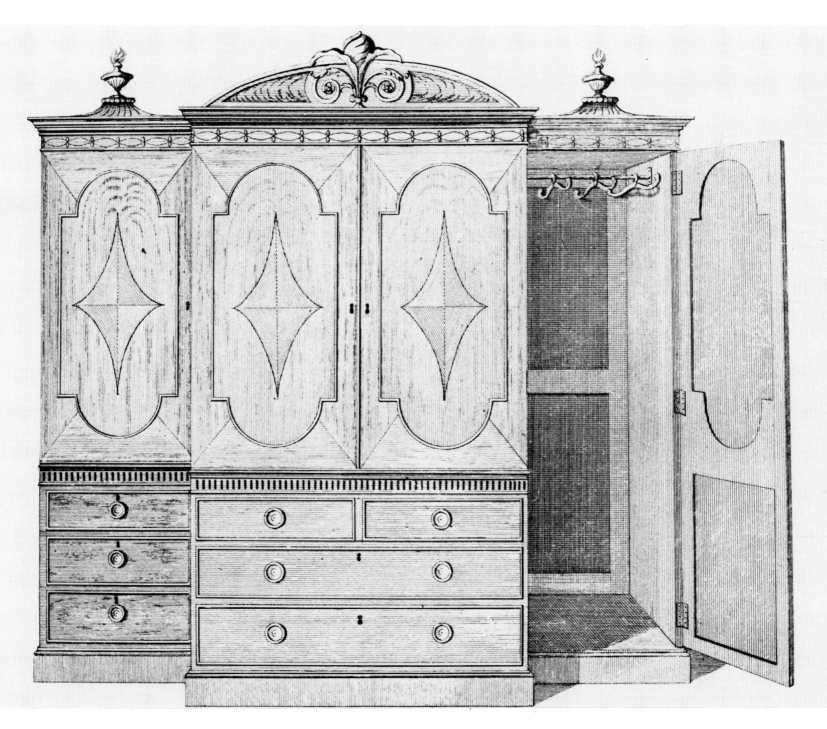

159 Wardrobe. Plate 86 in Hepplewhite's *Cabinet-Maker and Upholsterer's Guide*. Engraving dated September 1, 1787.

160 Wardrobe shown by Gambs of St. Petersburg at the 1851 Universal Exhibition, London. Engraving taken from the exhibition catalogue.

161 Part of the library at the Marbeuf town ▷ residence, built by the architects Legrand and Molinos. Plate XCV in Krafft and Ransonnette's work.

159   160

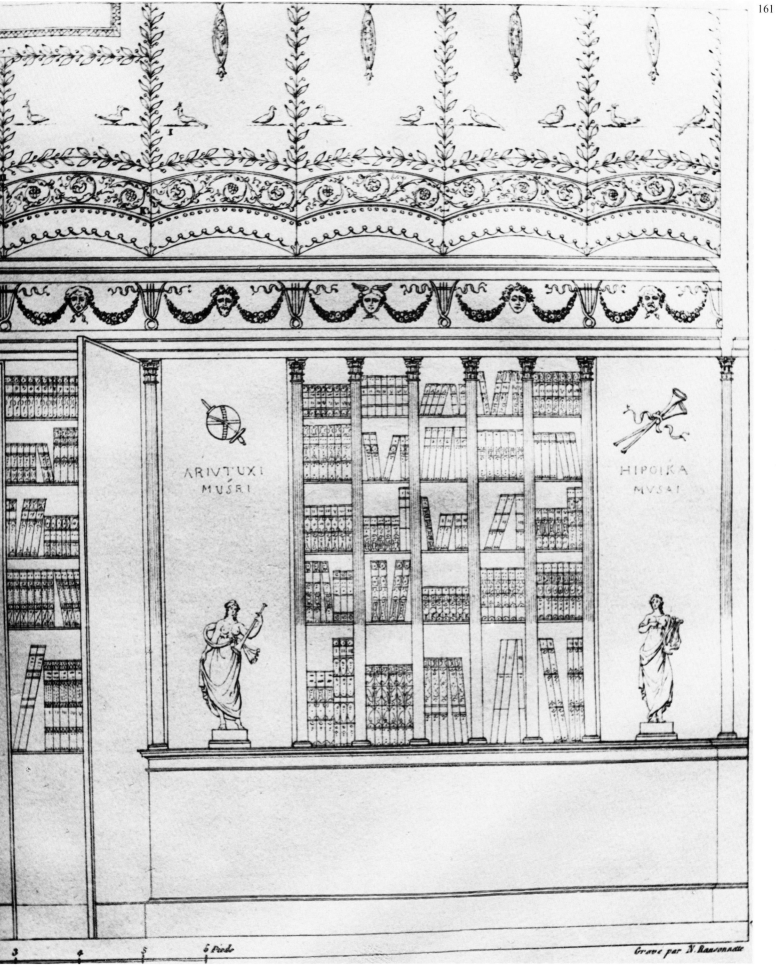

ARIVTUXI
MVŚRI

HIPOIKA
MVSAI

Gravé par N. Ransonnette

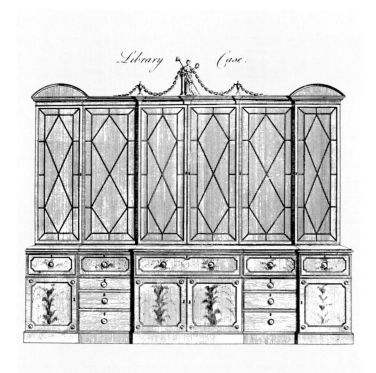

162

163

164

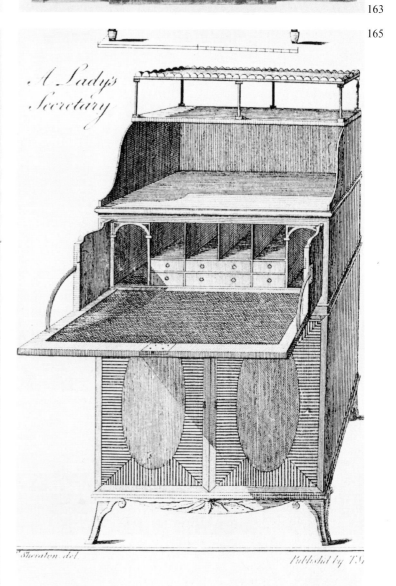

165

162 Bookcase. Plate 48 in Hepplewhite's *Cabinet-Maker and Upholsterer's Guide.* Engraving dated July 2, 1787.

163 Mahogany bookcase-cupboard inlaid with fillets and decorative details in black-stained wood. Sold at Christie's, London, June 25, 1981.
The central part projects further than the two flanking wings, a characteristic shared by other English bookcases. A similar bookcase sold at Christie's on December 1, 1977 was dated about 1810.

164 Bookcase-secretaire. Plate 28 in Sheraton's *Cabinet-Maker and Upholsterer's Drawing Book.* Engraving dated December 24, 1791.

165 "A lady's Secretaire." Plate 43 in Sheraton's *Cabinet-Maker and Upholsterer's Drawing Book.* Engraving dated September 27, 1792.

166 Mahogany secretaire with fillets and applied flutes in lemonwood and gilt bronze drawer handles and key plates; gray St. Anne marble top. Musée national du château de Pau.
This secretaire, which bears a Tuileries Palace stamp, used during the Empire period, was no doubt in one of the less important rooms in that palace. It must have been made in the revolutionary period or at the very end of Louis XVI's reign.

167 Satinwood and rosewood secretaire with angled corners, inlaid with three panels of black lacquer. Low Countries, late eighteenth century. Sold at Christie's, London, December 13, 1979.
In Holland, as in Italy, marquetry remained in fashion for a long time. Furniture with marquetry of large flowers, little different from that found on pieces dating from the mid-eighteenth century, was being made even at the beginning of the nineteenth century.

168 Secretaire-cupboard, veneered with mahogany and ebony; white marble top. Musées royaux d'art et d'histoire, Brussels.
This unusual piece of furniture is a secretaire to which another piece has been added at each side to form a cupboard. Although it closely resembles Louis XVI pieces in style, it is apparently of Dutch or Belgian origin. The lozenge-shaped ornamental motifs were fashionable at the end of the eighteenth century.

166

167

168

169 Mahogany *semainier* with chased gilt bronzes; front flanked by two balusters. Strasbourg Museum, Palais de Rohan.
This *semainier* which can be dated to 1823 was part of a suite of furniture made for the Comtesse de Faucigny-Lucinge (see Plates 126, 141, 194).

170 Mahogany tallboy *(semainier)* with chased gilt bronze mounts, the corners imitating pilasters surmounted with Egyptian heads; marble top.
Sold by Messrs. Paul and Jacques Martin, Galerie des Chevau-Légers, Versailles, April 29, 1979.

171 "Double chest of drawers." Plate 53 in Hepplewhite's *Cabinet-Maker and Upholsterer's Guide.*
Engraving dated July 2, 1787.

172 Library tables. Plate 50 in Hepplewhite's *Cabinet-Maker and Upholsterer's Guide.*
Engraving dated October 1, 1787.

173 "Tambour writing table." Plate 67 in Hepplewhite's *Cabinet-Maker and Upholsterer's Guide.*
Engraving dated September 1, 1787.

174 Cylinder-top desk, made in Paris for M.H. Plate 32 in Percier and Fontaine's *Recueil de décorations intérieures,* 1803.
The caption informs the reader that "this table... was executed at M. Jacob's factory in Paris; it is of mahogany, with bronze ornaments and different kinds of marquetry; inside are pigeon-holes, secret drawers and several very useful partitions."

169   170

171   172

173   174

175 Mahogany desk with nine drawers, rounded corners and leather top. England, Regency period. Sold at Christie's, London, June 25, 1981.

176 Figured mahogany *bonheur du jour* with gilt bronze mounts, stamped C. Lemarchand (died 1826). Musée des arts décoratifs, Paris.

177 Light wood *bonheur du jour* with marble top. Empire or Restoration period. Musée des arts décoratifs, Paris.

175

176   177

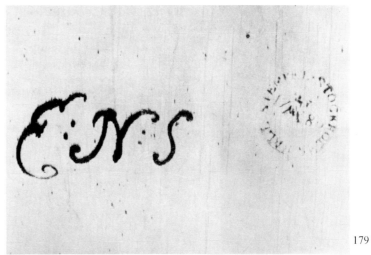

178

179

178 Mahogany chest of drawers with gilt brass handles and key plates. Porvoo Museum, Finland.
The chest of drawers is signed by the master cabinetmaker Erik Nyström of Stockholm and bears the city's stamp for the year 1782.

179 Erik Nyström's signature (E.N.S.) and the Stockholm stamp for the year 1782.

180 Swedish mahogany chest of drawers with gilt brass key plates and handles; gray marble top. National Museum of Finland, Pukkila manor.

180

181

182

181 Mahogany chest of drawers with gilt brass handles and key plates; gray marble top. Swedish. Armfelt Museum, Helsinki. This piece was originally at Joensuu (Åminne in Swedish), Haliko, Finland, and belonged to Count Armfelt, Gustave III's minister.

182 Mahogany and rosewood chest of drawers inlaid with lemonwood fillets. Inventory mark of the Tuileries Palace. Musée national du château de Pau.

183 Two chests of drawers (commodes). Plate 76 in Hepplewhite's *Cabinet-Maker and Upholsterer's Guide*. Engraving dated September 1, 1787.

184 Mahogany chest of drawers with gilt bronze mounts, stamped Beneman. Hermitage Museum, Leningrad.

183

184

185

185 Mahogany chest of drawers with gilt bronze mounts inlaid with Sèvres porcelain plaques. Hermitage Museum, Leningrad. This chest of drawers, which matches a secretaire also in the Hermitage, is not stamped and may therefore have been made after the furniture makers' guild was suppressed in March 1791. It is generally Louis XVI in style except for the frieze of classical figures and swans, two decorative themes which appeared only some years after the end of Louis XVI's reign. The lower frieze, which consists of two branches of laurel arranged horizontally on either side of a central rosette, could well be found on a piece of furniture made in the Empire period.

186 Mahogany secretaire decorated with ebony fillets and gilt bronze mounts. Victoria and Albert Museum, London.

187 Cupboard *(meuble d'appui)* of amboyna wood, bronze and gilt bronze; griotte marble top. Stamped Jacob Frères. Victoria and Albert Museum, London.

188 Mahogany cupboard *(commode à vantaux)* with gilt bronze mounts and black marble top. Stamped Jacob Frères. Musée national du château de Fontainebleau.

187 △

186   188

189

189 Mahogany chest of drawers with gilt bronze mounts. Drawing Room in the Charlottenzimmer, Residenz, Munich.
Most Directory and Empire commodes are more solid in appearance and less graceful than this example, which nevertheless exhibits the complete range of decorative motifs popular at the time, such as claw feet, Egyptian caryatids and gilt bronze drawer handles and key plates.

190 Mahogany chest of drawers with gilt bronze mounts and black marble top. Musée national du château de Pau.
This commode, with its two decorative columns on either side which are detached from the body of the piece, is the commonest model made at the end of the Empire and beginning of the Restoration periods.

191 Mahogany dressing table with gilt bronze mounts. Stamped by the Brussels cabinetmaker Chapuis. Musées royaux d'art et d'histoire, Brussels.
The lower part resembles the chest of drawers in Plate 190 and, although smaller, is probably contemporary with it. It differs in the large movable mirror added to the upper part, which seems out of proportion to the small piece of furniture supporting it.

192 Mahogany secretaire with gilt bronze mounts on the side columns, and gilt bronze handles and key plates. Underneath the marble top is a handwritten label inscribed "Marcion, no. 25" and an inventory mark of Napoleon's Elysée Palace (1809–15). Musée national du château de Pau.
This simple and well-proportioned secretaire is just as fine a piece as any made by the Jacobs. Marcion was one of the leading suppliers of furniture to Napoleon in the last years of his rule. The columns turned to resemble balusters are characteristic of Marcion's furniture. In the Empire period a white marble top is always an indication of high quality workmanship.

193 Mahogany secretaire with gilt bronze mounts. Musée des arts décoratifs, Paris.
This Paris-made secretaire was part of the same suite of furniture as the bed in Plate 127. Both must date from the first decade of the Restoration period.

194 Mahogany secretaire with gilt bronze mounts. Given to the Comtesse de Faucigny-Lucinge by Comte d'Artois (see Plates 126, 141, 169).
Strasbourg Museum, Palais de Rohan.

191

192

193

194

195

195 Satinwood and rosewood secretaire with gilt bronze mounts. Victoria and Albert Museum, London.

This secretaire, which bears the label of a maker or of a shop named John MacLane, must date from about 1810. Certain features, such as the shape of the doors and the legs and the gilt bronze beading emphasizing the moldings, would seem old-fashioned on a contemporary French piece.

The superstructure in the form of two shelves is an English type which Sheraton had shown in his *Cabinet-Maker and Upholsterer's Drawing-Book*, Plate 43, in an engraving dated September 27, 1792. On the Continent this arrangement was adopted much later. Upper shelves are found in most cupboards and on some smaller pieces of furniture made during Louis-Philippe's reign.

196 Pine cupboard decorated with pen-and-ink designs on a black ground imitating marquetry. The caryatids are of gilt bronze. England, early nineteenth century. Victoria and Albert Museum, London.

The proportions of this cupboard, which measures 89 cm in height, 114 cm in length and 34.50 cm in depth, are similar to those of contemporary French cupboards. However, the *bombé* front of this piece had long been out of fashion in France by this date.

197 Three-door cupboard of light wood and black-stained wood, by George Bullock. Victoria and Albert Museum, London.

Like most of Bullock's work, this piece displays excellent craftsmanship and rather overelaborate decoration, together with a certain lack of harmony of proportion. Bullock, who died in 1818, did not always work from his own designs. Three-door cupboards became fashionable in France during the Restoration.

196   197

198

198 Low bookcase of mahogany and lemonwood from the Duke of Orléans' apartment in the Tuileries Palace. Musée du Louvre, Paris.
This bookcase, which was made by Alphonse Jacob-Desmalter, doubtless dates from between 1837, the date of the duke's marriage, and his death in 1842.

199 Cupboard *(commode à vantaux)* of thuya wood and black-stained wood with gilt bronze mounts and a white marble top. Musée des arts décoratifs, Paris.
This attractive cupboard, dating from after 1827, is signed by the cabinetmaker Fischer. It is of refined and sober workmanship and classical in style. Its proportions are similar to those of the Duke of Orléans' low bookcases, likewise in the classical idiom, but it is also related to the less classical cupboard *(meuble d'appui)* made by Bellangé.

200 Cupboard *(meuble d'appui)* of black wood with gilt bronze mounts. Stamped Bellangé, cabinetmaker to the French king. Musée des arts décoratifs, Paris.
The upper drawer folds down to form a desk with small drawers of palisander wood. The lower part is a two-door cupboard with "English" drawers also of palisander wood. Alexandre Bellangé became cabinet-maker to the king in 1842 and the cupboard must therefore have been made after this date.

199   200

Seat Furniture

In the majority of cases seat furniture was designed as part of an ensemble comprising chairs, armchairs, stools and sofas, nearly always made to match. The furniture maker repeated the same decorative motifs and details on each piece. In cases where this was not done, confusion about dating can arise. There was after all no obligation to make chairs conform to a pattern. There are suites with armchairs with stuffed backs but chairs with carved backs. Other suites have some chairs with straight backs and others with S-shaped backs. There is no strict rule about suites of seat furniture, and the most sensible approach is to follow the evolution of forms for each subcategory. We shall apply this approach to stools and sofas, but shall not treat chairs and armchairs separately since they have so much in common.

Chairs and armchairs

Apart from chairs based on classical models (see Chapter I), chairs and armchairs made at the beginning of the nineteenth century were closely related to their eighteenth-century counterparts. The most striking example is the chair with a rectangular back, or "square" back as it was called by contemporaries. There is usually only one important difference between a Louis XVI-style chair *à la reine* and a chair made in the Directory period. It consists in the replacement of fluted back legs with saber-shaped ones. As time went by these saber-shaped legs were slightly inclined so as to improve the stability of the chair, at the same time giving it a lighter appearance.

One of the most constant characteristics of Empire and Restoration chairs is the saber shape[25] of the back legs. This gives a continuous S-shaped line to the back part of the chair or armchair, and makes a chair of this period attractive when seen from any angle. Saber-shaped legs naturally help to date a chair.

Saber-shaped legs on French chairs are probably based on antique models rather than on English eighteenth-century ones. However, the English chairs were made with backward-curving legs either at the back or the front. The most pleasing, such as the armchairs from the gallery at Corsham Court, Wiltshire (about 1760), already look like Directory chairs when seen in profile. Their inclined back and legs form a single continuous curve. True saber-shaped legs, which are curved rather than inclined and slope strongly backwards, were introduced at about the same time on both sides of the English Channel.

It is never easy to discover exactly when fashion changes. The transition from one style to the next never affects all craftsmen at exactly the same moment. Saber-shaped legs only became fully accepted around 1800, having appeared some fifteen years earlier without displacing the fashion for straight inclined back legs. Several securely dated chairs enable us to follow the evolution of the style.

In 1785 Monsieur, the king's brother (the future King Louis XVIII) received from Jacob through his financial secretary the following memorandum:[26]

24 April 1795

For Madame, at Montreuil[27]

Six chairs *à l'anglaise* in the new style, of mahogany; arched on plan and elevation; the backs curved and pierced, ornamented with carved moldings in the form of pierced sheaves; the back formed of ears of corn carved in low relief above flowerets; lower down laurel leaf ornament enriched with pearls and palmettes in the corners of the back; turned fluted front legs of waisted shape; back legs in the form of deer's legs. The whole polished *au tripoli*.

The expression chairs (or armchairs) *à l'anglaise,* as applied to chairs with carved backs, occurs in other memoranda by Jacob of about the same date and confirms the English origin of this type of chairback. It is also described as "fan-shaped" (in a document dated March 8, 1783), "in the form of openwork lyres" (April 24, 1785) or "carved with ears of corn" (October 17, 1785). The passage we quoted above dated 1785 seems to contain the first mention of the back legs of a chair being carved to imitate deer's legs. The expression refers to saber-shaped legs, which are also called Etruscan legs in other documents.

Until 1788 G. Jacob, in common with other Parisian carpenters, made chairs with straight fluted legs. Several chairs in Dugourc's album[28] have straight legs, combined with other features which prefigure the Directory style. Others have saber-shaped legs but the design still needs to be fully worked out.

After 1790 chairs commonly had at least two of their four legs shaped in this way.

There are still a great number of surviving chairs stamped *Assemblée Nationale* which are of this type. On July 9, 1789 the Estates General took the title of National Constituent Assembly. None of the chairs bearing this mark have a maker's stamp, which indicates that they were made after the suppression of the craft guilds in March 1791. The Constituent Assembly disbanded on September 30, 1791 but the assembly elected to replace it, called the Legislative Assembly, continued to be known officially as the *Assemblée Nationale*. It gave way in turn on September 20, 1792 to the National Convention. The chairs stamped *Assemblée Nationale* must therefore date from between 1791 and 1792.

In 1792 Georges Jacob had himself painted with his family by an otherwise unknown artist, Lepeintre, who signed and dated his picture.[29] The *ébéniste* is depicted seated in an armchair in the antique style with four saber-shaped legs, but as these chairs are shown from the front the legs are too indistinctly drawn for us to be certain of their shape. The same would have been true for Sheraton's chairs, had he not shown one in perspective (Pl. XXIV, dated August 1, 1792) and provided a view of the Prince of Wales's dining room (Pl. LX, dated January 16, 1793). In both plates the chairs have saber-shaped legs rather like those on an almost contemporary chair designed by John Linnel, who died in 1796.

By around 1795 saber-shaped legs are so commonly found that it seems pointless to single out examples. After 1800 it became the exception to make chairs with straight back legs. Jacob-Desmalter no longer bothered to give details in his bills (1803–13) of the shape of the back legs of his chairs, as they were always saber-shaped. However, he continued to describe front legs which could be made in various shapes. These will be shown in the pieces we have chosen to illustrate.

Throughout the Empire period most chairs had square backs. Those made by the Jacobs, with a few exceptions, had square or rectangular backs with an equal amount of wood left showing on each side of the back. Other furniture makers raised the top rail and gave it a slight curve; similarly the side rails were curved where they joined the seat. The chair then took on a form close to gondola-shaped examples 217, 218 made at this time.

The square-backed chairs described above were closely based on Louis XVI chairs. This was not the case for chairs with curved backs, which were popular throughout the Empire period and were still made after the Restoration. For contemporaries this shape had classical connections. An overdoor with a bas-relief from the Lakanal premises[30] shows the influence of the antique at this time. The bas-relief depicts two women in Greek costume seated by a flaming tripod altar. As was customary, the details of this sacrificial or ceremonial scene have been borrowed from antiquity. One of the women is playing a musical instrument, while the other is leaning towards the altar, allowing us to see the curved scrolled chair back.

Chairs of this form made in the Directory period are common but there are few securely datable classical prototypes. An armchair with a slightly curved back can be seen in a fresco from Boscoreale now in the Metropolitan Museum, New York. Armchairs, or rather thrones, their low vertical backs surmounted by a bird's head, are shown on archaic Greek vases.

Once again it is the eighteenth century rather than the classical period which provided the original shape. Scrolled curved backs can be seen on many wall sofas for window 219 recesses and on beds à la turque dating from Louis XVI's reign. In 1777 Georges Jacob made chairs and armchairs in gilded wood[31] for the Turkish room in the residence of the Comte d'Artois in the Temple quarter of Paris. These chairs have curved backs and legs which are almost saber-shaped but terminate in scrolls. They are close in style to their later counterparts made in the Directory period.

It is difficult to discover exactly when forms which had previously been called oriental began to be thought of as classical by designers and their clients. The chairs made in 220 1787 by Georges Jacob for Marie-Antoinette's dairy at Rambouillet are generally taken as the first example of this phenomenon. Jacob himself describes them on his bill as not of his own invention but "of a new form in the Etruscan style... after a design by sieur Robert." This "sieur Robert" is thought to be the painter Hubert Robert. Jacob and his sons must have liked these chairs at Rambouillet, which are attractive and novel in design, as they continued to use, 221, 222 simplifying them slightly, the palmette and strapwork motifs on the backs. The design of these chairs without doubt considerably influenced other furniture makers. The strongly curved chairback is a feature of many of Jacob's pieces, as well as those of other craftsmen. Yet even for the Rambouillet chairs there were precedents. In 1785 Georges Jacob sent the following invoice:

Memorandum concerning work carried out for and supplied to Monsieur at Versailles, on the orders of M. de Bard...   24 April 1785
Two large *voyeuse* chairs of new form, square, the backs of arched form, the uprights of the backs in the form of an inverted cross, the top rail scrolled and ornamented in the center with rosettes of sunburst form...[32]

These chairs have survived and have recently been acquired by the Museum at Versailles. The back is superbly executed, and is similar to the two *voyeuse* chairs illustrated in Plates 223, 224.

We shall doubtless never know who had the idea of making chairs and armchairs with scroll backs, a type that was extremely popular during the Directory and Empire periods. The first examples had high backs, which were so 225 strongly curved towards the rear as to threaten the equilibrium of the chair. These chairs are easily knocked over and the top rail broken. Many surviving pieces have been repaired. For this reason furniture makers were forced to reduce the weight of the overhang at the top of the chairback and to attenuate its curve. In doing this they achieved the S-shaped curve which gives Empire and Restoration chairs such a graceful and pleasing line.

The chairs and armchairs made for the Récamiers deserve special mention. Madame Récamier's apartment, furnished between 1798 and 1800 by the architect Berthault, a pupil of Percier, was one of the attractions of Paris, which all distinguished visitors wanted to see. The chairs, designed by Berthault and made by the Jacob brothers, were so much admired that they were soon imitated by all the fashionable furniture makers. Thanks to Madame Récamier herself, who kept the chairs all her life and left them to her descendants, some of them have survived. One is illustrated in Plate 226.

The copies mostly repeat the curved back, and the rather unusual and most attractive armrests in the form of sphinxes, which have a lighter appearance without their front feet.[33] None of the copies, however, even those from the Jacob workshop, such as the examples sold by Blache at Versailles on May 9, 1979, quite capture the refinement of design and execution of the originals.

Besides the almost exact copies which we have singled out, a number of chairs exist which appear to derive from Madame Récamier's chairs and armchairs. These include a small two-seater sofa in the Musée des arts décoratifs, Paris.[34]

All these chairs, which have an S-shaped curved back, thin straight armrests attached by a joint to the chairback, probably date from the first years of the nineteenth century. 227 A fine piece in the Musée des arts décoratifs, Paris, is in the same style.

There is only one remaining category of neoclassical chair of nineteenth-century date. This comprises chairs with a gondola-shaped back *(sièges en gondole)* which replaced the eighteenth-century cabriole chairs[35] and became increasingly popular in France at the end of the Empire period and after the Restoration. Both light and easily movable, they were as comfortable as larger chairs and took up far less space, especially in a small room such as a boudoir or a dressing room, where they were first used before being introduced into drawing rooms. In shape and construction the gondola-shaped chairs do not differ greatly from desk chairs. However, desk chairs made in the early 1800s, clearly hark back to their eighteenth-century predecessors, while gondola-shaped chairs have a more 228 shadowy origin. Large comfortable *bergères* or armchairs, which had rounded backs enveloping the sitter, were made during the reigns of both Louis XV and Louis XVI. Yet 229–233 there is no smooth transition from these amply conceived chairs to the small boat-shaped examples of the later period, especially as the backs of the earliest examples were horizontal, like the backs of some desk chairs.

It is probable that the designers who created the gondola-shaped chair, among whom Percier must be included, harked back as much to the curved backs of classical stone thrones (see p. 17) as to any eighteenth-century model. After 1808–9 most gondola-shaped chairs began to have curved backs.

Many details characteristic of chairs made during this period deserve to be mentioned, but we shall single out only one aspect: the form of armrests on armchairs and sofas. We shall discuss in turn examples of solid armrests, those with baluster supports and horn-shaped ones.

The form of armrest most often found during the Louis XVI period, the so-called *accotoir en console,* is rarely met with after the Revolution. It reappeared in a different guise in the Empire period. Arms usually terminating in a lion's head rested on a curved support in a shape which hardly merits the term console. A new version of the true console-shaped armrest became current in the Restoration period. In this version the armrest is often continued beyond the point where it is attached to the console, and terminates in a scroll which can be fairly elaborate. This type of armrest seems to have been invented in England, as it is found as early as 1800 on armchairs at Southill, a house redecorated and furnished by the architect Henry Holland. With various modifications these armchairs remained in use in England throughout the Regency period, and it is doubtless the English original that was adopted in Russia and other European countries. It is indeed doubtful whether France should be included, as the first French examples appeared much later[36] and attained their greatest popularity at the end of the Restoration period and during Louis-Philippe's reign.

From the end of the Louis XVI period baluster-shaped armrests became more common than those of the console type. They were by far the most popular of all in the Directory and Consulate eras.

The baluster support is sometimes placed some way back from the edge of the chair, but is more commonly found above the front leg, both being turned at the same time—a method of construction which increased the solidity of the chair. Since they comprised a single structural element, furniture makers soon gave them visible coherence by forming the front leg as one member, slightly tapering toward the bottom; a single of piece wood rises without interruption from the floor to the armrest. Sometimes the leg was turned; when rectangular in section it was surmounted by an Egyptian head.

Armchairs for use on state occasions were made by the Jacob brothers and later by Jacob-Desmalter. Their legs and armrests were in the form of a "double baluster," a design probably originating with Percier. The front legs of thrones designed by Percier are often of square or rectangular section and are ornamented in low relief. This type of leg was also adopted for armchairs.

It should be noted that despite the invention of new forms, armrests supported by a column or baluster which was quite separate from the leg still continued to be used, and were current throughout the Empire period and beyond.

We shall not describe in detail armrest supports carved to represent animals or chimeras. These were not widespread and normally are found only on furniture made for the luxury market. Seldom were they successful.

Horn-shaped armrests, which may terminate in spiral scrolls, are more common and seem to have been more important for the history of furniture. Once again prototypes can be found in Louis XVI's reign. Only one example, which is securely datable, has been chosen for illustration here. In 1784 Henri Jacob delivered armchairs of gilded wood to the Grand Duchess Maria Feodorovna for her own room at Pavlovsk. Henri Jacob probably did not invent this type of armrest. It can be seen in drawings by the ornamentalist Lalonde, and was used by other furniture makers such as J. B. Séné and Georges Jacob. Several armchairs made by Georges Jacob during the Revolution already had the horn-shaped armrests which we so much admire in the work of his sons.

Many English armchairs, smaller and lighter than their contemporary French counterparts, have similar armrests. The scroll terminal, which initially was restrained but later became more elaborate, probably originated in Great Britain.

In France spiral scroll armrest terminals were rare in the early period. The device reappears around 1808 and became very common during the Restoration period, when chairs with this feature were the most popular type, together with the gondola-shaped armchairs described earlier.

In the course of time the scroll became more and more elaborate so that it was sometimes exaggerated. The whorls of the spiral were opened out and the back itself became slightly curved.

In the Restoration period there were complex cross-currents in design and fashion. Other styles, such as Gothic, Renaissance and Louis XIV, coexisted with neoclassical, which itself was now interpreted in many different ways. There was a general and persistent tendency to produce heavier furniture of more complicated design. This was particularly true of pieces made for the luxury market.

This tendency was now new. It was already in evidence in the Empire period but became more marked during the second decade of the nineteenth century in both France and England. There was a conscious and noticeable change in taste in England, as can be seen from a passage by Sir Walter Scott written for the *Quarterly Review* in March 1828[37]:

> Our national taste indeed has been changed, in almost every particular, from that which was meagre, formal, and poor, and has attained, comparatively speaking, a character of richness, variety, and solidity. An ordinary chair, in the most ordinary parlour, has now something of an antique cast—something of Grecian massiveness, at once, and elegance in its forms. That of twenty or thirty years since was mounted on four tapering and tottering legs, resembling four tobacco-pipes; the present supporters of our stools have a curule air, curve outwards behind, and give a comfortable idea of stability to the weighty aristocrat or ponderous burgess who is about to occupy one of them.

Despite his appreciation of contemporary furniture, Scott dit not omit to remind his readers that excessive ornamentation was not in good taste.

France and other countries in continental Europe did not entirely escape this change in style, although it took some time to take effect. Many chairs made in France between 1820 and 1830 are as light and elegant in appearance as chairs of the Directory and early Empire periods.

Despite Sir Walter Scott's pronouncements, lighter looking chairs continued to be made in England. "Bedroom
267 chairs" were illustrated by Ackermann in his publication of 1814.[38] They were of an advanced design for the time and could easily be mistaken for models made around 1830. Italian makers in Chiavari were among those producing very light chairs, which were to be found in most drawing rooms alongside heavy upholstered ones.

Two of these light chairs are reproduced in Plates 268, 269. They are now in the Cinquantenaire Museum, Brussels. The style of the first is strongly influenced by English chairs, while the other conforms to a type commonly found on the Continent during Louis-Philippe's and Napoleon III's reigns. Both are painted black and are decorated with polychrome and gold motifs, a technique which became widespread after 1835–40. Once again it is difficult to overlook the English influence. Painted furniture was also popular in England at the beginning of the nineteenth century.

Sofas and daybeds

Sofas, referred to as *canapés* in early nineteenth-century accounts, inventories or bills, are usually six feet (about 1.90 m), occasionally eight feet, in length. Most were made with matching armchairs to form a suite, but occasionally sofas differed slightly from the matching chairs for practical reasons. For instance, as a sofa was always placed against a wall it would have been inappropriate to give it a curved back. Sometimes the furniture maker gave the sofa different details from its matching chairs, as in the case of a suite of which part is now at Fontainebleau and the rest at Pau. The armrests on the sofa terminate in an outward-turned scroll,
272 while those on the armchairs are more classical in design
214 and are in the form of columns supporting the arm.

As far as possible we shall confine ourselves to illustrating
270–275 sofas which match armchairs already discussed. Because of the size and weight of a sofa, the different elements of the carcase are generally larger and thicker than they would be on an armchair. This often had unhappy results, making the sofa heavier and clumsier in appearance than its matching chairs. Exceptions exist, showing that furniture makers were capable of solving the structural problems. It is worth noting that the earliest sofas are the most elegant.

Sofas of the type described above were not the only kind made. Others had a headrest at either end as high as the
276 back, like beds or alcove sofas of the Louis XVI period.

Small two-seater settees called *têtes-à-têtes,* which resemble large *bergère* armchairs, continued to be made in the Empire period, as did chaises longues and daybeds, which were given a variety of names.

A new type of sofa came into being during the First Empire. It was known as a *méridienne* and was also referred
277, 278 to in France as a *paumier* or *pommier*. It is a small sofa with three sides, each of different dimensions. It can be entirely covered in fabric, or else the wooden frame may be left exposed on at least one side. Despite its relative impracti-

cality—its size did not allow the user to stretch out fully —the *méridienne* was extremely popular for a long time. Fine examples were still being produced in France during 279–281 the Restoration period. They were usually placed near the chimney breast. The *méridienne* did not really take the place of the daybed, which continued to be made. It had either one or two bedheads and was similar to contemporary boat-shaped beds, although smaller and more delicate in appearance.

The English version of the *méridienne* is longer and less satisfying from an esthetic point of view, as its scrolls and curves are exaggerated. In an age dominated by classicism it has an almost baroque appearance. However, it is a true chaise longue which allows the user to lie at full length and 282 even rest his or her feet on its upholstered end. The scroll at the extremity was copied in France and can be found on Restoration daybeds with a single bedhead. The French examples are more classical in style than their contemporary English counterparts, which are overdecorated and heavy-looking.

The same taste for solid, heavy furniture is seen in English sofas. Their armrests have increased in size and the wooden 283 parts are elaborately carved, while the legs are short and squat. Their weight and volume are reminiscent of Bieder-meier furniture, which was fashionable in all continental countries except France, where it never attained any popularity at all. This is perhaps because numerous comfortable daybeds, consisting almost entirely of a 284 mattress and cushions, were made there from the eighteenth century onward. They were first used in rooms furnished in "Turkish style." These daybeds became even more popular in the Restoration period. They were often very large, but might be no bigger than a sofa. Almost invariably they were specially made to fit into a certain part of the room and were placed on a fixed wooden plinth. As they were almost impossible to move, they were certain to be replaced by other furniture in the course of time. The models which survive were often movable. They have a wooden chassis on wheels and a vertical back against which cushions were placed. The daybed which can be seen in Queen Hortense's boudoir was 56 probably of this type. Two examples made of light wood with carved backs are in the château at Pau. 285

All these daybeds were placed against the wall. When it became customary to put furniture in the middle of the room, there was a fashion for a sort of central daybed consisting of a stuffed backrest associated with a divanlike seat. This later became known in France as a *borne*. It had its greatest moment during Napoleon III's reign but had been invented long before. There was one in the Large Drawing Room in Brighton Pavilion designed by John Nash for George IV,[39] and another in Comte de Mornay's bedroom as it appears in a painting of 1832 by Delacroix. 76

The date of the first fully upholstered and covered day- 287 beds is uncertain. British interiors painted in the first and second decades of the nineteenth century seem to show this type, but it is not always easy to decide whether the daybed is upholstered or just covered with a dust sheet. The habit of leaving dust sheets in place except when guests were expected certainly made people accustomed to seeing large upholstered furniture in the center of a room. Here again England seems to have been the first country in Europe to adopt this way of arranging a room.

Stools

We have seen how architects and furniture makers were inspired by Greek chairs (pp. 11ff.). Other classical seat furniture, especially stools, also provided models.

Stools are undoubtedly the piece of furniture easiest to make. They are used by primitive peoples, to whom the Greeks and Romans were obviously closer than we are, since stools were in common in the classical period. On vase paintings and in sculpture even the gods are often shown seated on stools. On the Parthenon frieze Zeus himself deigns to use one, and Ares perches happily on another.

Folding stools of cloth or leather have always coexisted with proper stools, but in the eighteenth century these two types seem to have become somewhat interchangeable. Ordinary stools were made with X-shaped legs like those of folding stools. At the end of the Ancien Regime the word *pliant*, or more commonly *ployant*, was used to describe all sorts of stools, whether folding or not. This usage continued in the nineteenth century. Admirers of the Ancients naturally tried to imitate classical stools, but in practice they were inspired only by finely made folding stools (some of which must originally have been made in bronze). These were more attractive than ordinary wooden stools with large turned legs.

It was considered good form to have stools in one's bedroom or drawing room and to use them frequently. As in preceding centuries, stools were considered indispensable at court for reasons of etiquette. From the time of Louis XIV only a duchess had the right to sit on a stool in the presence of the king and his consort. The right to sit on a stool was seen in France as a privilege and the stool itself was considered as a seat of honor.

Up to a point Napoleon attempted to resurrect the etiquette of the Ancien Regime. This is why there are so many stools in his châteaux. However, he relaxed etiquette in favor of the female sex, for in the empress's great drawing room at the Tuileries there were seven large armchairs, thirty-six chairs and only five stools. This arrangement did not suit the duchess of Angoulême, Louis XVI's daughter, who occupied the empress's quarters after the Restoration of the Bourbons. In August 1816 Madame "expressed the desire that at the time of her return the thirty gilt wooden chairs in Her Majesty's drawing room should be replaced with stools according to etiquette."[40]

We can deduce from this pronouncement, which is less insignificant than it seems, the narrowness of spirit of members of the royal family. After 1830 the duchess of Angoulême was made responsible for the education of her nephew, Count Chambord, pretender to the French throne, who in 1873 felt obliged to renounce the throne over the question of the color of the flag.

Two or three types of X-shaped stools, originally designed by Percier and Fontaine, were produced in quantity with only slight variations. In one the four arms of the X are straight and are placed symmetrically in relation to a central rosette from which they appear to spring. These legs often look like two flattened balusters placed opposite each other. In the other type the legs curve 290 inwards so that, seen from the front, the piece seems to be made of two opposed semicircular elements meeting in the 286 center. The stools in the Council Chamber at Malmaison are of this type. Thomas Hope plagiarized this model, which he claimed to have designed himself. It is true that in 1807 England was at war with France, so that it would probably have been unwise of him to have acknowledged the source of his inspiration.

We reproduce here several early nineteenth-century 288–295 stools. All but two of these conform to the types described above. Three have their original coverings and fringes. These fringes, which were part of the architect's or designer's original specifications, are sometimes very effective, but they can also disguise unduly the structure of the stool.

201

202

201 Painted wooden chair, Louis XVI period, stamped Georges Jacob. Musée national du château de Pau.
During the Empire period this chair was in an antechamber of the Tuileries Palace.

202 Painted wooden chair, Empire period, stamped J. Louis. Musée national du château de Pau.

203

203 Gilded wooden chair, stamped Jacob-Desmalter. Musée Masséna, Nice.
This chair is part of a suite made for Cambacérès, the High Chancellor.

204 Mahogany chair with petit point upholstery, stamped Jacob-Desmalter. Private Collection.

There are at least two suites of furniture which include chairs of this model. One is at the Villa Marlia, near Lucca, and includes chairs with the same openwork detail on the lower part of the back. The other set in the Musée Masséna, Nice, only comprises armchairs and a sofa.

205

205–207 Three designs for chairs. Musée des arts décoratifs, Paris.

These three watercolor designs from Dugourc's album of 1790 are all by the same hand and were probably executed by the decorator Grognard.

206

207

208

208 Wooden chair marked *Assemblée Nationale*. Direction des musées de France, Louvre, Paris.
These chairs were mass-produced by a large number of different chairmakers. The back legs are saber-shaped, and the back with its grille pattern is slightly inclined. Dining room and desk chairs of the same type were made during the Empire period. The designer is unknown.

209 Measured drawing of chair. Plate 24 in Sheraton's *Cabinetmaker and Upholsterer's Drawing Book*.

210 Design for a chair. Pen-and-wash drawing by John Linnel. Victoria and Albert Museum, London.
John Linnel, one of London's best craftsmen in ebony, worked for Robert Adam and other architects or private individuals of distinction. He died in 1796, and this design may date from the last years of his life. The chairback is reminiscent of one on a Louis XVI chair: the turned front legs terminate in feet resembling a spinning top, while the rear legs are saber-shaped and are just like those made by contemporary French craftsmen in ebony.

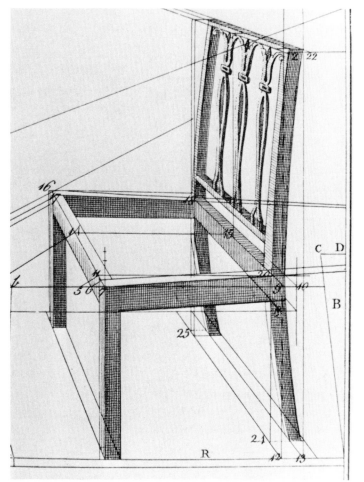

209 210

211 Chair of white-painted wood, partly gilt. Royal Palace, Brussels.
The label on this chair, which reads *Service de Mrs les Officiers à Laeken* ("The Laeken Officers' Suite") proves that it was at Brussels from 1805 or 1806. It is also stamped by Jacob-Desmalter and is a good example of his current production. The rear legs are thick and sturdy.

212 Chair of white-painted wood, partly gilt, stamped Jacob-Desmalter. Musée national du château de Pau.
This chair was made for the duke of Frioul's first drawing room at the Tuileries Palace, where he was grand marshal. It must date from 1810 and was once upholstered with a purple silk brocade that had gold floral motifs and a border of the same fabric.

213 Mahogany chair covered with silk brocade. Schloss Ehrenburg, Coburg.
Around 1815 Duke Ernest of Saxe-Coburg bought a quantity of furniture from Paris makers. This chair may be French.

211

212

213

214

215

216

217

214 Carved and painted wooden armchair covered with tapestry. Musée national du château de Fontainebleau.
This finely carved chair was made by the Jacob brothers. It was part of a large suite of salon furniture now divided up between Pau (see Pl. 272) and Fontainebleau. All the chairs are stamped with the mark of the Directory. Only the Fontainebleau ones are tapestry-covered.

215 Mahogany armchair, stamped Jacob-Desmalter. Private Collection.
The suite of salon furniture to which this armchair belonged was originally delivered to a man named Quevauvilliers. It is now the property of M. Dieudonné Duriez. The shape of this armchair is almost the same as that of examples from the Directory period illustrated earlier, but it is sturdier and less refined.

216 Wooden armchair (originally painted), stamped J. Louis. Musée national du château de Pau.
The Imperial furniture depository ordered a fairly large number of chairs with a square back such as one finds here. They were made by various chairmakers to Jacob's original design, but were less expensive.

217 Mahogany chair with pediment back. Schloss Ehrenburg, Coburg.
Like the chair illustrated in Plate 213, this one could be French. The front legs may be replacements.
The shape of the back, which is stylistically midway between the square and the boat-shaped back, dates from the beginning of the Empire period. The pediment on top is a sign of fine craftsmanship.

218

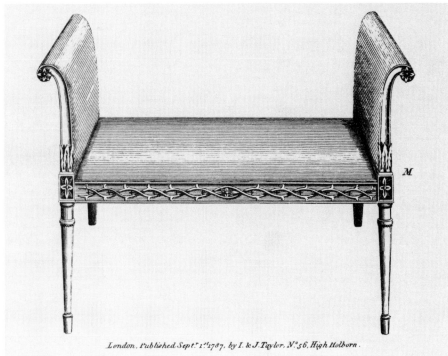

219

218 Mahogany *bergère* armchair, marked M. E. Private Collection.
Rounded and slightly curved chairbacks were common during the Empire period, but only two or three examples of this form survive from the Jacob workshop.

219 "Window stool." Plate 20 from Hepplewhite's *Cabinet-Maker and Upholsterer's Guide,* engraving dated September 1, 1787.

London. Published Sept.ʳ 1.ˢᵗ 1787, by I. & J. Taylor, N.º 56, High Holborn.

220 Carved chair of solid mahogany. Musée national du château de Versailles.
This chair was made for Marie-Antoinette's dairy at Rambouillet. It was made by Georges Jacob in 1787.

221 Mahogany armchair, stamped Jacob Frères. Musée national de la Malmaison.
A label reveals that this chair, together with others, was made for Maret, who was created general secretary to the Consuls after the *coup d'état* of 18 brumaire. His was a highly important post and it is possible that these armchairs were ordered to provide him with an office in keeping with his function. The chair is in the style fashionable around 1800.

222 Carved mahogany armchair, stamped Jacob Frères. Private Collection.
This armchair is similar in style to the one made for Maret, secretary to the Consuls (see Pl. 221), except for the front legs which are in the form of goats' hooves.

221 △

220   222

223 *Voyeuse* chair of carved wood, painted green, stamped Georges Jacob. Maurice Thenadey Collection, Paris.
The seat and upper part of the back are covered with leather. The front of the seat is slightly rounded, a feature commonly found on chairs made during the Revolution and in the Directory period (see Pl. 208) and rarely during the Empire period. The front legs terminate in goats' hooves and are turned outwards, whereas the back legs, which are strongly arched, terminate in a scroll—a rare and old-fashioned feature.

224 Mahogany *voyeuse* chair with pierced back, stamped Jacob Frères. Musée national du château de Fontainebleau.
Made for the empress's Second Drawing Room at the Tuileries Palace.

223, 224

127

225

226

227

228

225 Mahogany *bergère* armchair, stamped G. Jacob. Private Collection.

226 Mahogany and lemonwood armchair made for Madame Récamier. Private Collection.

227 Mahogany chair inlaid with mother-of-pearl and copper. Musée des arts décoratifs, Paris.
This chair was doubtless made to order for its original owner whose monogram is inlaid on the upper part of the back, and is of fine quality. It was probably created by an architect or designer. The handrests, in place of the usual armrests, are highly original but were doubtless fragile and impratical. They are not found on any other surviving chairs. The general outline and the curved back recall other chairs made around 1800.

228 Mahogany desk chair with leather-covered seat; stamped Jacob-Desmalter. Direction des musées de France, Louvre, Paris.

Originally made in the Empire period for a prince's room at Fontainebleau, the armchair has been used since the nineteenth century by the Keeper of Egyptian Antiquities in the Louvre Museum. It was in Champollion's office. Georges Jacob had already made desk chairs of the same form.

229 Design by Percier for the armchairs shown in Plate 230, published by H. Lefuel in his book on F. H. G. Jacob-Desmalter, Plate VIII.

230 Gilt wooden armchairs *en gondole,* decorated with swans painted white. Musée national de la Malmaison.
When they had to execute Percier's designs for armchairs, the Jacob brothers were faced with the problem of interpreting an armrest of animal or chimera form. If the animal is carved in the round, the armrest and chair both look heavy, but it cannot be too flat. None of the compromises adopted were successful, and well-executed chairs of this model are rare.

229

230

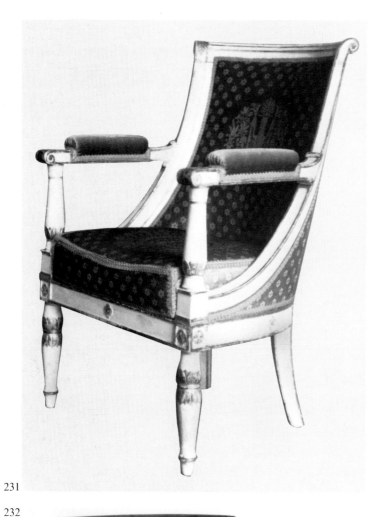

231

232

233

231 Armchair *en gondole,* of painted wood, partly gilt, stamped J. D. for Jacob-Desmalter. Schloss Nymphenburg, Bavaria.

232, 233 *Bergère* armchair and chair *en gondole,* of white-painted wood, partly gilt. Musée national du château de Versailles, Grand Trianon.
These chairs form part of a suite comprising a sofa, two *bergères,* four chairs and two stools, delivered on August 20, 1810 by the upholsterer Darrac for the bedroom at the Petit Trianon. They are not stamped but appear to have been made by Jacob.

234, 235 Chair and armchair *en gondole* of gilded wood. Musée national du château de Fontainebleau.
Delivered in 1808–09 by Jacob-Desmalter for the bathroom in the empress's small apartment, these chairs were covered in light blue grogram. The armchair has bronze armrests.

236 Mahogany chair *en gondole* by Jacob-Desmalter. Schloss Ehrenburg, Coburg.
This chair is the same model as those in the bathroom at Fontainebleau, but is of mahogany. It was probably acquired by Duke Ernest of Saxe-Coburg after 1815, and was formerly at the small castle of Rosenau.

237 Armchair *en gondole,* of light wood, inlaid with purple wood, covered with the original raspberry-colored tapestry. Musée Masséna, Nice.
The front legs and armrests *en console* are typical of the Restoration period.

234

235

236

237

238

239

240

241

238 Chair *en gondole*, of light wood, inlaid with purple wood. Roger Imbert Collection, Paris.
The earliest chairs *en gondole* had upholstered backs. During the Restoration period chairs with semiopenwork backs like this one appeared. These had a handgrip to make them easier to move around. The front legs are the same shape as those of the armchair in the Masséna Museum.

239 Armchair *en gondole*, of Brazilian rosewood, inlaid with lemonwood. Private Collection.
The arm of this chair extends beyond the armrest, a type of construction which became popular in France towards the end of the Restoration period. The form of the turned front legs is more elaborate than on Empire-period chairs.

240 *Bergère* of unstained wood, Louis XVI period, stamped by G. Jacob. Private Collection.
Georges Jacob made a large number of *bergères* like this one, nearly all distinguished by their generous size and fine proportions. The wooden parts of this chair were probably once painted.

241 Armchair of beech with cane seat, painted black and gilded. Victoria and Albert Museum, London.
This English armchair dates from the beginning of the nineteenth century. The decorative details of this well-balanced and elegant-looking chair are actually complex. Japanned chairs (that is those painted in Japanese manner) are as numerous in England as chairs painted white or gray are in France.

242 Painted wooden armchair. Municipal Library, Lyons.
This chair once belonged to a suite made for Cardinal Fesch, Napoleon I's uncle, who became Archbishop of Lyons in 1802. The square back is curved where it joins the seat and each armrest has a lion's head.

243 Gilded wooden armchair, covered with yellow *Gros de Naples* (corded silk) and brocaded with purple silk. Musée national du château de Fontainebleau, Second (Yellow) Drawing Room in the empress's apartments.
The chairs in this drawing room, which are of square form, were made by Jacob-Desmalter and date from 1808.

242 243

244 Cabriole chair, painted gray. Musée national du château de Pau.
This small armchair can be dated to the end of Louis XVI's reign or to the Revolutionary period on the basis of the baluster-shaped armrests, the trapezoidal back enclosed within columns and the lozenge-shaped motifs within square reserves on the front rail.

245 Two cherrywood *bergères* with baluster-shaped armrests and slightly curved backs. Musée national du château de Pau.
These chairs, which are part of a suite also comprising two armchairs and a sofa, bear only the inventory marks of Pau (1855 and 1896). They were probably purchased locally or at Bordeaux.

244

245

246 Carved and gilded wooden armchair. Royal Palace, Brussels.
The chair bears Jacob-Desmalter's stamp and a label inscribed "Laken. Grand cabinet de l'imperatrice. 6 fauteuils" (Laken. Empress's large room. 6 armchairs), proving that this chair has been in Brussels since 1805 or 1806. It is one of the chairs with double baluster legs and armrests produced in quantity by Jacob-Desmalter.

246

247

247 Painted white wooden armchair, partly gilt and upholstered with Beauvais tapestry. Musée national du château de Versailles, Grand Trianon Chapel.
This armchair of square form was part of a suite delivered in 1802 by the tapestry weaver Darrac. The chair itself was made by Pierre-Benoît Marcion.

248

249

250

251

248 Armrest on one of Madame Récamier's armchairs (see Pl. 226).
These well-proportioned chimeras or sphinxes are among the most elegant found on any chair.

249 Mahogany armchair, stamped by J.-B.-B. Demay. Musée national de la Malmaison (A. Kahn-Wolf gift).
The griffins are of ebonized and gilt wood.

250 Armchair in Egyptian taste, of black-painted wood, partly gilt. Victoria and Albert Museum, London.
Probably executed in 1806 for a drawing room at Frome Abbey after a design by George Smith dated 1804 and published in 1808 in his *Collection of Designs for Household Furniture* (Pl. 56).

The introduction of lions and chimeras into English furniture was no more successful than it was in France.

251 Beechwood armchair painted to imitate verdigrised bronze and decorated in gold. English, about 1810. Victoria and Albert Museum, London.
This chair shows French influence but is typically British in form. It is, however, less elegant than its predecessors.

252 Armchair of gilt wood stamped by Henri Jacob. Pavlovsk Palace, near Leningrad.
The scrolled armrests prefigure the "trumpet-shaped" armrests which were to become popular in France during the Revolutionary and Empire periods.
The suite of which this armchair is part was delivered in 1784.

252

253

254

255

253 Armchair of black-painted wood decorated with gilding; cane seat. English, about 1800. Victoria and Albert Museum, London.
This armchair with simple armrests again recalls French models with "trumpet-shaped" armrests.

254 Armchair of gilt wood covered with white and lapis lazuli-colored satin, brocaded in gold. Musée national du château de Fontainebleau, bedroom in the empress's small apartment.
Delivered in 1808 by Jacob-Desmalter, these chairs are among the earliest examples of chairs with scrolled armrests.

255–256 Armchair and chair from King Louis XVIII's room in the Tuileries Palace. They are of white-painted wood with gold decoration, upholstered with blue and black silk velvet. Musée du Louvre, Paris.
The Restoration government's strict program of economy succeeded in putting France's finances on a sound basis. Even the court, whose members had been so extravagant during the old regime, now kept its spending within reasonable bounds. For five years Louis XVIII slept in Napoleon's room in his bed, from which he merely stripped the Imperial emblems.
    In 1819 this room was partly refurnished. The poppy-colored velvet hangings were replaced by dark blue silk fabric, some of which survives. Jacob-Desmalter and Madame Morillon supplied some pieces of furniture. The name of the supplier of the chairs unfortunately remains unknown. It may be conjectured that they were delivered by the tapestry weaver Darrac according to a system often employed by the *Garde-Meuble*. As the chairs are not stamped, we may perhaps never know which chairmaker Darrac obtained them from. The form of these chairs is still in Empire style, but two of their details are typical of the early Restoration period: the shape of the front legs and the scrolled armrests of the armchair. The join between the scroll and the front rail of the armchair is more elegantly achieved here than on the earliest pieces of this type, such as those in the Empress Josephine's room at Fontainebleau (see Pl. 254). The upholstery of these chairs has been renewed, but follows strictly the original design. As on many Empire chairs, the trimming is a highly important element of the design.

257 Painted wooden armchair decorated with gilding; cane seat and back. English, about 1800. Victoria and Albert Museum, London.
The armrests recall French "trumpet-shaped" ones.

258 Mahogany armchair upholstered with Empire-period silk damask, gilt bronze mounts. Schloss Ellingen, Bavaria.
The top rail, which extends beyond the back of the chair and the saber-shaped legs still recall classical armchairs. The rather heavy armrests with their ponderous scrolls might indicate that the chairs in the same drawing room as this piece, which are attributed to the Paris cabinetmaker J.-J. Werner, are of somewhat more recent date than those in Louis XVIII's room. However, this is unlikely since the furnishing of Ellingen Castle, seat of the Prince-Marshal of Wrede, seems to have been completed by the time the duchess of Leuchtenberg saw it in 1818.

259 Walnut armchair from the Lyons region, with woven seat. Private Collection.
Although modest in appearance in comparison with the Prince of Wreda's chair, this armchair exhibits all the typical features of late Restoration style: armrests with open scrolls, curved back and front legs *en console*.

257

258

259

140

260 Carved and gilt wooden armchair, upholstered with Beauvais tapestry. Royal Palace, Brussels.

Two armchairs of this model stamped by Jacob-Desmalter and twenty-four stools were delivered by the tapestry weaver Darrac on August 25, 1810 for Napoleon I's Grand Cabinet at Trianon. The stools, which still have their original upholstery with a design of bees, are still at Versailles. The two armchairs were given by Louis-Philippe to his daughter Louise-Marie, who became queen of Belgium in 1832. Their tapestry coverings were rewoven or modified under Louis XVIII so as to "eliminate the emblems of the usurper," replacing them with the fleur-de-lys.

261 Carved and gilt wooden armchair. Royal Palace, Brussels. Stamped P. Marcion, this armchair dating from 1806 bears the following label:
"Imperial Furniture Depository,
Laeken Service
N° 100 Throne Room.
2 carved beechwood armchairs."
("Gard [e Meuble] imp[érial] Service de Laeken N° 100 Salle du Trône 2 fauteuils en bois de hêtre sculpté.")

260   261

262 *Bergère* with pediment and armrests, of carved and gilded wood upholstered with cut green velvet. Musée national du château de Fontainebleau.

This *bergère* is part of a suite of furniture made for the second drawing room in the emperor's lesser apartments, installed in 1810. Only the chairs are stamped P. Brion but there is no doubt that Pierre-Gaston Brion, one of the best sculptors in wood of the Empire and Restoration periods, was responsible for the entire suite. He is known to have delivered a similar set of drawing room furniture to the Imperial *Garde-Meuble* in December 1811. This furniture is now in Louis-Philippe's great drawing room in the Trianon. Another set of furniture of the same model is in the château at Chimay, Belgium.

263 Armchair of carved and gilded wood. Royal Palace, Brussels.

French armchair dating from the 1820s. Heavy forms and elaborate decoration have here been taken to an extreme. The armrests are highly exaggerated. The back, which flares at the base, and the scrolled front legs are reminiscent of some of Werner's armchairs.

The silk upholstery with its motif of crowns was rewoven at Lyons after a fabric used for curtains which may still be seen in Brussels.

264 Chair *en gondole,* of exotic wood (abura wood) and gilt wood. Victoria and Albert Museum, London.

This sumptuous and somewhat overelaborate chair *en gondole* was delivered in 1823 by the tapestry weavers Morel and Hugues to the duke of Northumberland.

Chairs intended for display made at this period often exhibit a grandiloquence which can only be considered as a defect. With its unusual form, this chair can only be compared with a *bergère* and armchair of similar shape illustrated by Percier and Fontaine.

It is interesting to note that, ten years after the appearance of the second edition of the *Recueil de décorations intérieures,* this publication still enjoyed great esteem in Great Britain.

262

263

26

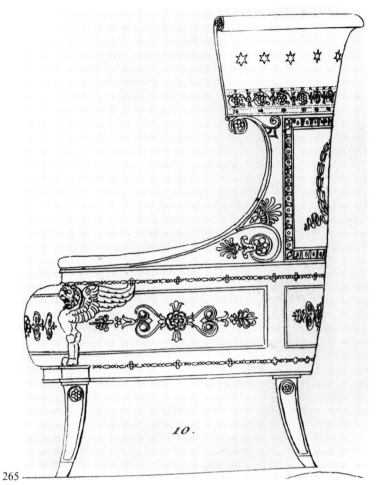

265

266

265 Armchair executed by the Jacob brothers for the bedroom of *Citoyen V*, Paris.
Engraving from Percier and Fontaine's *Recueil de décorations intérieures*.

266 Side view of a *bergère*. Engraving from the same publication.

267 Bedroom chairs. Engraving published in the periodical edited by Rudolf Ackermann, *Repository of Arts, Literature, Commerce, Manufactures, Fashions and Politics*, Vol. XII, 1814.

267

268   Chair of painted and decorated wood with upholstered cane seat. Musées royaux d'art et d'histoire, Brussels.

269   Chair of black-painted wood, decorated in colors with gilt ornaments and fillets; upholstered seat. Musées royaux d'art et d'histoire, Brussels.

270 Sofa. Plate 23 in Hepplewhite's *Cabinet-Maker and Upholsterer's Guide,* dated October 1, 1787.

271   Sofa of cherrywood with baluster-shaped armrests and slightly curved back. Musée national du château de Pau.
See Plate 245 for two *bergères* from the same suite.

272   Sofa of carved and painted wood, stamped Jacob Brothers. Musée national du château de Pau.
This sofa bears an inventory mark used by the *Garde-Meuble* in the Directory period and must therefore have been made between 1796, when the Jacob brothers firm was established, and late 1799, when the *coup d'état* of 18 brumaire an VIII (November 9, 1799) ended the Directory. See Plate 214 for an armchair from the same suite.

268   269

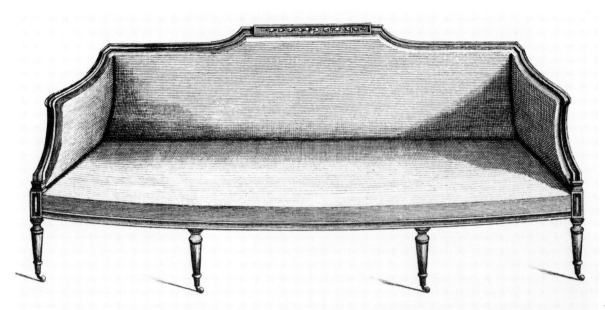

270

271

272

273

274

273 Sofa of carved and gilt wood, stamped P. Marcion. Royal Palace, Brussels.
This sofa bears a label inscribed *"Laeken nº 500 premier salon de l'Imperatrice."* It must therefore have been at Brussels since 1805 or 1806.

274 Sofa of carved and gilt wood upholstered with Beauvais tapestry, stamped Jacob-Desmalter. Royal Palace, Brussels.
This sofa, from the Empire period, was moved to Brussels in 1832 after Queen Louise-Marie's marriage. It is upholstered with a Restoration tapestry woven after cartoons by Saint-Ange or Dugourc, designers at the *Garde-Meuble.*

275 Sofa of carved and gilt wood, stamped Jacob-Desmalter. Musée national du château de Fontainebleau.
Like the armchair in Plate 243, this sofa was part of the furniture made for the Second (or Yellow) Drawing Room in the empress's small apartment at Fontainebleau.

275

276

277

278

276 Sofa of painted wood, partly gilt. Musée national du château de Versailles, Grand Trianon.
This unstamped sofa was delivered by the tapestry weaver Darrac on August 20, 1810 for the boudoir at the Petit Trianon. Of normal size (it measures 1.85 m), it is in the form of an elongated daybed and has matching chairs *en gondole* and armchairs (see Pls. 232, 233).

277 Sofa *(pommier)* and stool with carved and gilt legs, upholstered with green cut velvet. Musée national du château de Fontainebleau, second drawing room in the emperor's small apartment.
The suite of furniture was installed in 1810. The wooden parts of these pieces were made by Brion, who stamped only the chairs. A *bergère* from the same suite is shown in Plate 262.

278 Walnut sofa. Musée national du château de Pau.
The shape of this sofa is almost the same as that of the preceding piece. The sofa at Pau lacks the fringe which should hide part of the legs.

279

279 Walnut daybed *(méridienne)*. Private Collection.
Daybeds of this shape were already being made in the Empire period. However, the form of the legs on this example indicates that it was made later, during the Restoration era. The lower side could at one time be lowered so that one could stretch one's legs on it.

280 Daybed of burr ash, inlaid with amaranth. Restoration period. Roger Imbert Collection, Paris.
This attractive and comfortable daybed has a rounded end partly extending beyond the sofa back. This form was uncommon in France but can be seen in the daybeds dating from around 1819 in Sir John Leicester's Gallery (see Pl. 68).

281 Daybed of palisander wood, inlaid with fillets of lemonwood. Private Collection.
The form of this boat-shaped daybed with its matching ends is unusual. The piece was part of the same suite as the chair in Plate 305 and the armchair in Plate 239.

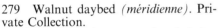

280

281

282

283

284

282 Chaise longue of carved and gilt beech. Victoria and Albert Museum, London.
This chaise longue was part of a suite delivered in 1805 by Gillows of Lancaster (one of the most important British furniture-making concerns of the period) for Kimmel Park, Denbighshire (Wales).

283 Part of a sofa. Anonymous drawing dated 1845. Victoria and Albert Museum, London.
A drawing of a sofa by Sir Charles Barry (1795–1860) which is very similar to the one illustrated here is in the library of the Royal Institute of British Architects.

284 Madame Bonaparte seated on a divan. Painting by François Gérard, 1800–01. Musée national de la Malmaison.

285 Detail of a divan of maple, inlaid with amaranth. Restoration period. Musée national du château de Pau.
The divan, which is on castors, has a pierced back formed of the same three elements as are shown in this detail. Three large cushions are supported by the back. The palmette motifs can only be seen if the cushions are removed.

286 Stool. Engraving from Percier and Fontaine's *Recueil de décorations intérieures,* Pl. 39.

287 Wooden sofa, fully upholstered by fabric; carcase stamped Jeanselme. Musée national du château de Versailles, Grand Trianon.
Two sofas of this model were delivered on March 31, 1838 by the tapestry weaver Laflèche for Louis-Philippe's large drawing room at Versailles. They were described precisely by Laflèche as follows:
Two beechwood sofas measuring 3.20 meters, their legs of palisander wood, shod with copper castors, stuffed with horsehair and covered with linen and spiral sprung; upholstered in yellow cannetillé, brocaded in blue ... yellow silk ... fringe with yellow and blue torsades [twisted fringe] ... buttoned and trimmed.
Archives nationales, O⁴ 1768.

285

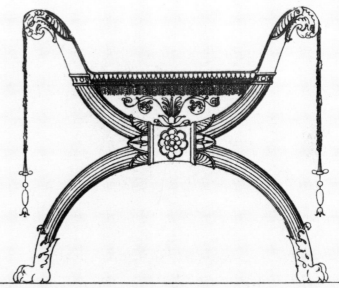

286

287

288 Stool of carved gilt wood, stamped by Jacob Brothers. Royal Palace, Brussels.
Another stool from the set bears the gilder Chatard's label and is inscribed: "For the chapel, Laeken" *(Service de la chapelle, Laeken)*.

289 Stool of carved gilt wood. Royal Palace, Brussels.
This unstamped stool can be attributed with certainty to Jacob, as various details on this stool reappear on other stools he made. The uncarved parts of the chassis must at one time have been covered with a fringe.

290 Stool of carved gilt wood, covered with tapestry. Royal Palace, Brussels.
This stool, with its X-shaped chassis, is formed of four baluster-shaped elements placed opposite each other and is one of the most common types of stool to be made during the Empire period. It bears the stamp of Jacob-Desmalter and is based on a design by Percier. It was taken to Brussels in 1832 together with Queen Louis-Marie's furniture.

291 Stool of gilt wood; original cream embroidered silk covering with green fringe and green and cream tassels, stamped Jacob-Desmalter. From the château at Saint-Cloud. Victoria and Albert Museum, London.
Seven stools were commissioned by the architect Poyet to his own designs on the occasion of Napoleon's coronation and reception by the *Corps Législatif*. The stools are described as follows in Jacob-Desmalter's estimate and bill of costs:
"Seven finished stools, with very elaborate crossed saber-shaped legs, carved and gilt, bronze-colored grounds
... at 380 fr....2660
Apart from one detail (the bronze-colored grounds), the description accords perfectly with the stool illustrated, the original covering of which has survived in a remarkable state of freshness.

288

289

290

291

292 Stool of white-painted wood with gilt relief ornament; edges of stool legs gilt. Musée national du château de Versailles, Grand Trianon.
In 1810 this stool was placed in the gallery of the Grand Trianon together with 47 other stools, eight benches and 16 console tables. All this furniture was made by Pierre-Benoît Marcion.

293 Stool of carved gilt wood, upholstered with Beauvais tapestry. Musée national du château de Versailles, Grand Trianon.
Twenty-four stools of this type were delivered on August 25, 1810 by the tapestry weaver Darrac for the Emperor's Grand Cabinet at Trianon. The wooden parts of the stool were probably made by Jacob-Desmalter, whose stamp can be found on two armchairs from the same suite now in Brussels (see Pl. 260). The stools have their original tapestry upholstery decorated with a bee motif. Such

textiles are rarely found, as most Imperial emblems were destroyed after the restoration of the monarchy.

294 Stool of cherrywood and ebonized wood. Nymphenburg Castle, Bavaria.
This most attractive stool in Biedermeier style has retained its original leather upholstery and fringe.

295 Stool of lemonwood, stamped Jeanselme. Jean Chélo Collection, Paris.
This Restoration stool, dating from after the establishment of the Jeanselme concern in 1824, retains the form of stools designed by Percier and Fontaine, who were inspired by classical X-shaped stools. Here, however, the equilibrium between the upper and lower arms of the X has been disturbed.

292

293

294

295

Reciprocal Influences between France and England

In the preceding chapters we have often had occasion to discuss the reciprocal influence which England and France have had upon each other's furniture styles. It may be helpful at this point to discuss this influence in some detail.

In the eighteenth century and at the beginning of the nineteenth the two countries were often in conflict. They were at war with each other from 1743 to 1748, 1754 to 1763, 1778 to 1783, 1792 to 1802, and 1803 to 1814. Yet at the same time the two nations were drawn to each other and each time peace was declared intellectual and artistic relations were immediately resumed. Despite the vicissitudes of politics, the two countries were surprisingly close.

The adoption by the French of English domestic habits has a special relevance for our study of furniture. The French copied vegetable gardens, dining rooms (rooms used exclusively for eating were first known in England), mahogany furniture, and seats with pierced and carved backs.

French furniture makers do not, however, seem to have used English designs, nor to have copied English furniture styles, to the extent that might be expected. Although it is easy to show the influence of English furniture treatises in places as far apart as northern Germany and the duchy of Tuscany, it is only with difficulty that one can find two or three cases in France of direct imitation of English furniture.[41]

This can be explained chiefly by the fact that Hepplewhite's *Cabinet-Maker and Upholsterer's Guide* did not appear until 1788 (second edition, 1789, third edition, 1794) and Sheraton's *Drawing Book* was published only in 1793. This meant that the works did not become known in Paris until after the Revolution and the war which ensued. It should be added that Parisian cabinetmakers ruthlessly imitated their rivals but took little notice of foreign styles.

On the other hand, French influence made itself felt in Britain by way of actual pieces, and is therefore easily traced. It became evident as soon as the neoclassical style took hold in both countries. Several of Robert Adam's clients are known to have ordered tapestry chair covers from Paris for which chairs with upholstered oval backs were specially designed. They were similar to Louis XVI-296 cabriole armchairs. An armchair like the one from David Garrick's drawing room is so closely related to contemporary French *bergères* that it must have been based on them. Every English ambassador in Paris bought furniture there, and the English bought more extensively than anyone else at the sales held during the Revolution when most of the furniture from royal palaces and châteaux was sold, together with property which had belonged to emigres.

Two leading eighteenth-century English architects, Sir William Chambers (1726–96) and Henry Holland (1745–1806) were connoisseurs of French art. Holland, the Prince of Wales's architect, bought French furniture through Daguerre for his royal master. He employed French designers, artists and craftsmen chosen from among the many who had come to London after the Revolution. Guillaume Gaubert, who later called himself a "furniture maker," was Holland's foreman; Jean-Pierre-Théodore Trécourt was a designer who seems to have been one of Holland's principal assistants (when Trécourt died in 1796, Holland spoke of retiring); Jean Dominique was a bronze caster and gilder; Jean Prussurat was a wood-carver, Alexandre-Louis Delabrière a painter-designer who had worked for Bélanger at Bagatelle; and François Hervé was a chairmaker who may have been responsible for the armchair reproduced in Plate 297, which has both French and English characteristics.

A sketch by David Wilkie (1785–1841) for a picture of 298 1813 indirectly confirms that there was a wealth of French furniture in England at the beginning of the nineteenth century. Only a small screen at the back of the picture, which is typically English, shows that it does in fact depict an English interior. The bookcase could have been made in either England or France and the two other pieces of furniture, a Directory or Empire period armchair and a Louis XVI cylinder-top desk, are incontestably French.

The renowned books of models for furniture makers issued under the names of Hepplewhite and Sheraton, which are the most valuable documents we possess for the history of English furniture, provide evidence of the importance of French influence. A great number of French terms are used, such as "tambour writing table," or "cylinder" for a *bureau à cylindre,* "cabriole chair" for a *fauteuil en cabriolet,* as well as "confidante," "duchesse," "commode," "bidet," "chaise longue" and "girandole." As we have seen, many pieces were inspired by French furniture, including chairs. Sheraton and Hepplewhite, especially the former, illustrate several armchairs and sofas directly based on contemporary (or even earlier) French 299–301 examples. Sheraton's book is full of references to France and French fashions. Even though there is a far greater quantity of purely English furniture in the work, French influence is clearly present. It was to remain important 302–304 throughout the Empire period until well into the second decade of the nineteenth century.

The year 1815 marked a turning point in furniture making as in the political sphere. French fashions, furniture and luxury items could now be exported and even found their way to England,[42] but more often the traffic was in the other direction. For the first time English styles in furniture were adopted across the Channel. The elegant French chairs of the Restoration period were to a large extent the descendants of English early nineteenth-century Regency chairs. 305–307

296 *Bergère* of beech, painted green. Victoria and Albert Museum, London.
This chair belonged to David Garrick (1717–79).

297 Lyre-back mahogany armchair, with copper rods below the armrest. Victoria and Albert Museum, London.
This chair is related to Louis XVI chairs (see, for example, the armrests on the pieces by Henri Jacob at Pavlovsk, Pl. 252) and is constructed in the same way. The top rail is fixed to the inner edge of the vertical members, whereas on English examples it extends beyond them. However, the chair also displays some English characteristics such as the upholstery on the front of the seat and the low, rather squat, back. On the evidence of the saber-shaped rear legs, the chair cannot have been made before 1790. It is thought that it may be the work of a French craftsman active in London.

296   297

298 View of part of a library or study. Painting by David Wilkie (1785–1841). Victoria and Albert Museum, London.
This is a preparatory study from life for a painting of 1813 by Wilkie entitled *The Letter of Introduction*.

299 Chair and armchair. Plate 9 in Hepplewhite's *Cabinet-Maker and Upholsterer's Guide* dated September 1787.
The left-hand chair, with its barred back and columnar side rails, is reminiscent of contemporary French chairs.

298

299

300   Drawing room armchairs. Plate 6 in the appendix to Sheraton's *Cabinet-Maker and Upholsterer's Drawing-Book,* 1793.
The circular seat, chairback, armrests and their baluster supports are derived from French chairs of the Louis XVI period.

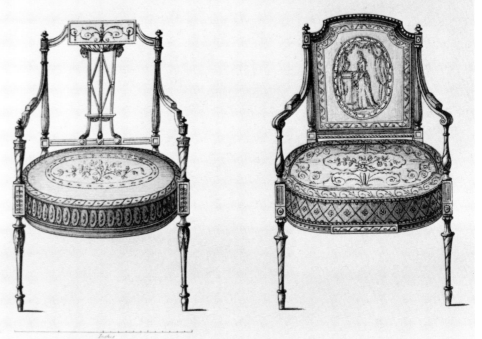

300

301

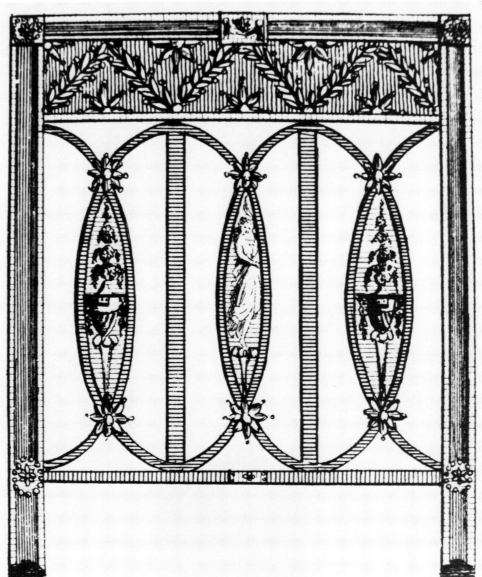

301   Chairback. Detail of Plate 13, 3rd edition of Hepplewhite's *Cabinet-Maker and Upholsterer's Guide,* 1794.
Following Sheraton's suggestion in the introduction to his own work that Hepplewhite's chairbacks were old-fashioned, the editors of the *Cabinet-Maker and Upholsterer's Guide* introduced more modern ones in the third edition. Of the twelve chairbacks shown in Plates 12 and 13, seven are of square form with a straight top rail. This was a new type for Hepplewhite, but can be found on the majority of French chairs in production at that time.

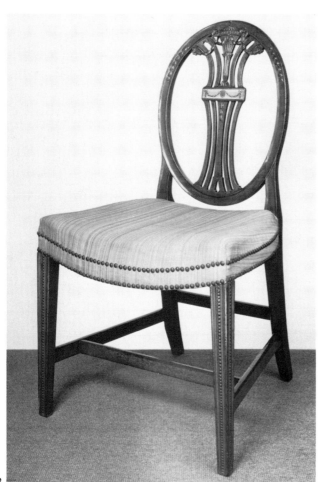

302–304 Three English mahogany chairs dating from 1785–95. Victoria and Albert Museum, London.
The front of each of these chairs is entirely covered with fabric. Plates 4 and 1 in Hepplewhite's book, the first edition of which was published in 1788, provided the inspiration for the chairbacks in Plates 303 and 304.

302

303

304

305 Mahogany chair, inlaid with copper fillets, upholstered in leather; stamped Jacob-Desmalter (1813–25). Musée des arts décoratifs, Paris.
This chair was formerly in the dining room of the château at Neuilly, the property of the Duke of Orléans, later King Louis-Philippe.

306 Mahogany chair, stamped by J. Louis. Direction des musées de France, Louvre, Paris.

307 Chair of palisander wood, inlaid with fillets of lemonwood. Private Collection.
Turned front legs never went out of fashion, but during the Restoration period they were enriched with deep flutes, gadroons and elaborate moldings. This chair, which must be of more recent date than the preceding examples, is part of a suite of furniture for a bedroom comprising a bed, bedside table, wardrobe with mirror, two armchairs *en gondole,* a daybed and four chairs of this model.

305

306

307

IV Neoclassical Furniture in the Rest of Europe: Influences and National Characteristics

German Furniture, 1790–1815

Any discussion of early nineteenth-century German furniture must begin with a mention of David Roentgen's semi-industrial workshop, the first of its kind, which manufactured luxury furniture between 1772 and 1795. His success was due principally to his commercial acumen. He sold furniture to the most powerful sovereigns in Europe and later to many other important people. The technical and mechanical quality of his furniture contributed to his success as much as its richness and monumental character. From a stylistic point of view his furniture must be considered as wholly German. It did not affect the style of furniture made elsewhere for a considerable time. It was

350 copied only in Germany, where the taste for huge secretaires decorated with arches, columns, entablatures and other motifs borrowed from architecture lasted until around 1830.

The style of Roentgen's furniture evolved in rather the same way as Louis XVI furniture. Decorative elaboration gave way to a certain severity. Beautiful marquetry, which had won Roentgen his first clients, was replaced not long after 1780 by mahogany with inlays of pale wood. Roentgen was one of the first, if not the first, to introduce this kind of furniture and to make it fashionable. Huge desks, veritable edifices of wood and bronze often surmounted by statues, were gradually replaced by desk tables of much simpler form. Even if Roentgen did not completely abandon decorative superstructures, he certainly cut down on them.

308–310 The latest of his desks, three of which are reproduced, were as plain as contemporary French furniture. His commodes and smaller pieces of furniture were even plainer.

Roentgen was a unique phenomenon in Germany. Aside from several pieces made by German furniture makers working in St. Petersburg and some Swedish commodes which are very similar to German examples, it seems that Germany exported neither her furniture nor her style.[1] Like Italy, Germany was deeply affected by the baroque. Both countries reacted against this style more slowly than France did. For models in the new neoclassical style German makers looked to France and England, the wealthiest and most highly developed countries in eighteenth-century Europe.

In general long-established north German merchants who had trading links with England were oriented towards London, whereas the princes in the west and south of Germany looked to France. However, there were many exceptions to this rule: Hepplewhite's and Sheraton's

influence spread as far as Saxony or even in some cases to Switzerland, while Italian and French artists working in Germany, of whom there were many in the eighteenth century, took the art of their native land to such places as Berlin and Dresden.

It should also be noted that British influence made itself felt in Germany before the French Revolution, and that Napoleon's conquests led to the diffusion of French artistic styles.

The gradual substitution of French fashions for English ones can be seen in a well-known German periodical, *Journal des Luxus und der Moden,* published at Weimar. The editor, Friedrich-Justin Bertuch, included in each number furniture and objects in the latest style, rather as La Mésangère was to do in France. In the first few years the furniture was nearly all English but later German and English pieces predominated. French furniture was illustrated in 1792 but then did not appear again until 1802. From that year until 1805 the *Journal* reproduced French and German pieces in equal number and after 1806 published only Empire furniture.

Some of Bertuch's opinions about furniture should not be taken too seriously. For instance he calls a commode made in Weimar in 1785 "English," even though it is far closer to French commodes than English ones. However, the résumé we have given retains a good deal of truth.

While France was experiencing the Revolution and the subsequent establishment of Napoleon's Empire, Germany suffered a series of vicissitudes. Austria and Prussia were both defeated several times and lost a great deal of territory. During the years of peace they concentrated on rebuilding their armies. Free ports in the north were cut off from their markets and sources of raw materials, so that their prosperity became no more than a memory. A longing for peace and restoration of free trade made itself felt. Even before the abolition of the Holy Roman Empire, the ecclesistical states in the west and center of Germany were secularized, as were the great abbeys. Bishops and members of the religious communities had been the principal customers of eighteenth-century craftsmen.

Only the south German states such as Baden, Bavaria, and Württemberg, which had allied themselves with Napoleon, grew stronger and benefitted from the changed political situation.

These states, along with the kingdom of Westphalia which was created in 1807 for Napoleon's younger brother, and curiously enough Würzburg, where the Austrian emperor's brother, Archduke Ferdinand, ruled from 1806, had the best Empire furniture in the finest interiors anywhere in Germany.

Württemberg

Duke Frederick II came to the throne in 1797. He later became Napoleon's ally and took the title king of Württemberg. Soon after 1797 the Duke appointed the architect Nikolaus Thouret to carry out renovations at most of his castles, in particular at the New Palace in Stuttgart and at the castle of Ludwigsburg.

Despite his name, Nikolaus Thouret, or Touret, was a German. He was born in Ludwigsburg in 1767 and died in Stuttgart in 1845. After being trained as a painter in Ludwigsburg he was sent to Paris by the duke of Württemberg to continue his studies in the studio of J.-B. Regnault. He remained there from 1789 to 1793, and then obtained permission to go to Rome, where he studied architecture.

After being recalled by Frederick-Eugene in 1796, Thouret was first employed at Hohenheim. Goethe admired his interiors and recommended him for a post at Weimar, where he stayed from 1798 to 1800. He also worked at Ludwigsburg from 1798 and soon became the new duke's favorite architect. Frederick ennobled Thouret in 1810 and continued to employ him on various projects throughout his reign.

Thouret's four-year sojourn in Paris formed his taste. His first works demonstrated that he had totally assimilated Parisian architectural and decorative styles. He was as competent as his French counterparts without being in the least plagiaristic.

The New Palace at Stuttgart was destroyed in the last war, but fortunately the castle at Ludwigsburg survives. Here Thouret decorated about twenty rooms. Some of these are untouched, while others have been furnished with pieces by Thouret from the palace at Stuttgart. The king's and queen's quarters form one of the most attractive and complete sets of apartments in Empire style.

Thouret's furniture, which is very well made, is so close to contemporary French style that the two are not always easy to distinguish. The secretaire illustrated in Plate 311 could have been made in Paris. Not long ago a commode which must have come from Stuttgart or Ludwigsburg, 312 where there are two identical specimens, was sold on the 313 Paris market and described as "attributed to Jacob." The description was perfectly understandable.

One room and several ceilings at Ludwigsburg are decorated with pretty mural paintings, also carried out according to the designs of Thouret, who was of course a painter as well as an architect. The seats are less well made, and may have been designed by a different artist. They were probably executed by a different craftsman. Thouret was assisted by an excellent furniture maker called Johannes Klinkerfuss,[2] a pupil of Roentgen who became *ébéniste* to the court of Württemberg in 1799. He was responsible for the bookcases in the *Registraturzimmer* at Ludwigsburg castle, and probably also for the majority of the furniture in the royal castles. The chairmakers lacked his skills, as did the sculptors who made papier mâché models of the griffins and lions forming the legs of some of the tables at Ludwigsburg.

Würzburg and Frankfurt

Grand Duke Ferdinand of Tuscany, brother of the Austrian emperor, lost his Italian possessions to Napoleon. After the Peace of Pressburg in 1806 he was given a principality in Germany specially created for him, mainly on land which was formerly part of the archbishopric of Würzburg.

Soon after going to live in the palace, which had once belonged to the prince-bishops of Würzburg and had been painted with frescoes by Tiepolo, he began to redecorate it in the style of the day. Other neighboring German princes were doing the same in their palaces.

It might have been supposed that Ferdinand would have disliked France and French art, but political circumstances do not necessarily affect artistic outlook. The taste of the day was French and Ferdinand patronized an immigrant French architect living at Frankfurt called Nicolas-Alexandre de Salins de Montfort.

The new rooms at the Residenz were hung with silk in Empire style. Some of the seat furniture and other pieces were ordered from Paris manufacturers. Salins took on Ludwig Rumpf, a Frankfurt upholsterer whom he probably already knew, and designed furniture which was executed by a young Frankfurt *ébéniste*, Johann Valentin Raab, who 94 had recently qualified as a master. According to some authorities, an older craftsman, the joiner Philipp Carl Hildebrandt, was also involved in furnishing the palace. However, others maintain that Hildebrandt died in 1805. We do know that there are chairs by him at Würzburg, for 314 Hildebrandt, like his French counterparts, was in the habit of stamping his chairs. Raab also stamped his work and it is possible that both men had been apprenticed in France. This theory is difficult to substantiate in Hildebrandt's case since his career was so brief. It seems quite plausible that Raab, who was active until 1839, was trained in France, as his chairs and other furniture are all close to contemporary French models.

Furniture made for Jérôme Bonaparte, king of Westphalia

In 1807 Jérôme and his wife Catherine of Württemberg moved into the palace at Cassel, which was almost empty. Catherine asked her father King Frederick to send her the architect Nikolaus Thouret, but the king would not part with him as he was in great demand at Stuttgart.

Instead of Thouret, Jérôme and Catherine took on Louis Catel, who had worked at the castle in Berlin and was in Paris in 1807. He was employed at Brunswick but did not stay there long as from 1811 he was with his brother in Italy.

It is not clear whether he worked anywhere else besides Brunswick. There are no details of the work carried out at Cassel by the young Leo von Klenze, who was also taken on as an architect by King Jérôme. Lack of information on these points is all the more regrettable since the Empire furniture made during Jérôme's reign is among the finest produced anywhere in Germany at this period.

The palace at Cassel was destroyed in the last war and the remaining furniture is now dispersed between Wilhelmshöhe, Homburg and La Fasanerie, near Fulda, which makes it difficult to study the pieces in relation to each other. It is not easy to decide whether the furniture is in fact

German. The same problem is also encountered at Hesse, Munich and Stuttgart, since it is known that Jérôme and Catherine ordered some furniture locally and other pieces from Paris.

Some surviving furniture is signed. There is a large desk by Friedrich Wichmann on which the inscription records that he was a sculptor and had a furniture factory at Cassel. The desk is a highly luxurious item but is incredibly heavy in appearance and unlike anything made in Paris. A master joiner from Cassel, Carl Lauckhardt, delivered a series of mahogany chairs which are signed underneath the seat rail. It is possible that they were actually designed by an
315 architect. The large griffins supporting the armrests look as if they are the work of a sculptor.

However, these armchairs have other characteristics in common with certain chairs made at Cassel during Jérôme's reign, some of which are very close to French examples.

The armchair and chair illustrated in Plates 316, 317 seem to be of German origin. They are slightly less finely detailed than chairs made in Paris.
318 The small sofa (one of a pair) combines an accumulation of ornamental motifs, each of which could be found on a piece of French furniture. However, here they are combined in an unprecedented and not entirely successful fashion.
319, 322 Some commodes, console tables and stools, a shaving table and a daybed are barely distinguishable from contemporary French furniture. Yet in our present state of knowledge it would be rash to categorize them as French. It would also be hard to maintain that they were made by different craftsmen from those responsible for the chairs discussed earlier, since the bronzes on most Empire furniture at Cassel are all in the same style.

Bavaria

The strangest example of French cultural influence occurred in Bavaria in the early years of the nineteenth century. It affected both the royal family and the government in Bavaria.

In 1799 a member of the younger branch of the house of Zweibrücken succeeded to the Wittelsbach possessions, which had been shared out between various branches of the family since the Middle Ages. The electors palatine and later the dukes of Zweibrücken had long been involved in the affairs of their French neighbors. Part of their territory was in Alsace, so that during the eighteenth century they became as much French as German.

Duke Christian IV (1722–75) had an apartment at Versailles and a house in Paris. His nephew and successor, Charles Augustus, built a castle at Carlsberg, equipping it at great expense with furniture, sculpture, works of art and fabrics ordered from Paris and Lyons.

On the death of Charles Augustus in 1795 his brother Maximilian Joseph became duke of Zweibrücken and next in line of succession to his cousin, Charles Theodore, elector of Bavaria.

Four years later he inherited what remained of the Wittelsbach lands: that is, Bavaria and the part of the Palatinate on the right bank of the Rhine, since France occupied nearly all the German territory on the river's left bank. She went on to annex these areas of the Rhineland by the Treaty of Lunéville in 1801.

Like his brother, Maximilian Joseph had had French tutors. As he was destined for a military career, he had been educated as an officer at Mézières military academy. In 1770 King Louis XV made him colonel of the Alsace regiment. This German unit was traditionally in the service of France and was commanded by a prince of the house of Zweibrücken.

The regiment was based at Strasbourg, where Maximilian Joseph was in almost permanent residence between 1776 and 1789. He owned the Hôtel des Deux-Ponts, which he had completely refurnished at the time of his marriage in 1785.

In 1789 Maximilian Joseph was made lieutenant general by Louis XVI, but he left Strasbourg at the end of the year as a result of the revolutionary disorders, going to Darmstadt with his family and later to Mannheim. He was then forced to flee to Ansbach to escape the advancing revolutionary army. Despite his experiences during the Revolution, Maximilian Joseph remained French in outlook.

As soon as he settled in Munich, Maximilian Joseph made Baron Montgelas his chief minister. Montgelas, the son of General Montgelas, a Savoyard in Bavarian employ and his Bavarian wife, was French-speaking like his king. He too had been mainly educated in France, at Nancy and Strasbourg. He remained minister for eighteen years and many years later wrote his memoirs in French.

The king and his minister transacted their business in French, and that language was also spoken by the prince within the family circle. Maximilian's second wife, who was a princess of Baden by birth, had not lived with him in Strasbourg yet she wrote to her mother in French. The king (Maximilian Joseph became king of Bavaria in 1806) had his official portrait painted by Stieler in 1814. At this time he was no longer an ally of France —indeed he was officially hostile to the country—but in the portrait he is shown with three bound volumes beside him. Their French titles are significant: the works of Tacitus, Buffon and Montesquieu.

The king and his family surrounded themselves with things French. Some of these objects were presents from Napoleon, such as a small mahogany table decorated with pewter and ebony inlays and with Sèvres porcelain plaques, 108
and two fine services of Sèvres porcelain. Other things had been in residences and castles formerly belonging to the Zweibrücken family, in particular in their Strasbourg residence, from which the future king gradually removed the furniture once he had left France. Other pieces came from Carlsberg castle, near Homburg in the Sarre region. Christian de Mannlich, who was the duke of Zweibrücken's architect (he was Maximilian Joseph's elder brother), managed to save the pictures and furniture before the French revolutionaries burned the castle. At Munich one can still see an impressive state bed and a throne both ordered from Georges Jacob by Duke Charles Augustus, chairs by the same maker, console tables, some by Weisweiler, and clocks and bronzes in Louis XVI style which are clearly French.

Many other pieces of furniture were ordered or acquired by the king and queen during their reign, particularly during their visit to Paris in 1810 on the occasion of Napoleon's wedding. On the queen's program were visits to the furniture maker Jacob-Desmalter, the bronze founders Thomire and Ravrio, the Mont-Cenis glassworks, the Sèvres porcelain factory, as well as to porcelain factories in Paris owned by Dagoty, Nast, Dihl and Neppel.

The porcelain now at Munich and Nymphenburg includes a Dagoty dinner service, a large service with printed decoration by Stone, Coquerel and Legros d'Anizy, two huge Sèvres vases with portraits of the king and queen which were ordered from the factory in 1805 through the Bavarian ambassador in Paris, an enamel service of 502 pieces made by Odiot and Biennais, and numerous ormolu candelabra and clocks.

It is not always easy to determine the origin of furniture without maker's marks. Most Empire chairs and other furniture are so French in appearance that a Paris or Strasbourg origin seems likely. However, there may have been other reasons for their French aspect.

The Residenz in Munich was unsuitable for occupation by a large family such as Maximilian Joseph's. As soon as he moved in the monarch decided to construct new buildings, a project which he entrusted to Charles-Pierre Puille, a Frenchman who had already worked for Maximilian Joseph in Strasbourg. Puille was in charge of court buildings, a post he held between 1799 and 1804. On the evidence of his two surviving drawings, Puille's style was entirely French and close to the Louis XVI style. He died in 1805 and was replaced by a German, Andreas Gärtner, who had worked at Versailles and Paris for several years before becoming director of buildings to the elector of Trier. He went on to collaborate with Peyre the Younger on plans for the elector's castle at Coblenz.

Our knowledge of the royal apartments in the Munich Residenz and at Nymphenburg is based chiefly on an album of watercolors (the *Wittelsbacher Album*), given to the king by his wife as a birthday present in 1821. The album contains accurate paintings of the reception rooms as well as of the small private rooms occupied by the royal family. Some rooms furnished by Gärtner were decorated in French Empire style and hung with silk from Lyons. Others were done in a mixture of Louis XVI and Empire-style furnishings.

This album, which was published in 1979 by H. Ottomeyer,[3] shows the original position of many of the chairs and other pieces of furniture and works of art, which are no longer on exhibition or have been moved to other rooms. As one might expect, the album gives no details of the provenance of the pieces.

They came from a variety of sources. Among the surviving items of furniture are gilt wooden chairs for state occasions convincingly attributed to Gärtner. These can be found in the Council Chamber, in the drawing room and in 320, 321, 323 Queen Caroline's bedroom at the Residenz. Other pieces that have come down to us are French: two commodes, a 189 black table now in the Blue Drawing Room at Nymphenburg, and the chairs in the room containing the portraits of 231 young women which were commissioned by Ludwig I. Numerous other chairs and pieces of furniture must be 340 either German or Austrian. These include the queen's bed from Nymphenburg, and the furniture from the queen's study, which is of light wood. Some pieces are difficult to attribute. Among them are a sofa and two armchairs based 324-328 on classical originals which also have French antecedents.

They were formerly in the queen's boudoir. The shape of the legs of these two armchairs is reminiscent of the legs of a series of mahogany chairs, most of which were in the Blue Drawing Room at Nymphenburg between 1808 and 1814. 329, 330 Some used to be in the queen's studio at Nymphenburg. These chairs, which are of high quality, were of a type in 331–333 widespread use in France. However, their method of construction is rather special and rules out their attribution to a Paris maker. It seems most likely that they are of German origin, but if so they are almost unique. The two console tables which have always been in this room are also of a type which was highly unusual in Germany. They have columns supported by gilt bronze zephyr heads and are very similar to a small Empire console table in the museum at Agen, France.

Prussia and Eastern Germany

At the end of his life Frederick the Great became very thrifty, and died amidst rococo interiors dating from his youth. His death in 1786 was the signal for building to be resumed in Berlin. However there was no famous architect in the capital at that time, so that Frederick William II was obliged to summon Friedrich Wilhelm Erdmannsdorff from Dessau, Carl Ferdinand Langhans from Breslau and Johann Gottfried Schadow from Rome. Together these three transformed the city in the last years of the eighteenth century. Erdmannsdorff (1736–1800) and Langhans (1732–1808) were both already over fifty. Erdmannsdorff was responsible for furnishing the king's apartment in the royal palace in Berlin, but did not like the city and left after two years. Langhans had a more modern outlook. He was more successful and was put in charge of architectural work at court. The Brandenburg Gate was designed by him, as was the theater which burnt down in 1817. The apartments he decorated have been destroyed. They are known only from drawings and photographs which lead one to deplore their disappearance. These interiors were in a distinguished and sober style typical of the late eighteenth century.

Had he lived, the architect Friedrich Gilly (1772–1800) would have been the most remarkable of his time. He was descended from a Huguenot family which had emigrated to Prussia at the end of the seventeenth century. He was the pupil in turn of his architect father and then of Erdmannsdorff and Langhans, but it was in Paris and London, which he visited in 1798, that he became a fervent apostle of the pure classicism adopted by David and his young architect contemporaries.

Friedrich Gilly left some designs for furniture but his importance for art history lies in the influence he exercised on the two young architects who were to become the foremost of their generation: Karl Friedrich Schinkel (1781–1841) and Leo von Klenze (1784–1864).

So many buildings in Berlin were destroyed as a result of the last war that only a few dating from our period now remain.

A small castle built in 1796 on Peacock Island (*Pfaueninsel*), in the Havel in Berlin, has survived. The furniture, most of it mahogany, includes a bed with two scrolled headboards and rounded pediments, surrounded by circular fluted pillars like those on a Louis XVI bed. Solid and rather heavy chairs with polished legs of square section are ornamented with "antique nails" at the junction of the leg and the seat, rather like those used by Paris chairmakers instead of the rosette which had previously been carved on this part of their chairs; however, the carved chairback is probably based on English models. Other chairs in Berlin, Saxony and Thuringia have similar characteristics. Their legs are straight, simple and square in section, a feature soon to be found on Biedermeier chairs. The motifs carved on the backs are reminiscent of those on English chairs.

Chairs and other pieces of furniture designed by architects are often more original but not always more successful than those designed by furniture makers themselves. The sculptor Gottfried Schadow, who assisted Langhans, designed a great deal of furniture, some of which survived at Potsdam until recently. His work included a console table ornamented with griffins which were quite well conceived, and some heavy armchairs in Louis XVI style. These are overloaded with decoration and were quite different from the chairs being made in Paris under the Directory.

Two chairs designed by Schadow in 1808 are more 334 successful in appearance, even though they were probably never actually executed as all artistic activity ceased after Prussia's defeat in 1806. The young Schinkel, who returned to Prussia in 1805 after more than two years abroad, only managed to survive on the strength of his talent as a painter. An exhibition of his paintings in 1810 enabled him to establish contact with the court and to obtain an official post which marked the beginning of his career. Among the modest commissions he carried out at this time was the design of furniture for Queen Louise's bedroom at Charlottenburg. The pieces included a bed and two bedside tables in pearwood which are highly original. The sinuous lines of the bed are almost art nouveau in feeling.

Most of Schinkel's work dates from after 1815. There was far more artistic activity in Prussia and in Germany as a whole in this period than in the preceding years.

308

308 Desk by David Roentgen. Oak veneered with birch, gilt bronze mounts. H. 124 cm., W. 140 cm., D. 81 cm. About 1785–90. Badisches Landesmuseum, Karlsruhe. Comparable examples can be found in the castle at Weimar and in the Bavarian National Museum, Munich.

309 Desk by David Roentgen. Mahogany and oak veneered with mahogany, gilt bronze mounts. H. 120 cm., W. 164 cm., D. 89 cm. Schloss Wilhelmshöhe, Cassel.

310 Desk by David Roentgen. Mahogany, oak and pine veneered with mahogany, gilt bronze mounts. H. 113 cm., W. 136 cm., D. 83 cm. About 1790–95. Schloss Wilhelmshöhe, Cassel. There are comparable examples in the Hermitage Museum, Leningrad and in the Neues Palais, Potsdam.

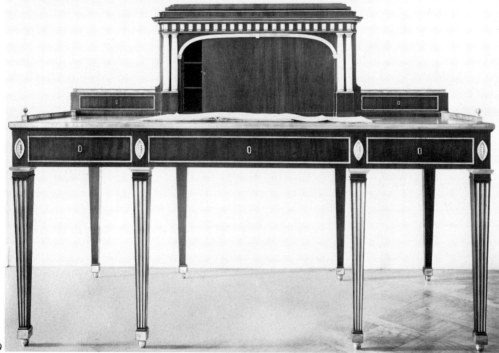

309

310

311 Mahogany and pine secretaire, ▷ veneered with mahogany, gilt bronze mounts. H. 130 cm., W. 80 cm., D. 46 cm. Stuttgart, Landesmuseum (formerly Schloss Ludwigsburg). Designed by Nikolaus Thouret.

312

312 Two-door commode of mahogany and oak and pine veneered with mahogany, gilt bronze mounts; Sulzer anhydrite marble top. Schlossmuseum, Ludwigsburg. Designed by Nikolaus Thouret.

313 Two-door commode of mahogany and mahogany veneer, gilt bronze mounts. H. 95 cm., W. 142 cm., D. 54 cm. Sold at the Palais Galliera, Paris, on June 15, 1971, when it was attributed to "the Jacobs."

314 Two chairs from the Residenz, Würzburg.
The left-hand chair, which is of cherrywood, is by Philipp Carl Hildebrandt (1753–1805), a Frankfurt chairmaker who stamped his pieces in imitation of his Parisian counterparts. This chair could pass for an example of French craftsmanship were it not for the straight tapering front legs, which are square in section. These legs are often found on chairs of German make but rarely on French ones.
The other chair is more directly inspired by French models. Its "pierced plank" back is a simplified version of a chair now in the Musée des arts dècoratifs, Paris (see Pl. 227). The chairmakers doubtless worked from engravings, not from the actual model.

313

314

315 Mahogany armchair, with gilt ▷ bronze mounts and ornamentation of gilt wood; original red and gold silk upholstery. Signed by the master chairmaker Carl Lauckhardt. 1807–13. Schloss Wilhelmshöhe, Cassel.

316 Mahogany armchair with square back curving towards the base and armrests of double baluster form, gilt bronze mounts; original blue silk grogram upholstery. 1807–13. Schloss Wilhelmshöhe, Cassel.

317 Mahogany chair with S-shaped back, gilt bronze mounts, original silk upholstery. 1807–13. Schloss Wilhelmshöhe, Cassel.

318 Small mahogany sofa with gilt bronze mounts. The rear left column-shaped member is surmounted by a gilt bronze Victory, whilst its counterpart at the front is surmounted by a helmet of carved gilt wood; original purple silk upholstery. Schloss Wilhelmshöhe, Cassel.

315

316

317

318

319

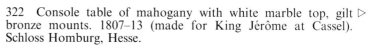
322 Console table of mahogany with white marble top, gilt ▷ bronze mounts. 1807–13 (made for King Jérôme at Cassel). Schloss Homburg, Hesse.

319 Mahogany stool, gilt bronze mounts. 1807–13 (made for King Jérôme at Cassel). Schloss Homburg, Hesse.

320 Chair of a member of the Bavarian State Council, of gilt wood. Residenz, Munich.
The Council, under the presidency of the king, sat in a room furnished and decorated around 1809–10. On the basis of various details, particularly the carving, the chairs of this series can be related to chairs attributed to Gärtner (Pls. 321, 323).
The strongly curved top rail is found also in other luxurious contemporary suites: for example, on the chairs in the Emperor Napoleon's drawing room at the Trianon (1811).

321 Armchair of gilt wood from Queen Caroline's drawing room. Residenz, Munich.
The design of these armchairs is plausibly attributed to the architect Andreas Gärtner, who worked in France for some years before being appointed director of building works to the elector of Trier. Gärtner probably obtained this position through the recommendation of Antoine-François Peyre who had been requested by the elector to supply plans for Coblenz Castle. After the electorate was abolished, Gärtner took up a similar position at the court of the Prince-Bishop of Würzburg, and, in 1804, with the elector of Bavaria.
The "dark blue silk with a gold-colored design" intended for these chairs was ordered from Lyons in 1809. The chair shown here was enlarged when it was used as King Maximilian Joseph's throne.

320

321

323

324

325

323 Armchair from Queen Caroline's bedroom. Residenz, Munich.

These gilt wood armchairs must date from around 1810. They are attributed to Gärtner. The crimson damask upholstery was made around 1815–20.

A group of French Empire chairs recently sold on the Paris market had armrests supported by eagle heads similar to those on this armchair (see *Connaissance des arts,* July 1965, no. 161).

324 Mahogany armchair inlaid with ebony, gilt bronze mounts. Residenz, Munich.

In 1820 this chair, together with another and a sofa, was in Queen Caroline's dressing room *(Ankleidezimmer)* at Nymphenburg.

Stone armchairs or thrones used outdoors in various public places are almost the only chairs that have survived from antiquity. They aroused understandable interest in artists working during a period when everything from the classical era was regarded as worthy of admiration. This armchair resembles one of these thrones by virtue of the ebony ornamental motifs, which are similar to low relief ornament decorating stone thrones (see Pl. 326). However, the latter are heavy and immovable by nature, so that the idea of imitating them in wood was unlikely to succeed and was rarely attempted.

The two armchairs in Munich, which derive directly or indirectly from a design by Charles Percier (see Pl. 327) are relatively successful, thanks to their classical-style legs.

325 Armchair in Plate 324, shown *in situ* at the Residenz, Munich.

There are enough similarities between the rather unusual form of this sofa and an engraving published in 1803–04 by La Mésangère to suggest that the engraving, or the drawing which preceded it, was the source for the design of the sofa. It is unlikely that the three pieces were made before 1804. See Plate 328.

326 Classical marble throne. Drawing after S. Risom, "Le siège du prêtre Dionysos Eleuthereus au théâtre d'Athènes" in *Mélanges Holleaux,* 1913, pp. 258 ff. *et seq.*

327 Engraving. An engraving published in the 1801 edition of Percier and Fontaine's *Recueil de décorations interieures.*

This engraving reproduces one of the four paintings which hung in the studio of Isabey, the miniature-painter. They depicted Architecture, Painting, Sculpture and Engraving. The engraver has forgotten the right front leg of the seat, part of which should be visible.

328 Design for a sofa published in *Meubles et objets de goût,* 1803–04, supplement to La Mésangère's *Journal des dames et des modes.*

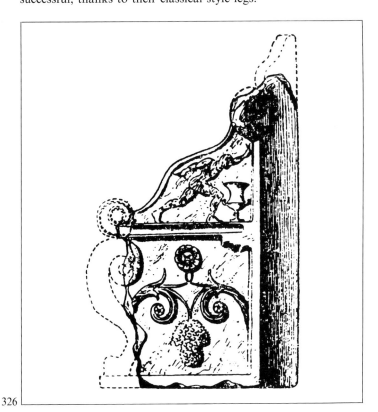

326

GRAVURE

327

328

329

329 Blue Drawing Room, Schloss Nymphenburg, Bavaria.
This room, once Queen Caroline's reception hall, was furnished between 1808 and 1814. From a watercolor by Friedrich Ziebland showing it as it was in 1820 we may see that the console tables and mirrors between the windows, the wall hanging (recently refurbished) and the curtains suspended from gilt wooden arches are still identical or similar. The chairs (see also Pl. 330) were originally all ranged along the walls, leaving the center of the room free. The French table that is there now comes from the queen's study.

330 Chair from the Blue Drawing Room, Schloss Nymphenburg, Bavaria.

This mahogany chair, decorated with copper fillets, is part of a suite of which most pieces were placed in Queen Caroline of Bavaria's Blue Drawing Room (reception hall) between 1808 and 1814, while others were in her gallery of drawings (*Zeichenkabinett*) in the Residenz, Munich.

331 Mahogany chair with openwork back. Residenz, Munich.
The form and detailing of this chair are both similar to chairs in the Blue Drawing Room at Nymphenburg Castle, and it can therefore be dated to 1808–14.
The lower rail of this chair can be related to a design published in 1797 in the *Magazin für Freunde des guten Geschmacks* (see Pl. 332) and also to a miniature of Madame Récamier, who can be seen seated on a similar chair in Plate 333.

330   331

332 Chairback. Engraving published in the *Magazin für Freunde des guten Geschmacks,* Leipzig, 1797, no. 3, fasc. 4.

333 Madame Récamier. Miniature portrait by Jean-Baptiste Augustin. Gouache on ivory, signed and dated 1801. Cabinet des dessins, Musée du Louvre, Paris.

334 Designs for chairs. Drawing dated September 5, 1808 and signed by Gottfried Schadow. Plansammlung der Fakultät für Architektur, Technische Universität, Berlin.

332

333

334

Vienna and the Biedermeier Style

Austria, like all continental countries, adopted the Empire style unreservedly. The style remained in fashion in Austria as long as it did in France and Russia, but it was quickly modified. Alongside furniture in classical style which was often both simple and elegant, pieces soon began to be made in Vienna which were quite original. They were based on Empire models but were more baroque in feeling, as if artists had been waiting to return to the curves and mannerisms of baroque and rococo art which had obtained such a hold on their forebears.

335 A design for one of twenty armchairs by Gottfried August Pohle dated 1806 survives in the Österreichisches Museum für angewandte Kunst, Vienna. The chairbacks are so bizarre and fantastic and differ so much from what was being made elsewhere at this time that it is difficult to believe the evidence of the dated drawing, and hard to credit that the chairs could actually be executed. However, chairs of this kind can indeed be seen in Vienna and the example chosen is not an isolated one. Three years later, in 1809, a Viennese architect, Georg Pein, published a book on
336 interior and exterior decoration.[4] It contains two designs for armchairs which are unlike Pohle's pieces but are equally original.

It was doubtless difficult to make substantial modifications to the design of tables, commodes or desks without affecting their function. However, attempts were made. One
337 example is the secretaire in the form of a mandolin resting on lion's paw feet in the Österreichisches Museum für angewandte Kunst. A *semainier* which is wide at the top and narrow at the bottom was made for the palace of the princes
338 of Thurn and Taxis at Regensburg. It shares the same unexpected and illogical quality of design which prevented such furniture from gaining currency. In general Viennese furniture makers were more reasonable, even though they took greater liberties in their designs than their foreign counterparts.

The secretaire in Plate 337 dates from around 1810, while the *semainier* was made about 1815. Like Pohle's and Pein's chairs these pieces are in the Biedermeier style, which was born in Vienna. The most typical shapes, as well as the most extravagant ones, originated there. After 1815 the style spread from Vienna to all German-speaking countries and even as far as Scandinavia.

The spread of the style marked the diminution of French influence in Germany and the consequent strengthening of Austrian influence. This was the result of Napoleon's defeat and the Congress of Vienna in 1814–15. The princes and diplomats assembled in Vienna made purchases or placed orders in the same way as the Allied leaders had done in Paris in 1814.

At this time Vienna was the home of a considerable number of craftsmen. There were 875 independent master furniture makers in Vienna in 1816; by 1823 the number had increased to 951. Viennese furniture was exported in quantity and today much furniture previously considered to be German has been reattributed to Austria. There are many examples of early nineteenth-century furniture in the
47, 339 Saxe-Coburg residences at Gotha, the Thurn and Taxis palace at Regensburg and Bavarian royal palaces and castles.

In Germany the Viennese style combined with local traditions which had been affected by French influence. In northern Germany and Scandinavia the Biedermeier style competed with English fashions.

In general terms German furniture was more classical than Austrian. Some pieces were almost French in style. We 340 have mentioned this tendency in our discussion of the work of Johann Valentin Raab, one of the leading Frankfurt chairmakers. One of his armchairs is reproduced in Plate 341. Similar pieces can be seen in the castle at Nassau, which was refurbished between 1814 and 1819 by Baron Stein. These may be by Raab, as Nassau is not far from Frankfurt.

However, Raab was not the only craftsman who was influenced by Parisian makers. Leaving aside certain chairs in Coburg which may be of French origin, as Duke Ernest I 213, 217 ordered furniture from Paris as well as Vienna, much German furniture, as we have said, is reminiscent of contemporary French pieces. That designed by Leo von 342–344, 421 Klenze, a pupil of Percier and Fontaine who became Munich's most famous architect, falls into this category; other examples include the chairs made between 1815 and 345 1820 for Maximilian Joseph's bedroom at the Residenz, and an armchair dating from 1840 which was made by Franz 347, 348 Xaver Fortner, a master chairmaker working in Munich who is renowned for his marquetry.

The epithet "Biedermeier" can hardly be applied to Schinkel's highly original furniture, nor is it a suitable 349 stylistic description of furniture designed by architects such as Alexis de Châteauneuf, who worked mainly in Hamburg. Indeed the term should not be too loosely used. Only two types of furniture are characteristically German: monu- 350 mental secretaires with elaborate superstructures, which probably derive from David Roentgen's large desks, and large sofas with high backs and elaborate scrolled armrests. These "Biedermeier" sofas became more and more rounded 351–354 in outline after 1830. Ten or fifteen years later they had the exaggerated and ridiculous curves of the neorococo style. 355

In contrast chairs remained elegant and light in appearance for a considerable time. They were fairly simple, sometimes based on Viennese models or else copies of 356–358 English or French chairs.

In conclusion we may look briefly at the work of Michael Thonet, who established a business which was to expand rapidly in the second half of the nineteenth century. Thonet was born in 1796 at Boppard on the Rhine. He became a craftsman in his home town where, around 1836, he began to use bentwood for his chairs. Thonet did not actually invent the technique of steaming wood before shaping it, for this method had been used earlier by wheelwrights and in shipbuilding. But he applied the idea to chair manufacture, which he was able to put on an industrial basis by the use of certain interchangeable elements.

Metternich saw Thonet's furniture at an exhibition and invited him to move to Vienna, where in 1842 he received a permit to make furniture. His firm soon became very successful.

Two chairs by Thonet are illustrated here. The first dates 359 from before the factory's removal to Vienna and bears the label of a furniture retailer in Coblenz. It is made of thin pieces of wood which have been bent and stuck together. The second chair is of a type which was to become a classic 360 and is still being made today.

335 Two designs for chairs. Gottfried August Pohle, Vienna, 1806. Österreichisches Museum für angewandte Kunst, Vienna. Only two designs are reproduced here from a sheet of twenty. The legs of Pohle's chairs are unremarkable; the designer's imagination is shown only in the form of the chairbacks.

336 Design for a chair.
The Viennese architect Georg Pein, author of a work on interior and exterior decoration, makes reference to antiquity, which he claims never to lose sight of, but at the same time claims artistic liberty not to copy slavishly his classical forebears. His designs for the use of craftsmen are in fact idiosyncratic and resemble neither classical furniture nor that made by his Viennese contemporaries.

This drawing for an armchair, one of two designs published by Pein in 1809, only vaguely resembles classical thrones or curule armchairs made during the Directory and Consulate periods. The delicate rounded forms are already typical of the Viennese Biedermeier style.

337 Secretaire veneered with mahogany and maple, carved and gilded, gilt bronze mounts. Vienna, about 1810. Österreichisches Museum für angewandte Kunst, Vienna.

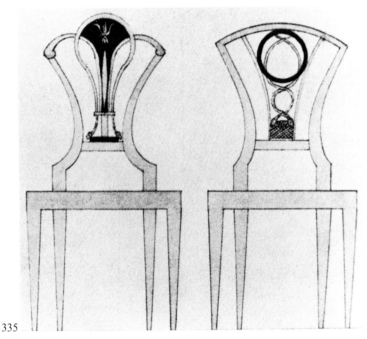

335

336

337

338 Chest of drawers *(semainier)* veneered with mahogany; gilt bronze key plates. Palace of the Princes Thurn and Taxis, Regensburg.
The Austrian Museum of Applied Arts has more than 2,500 designs for furniture from Joseph Danhauser's factory, the leading concern in Vienna at the beginning of the nineteenth century. One of the drawings corresponds to this chest of drawers which, therefore, was probably made in the Danhauser workshops.

339 Armchair from Rosenau Castle, ebonized wood. Vienna, Friedrich Hasselbrink. Schloss Ehrenburg, Coburg.
This armchair was one of 95 items of furniture ordered in 1816 from the Viennese maker Hasselbrink for the small castle at Rosenau, near Coburg. Despite appearances, this is probably not a desk chair. Two armchairs of this type can be seen either side of a sofa in a drawing room in Bürglass Castle at Coburg painted in 1832 by Heinrich Krüppel the Younger. This gouache was illustrated by Lorenz Seelig in "Wiener Biedermeier in Coburg," *Alte und moderne Kunst,* 1981, no. 178/179.

338   339

◁ 340 Queen Caroline's bedroom, Schloss Nymphenburg, Bavaria. Like the Blue Drawing Room (Pl. 329) this room has retained its Empire furnishings dating from 1817–18. The bed, which was probably made in Austria, was, however, placed across the room and paired with a twin bed. The mahogany chairs are similar in style to those in the Blue Drawing Room. Their console-shaped front legs are one of the earliest securely datable examples of the form commonly found in the Restoration.

341 △

341 Mahogany armchair. Frankfurt, Johann Valentin Raab. Schloss Homburg, Hesse.

The armchairs from the empress's dining room at Compiègne, designed by Jacob-Desmalter in 1810, are probably the earliest securely datable example of the use of curving armrests terminating in jagged leaves such as those on this chair. The leaf motif was to enjoy great popularity in France at the end of the Empire period and during the Restoration era.

Raab's chairs, which are well balanced and agreeably curved, are among the most successful of their kind. They must have been made at about the same time as the cherrywood armchairs of the same model but with differing armrests at Nassau Castle, which was redecorated for the Baron von Stein between 1814 and 1819.

342 Console table from Leuchtenberg Palace, Munich. Painted wood, partly gilt. Bayerische Verwaltung der staatlichen Schlösser, Munich.

In 1816 Eugène de Beauharnais, the former viceroy of Italy, was made duke of Leuchtenberg by his father-in-law, King Maximilian Joseph. The construction of Leuchtenberg Palace, designed by the architect Leo von Klenze, began the same year and was completed in 1818.

On the evidence of the duchess of Leuchtenberg's diary, the furnishing of the castle had not been carried out by September 18, 1818 when, after having visited Ellingen Castle, the Princess wrote; "Our furnishings will be much more modest, but we will be pleased with them." Following Percier's example, whose pupil he had been, Klenze himself designed the furniture for the rooms that he had been commissioned to decorate. However, we know that Jean-Jacques Werner, a Paris interior decorator and furniture maker, also received an important order for Leuchtenberg Palace. This console table, therefore, may have been designed either by Klenze, which seems more likely, or by Werner. It must date from around 1820.

The letter "E," for Eugène, carved in the middle of the frieze, was later altered to "L," for Ludwig I of Bavaria.

342

343   Console table of gilded wood, designed by Leo von Klenze between 1826 and 1830. Residenz, Munich.
Despite its relatively late date, Klenze has designed this table in a strictly Empire style.

344   Lyre-back chair. Bayerische Verwaltung der staatlichen Schlösser, Munich.
The discreetly classical form and slightly more abundant decoration than was used in the Empire period are both typical of Leo von Klenze's furniture.

345   Mahogany sofa, upholstered with Beauvais tapestry. Residenz, Munich.
King Maximilian Joseph of Bavaria's bedroom at the Residenz, Munich is shown in a watercolor of 1820 by Wilhelm Rehlen. A suite of chairs, similar in design to the suite to which this sofa belongs, can be seen in the watercolor, although it appears to be of maple or of figured birch. This suite survives but lacks its upholstery. There are two possible explanations: either the mahogany chairs replaced those of indigenous wood around 1820 and inherited their upholstery, or else the two suites were ordered at the same time and the first subsequently lost its upholstery. One thing is certain: both suites were intended for King Maximilian Joseph. Moreover, all the seat furniture belongs to the Bayerische Verwaltung der staatlichen Schlösser, successor to the Royal furniture depository.
It is likely that these pieces of furniture were made in Munich between 1815 and 1825, the year of the king's death.

346   Cherrywood chair. Empire or Biedermeier period. Homburg Castle, Hesse.

343

344

345

346

347, 348 Armchair *en gondole,* of palisander wood, inlaid with pewter, copper, mother-of-pearl and ivory. Neues Schloss, Baden-Baden (formerly at Karlsruhe).

Signed and dated 1840, this armchair was made in the workshop of Franz Xaver Fortner, a master furniture maker in Munich who employed thirty journeymen in 1842. He had won the highest honors at various exhibitions held in Germany, where he was particularly recognized for the quality of his marquetry and inlaid work, which was of the highest standard. The shape and material of this chair — palisander wood was extremely fashionable between 1830 and 1840 — are no different to those of contemporary French chairs *en gondole,* but French marquetry is generally more restrained in character. The petit point upholstery is also of the period.

347 348

349

350

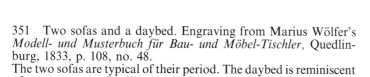

351

349 Armchair from the palace of Prince Karl of Prussia, gilt wood. Verwaltung der staatlichen Schlösser und Gärten, Berlin. Despite the relatively late date when the architect Schinkel designed this armchair (1828), he made serious attempts to imitate classical models. The slender, straight armrests terminating in an animal head and resting on small figures of sphinxes, could have been taken directly from a Greek throne, were they not placed too high. On antique chairs, "armrests" served to anchor the movable seat cushion rather than to support the arms of the sitter. The massive front legs, which are of square section, also derive from Greek or Roman thrones, but Schinkel has given them a lighter appearance by making them taper towards the foot. In the final analysis this armchair displays more modern characteristics than it does classical ones. It is original, but heavy in appearance.

350 Secretaire veneered with light woods; small columns, key plates and handles of ebonized wood. Thuringia, about 1820. Private Collection, Bremen.
Unlike French and Italian secretaires which are always flat on top, most German examples dating from the early nineteenth century were crowned with superstructures of various sizes. German secretaires were often conceived as veritable edifices with pilasters or columns of differing heights, plinths, cornices, an occasional pediment, or, as in this example, a relieving arch, which is, of course, artificial. The secretaire tapers slightly towards the top.

351 Two sofas and a daybed. Engraving from Marius Wölfer's *Modell- und Musterbuch für Bau- und Möbel-Tischler,* Quedlinburg, 1833, p. 108, no. 48.
The two sofas are typical of their period. The daybed is reminiscent of contemporary English and French examples.

352 Design for a sofa. Engraving from Friedrich Wilhelm Mercker's *Practische Zeichnungen von Möbel im neuesten und geläutersten Geschmacke,* Leipzig, 1831.

353 Sofa of white-painted wood. Formerly in the Music Room in Queen Charlotte's apartments at the Residenz, Munich. The remainder of the suite of furniture to which this sofa belonged has been lost.

354 Part of sofa of palisander wood, decorated with fillets of light wood. Claw feet, rosettes of carved wood. Germany (?), about 1835–40. Private Collection, Finland.

355 Sofa of ebonized wood. National Museum of Finland, Louhisaari Castle.
The undulating lines of this sofa suggest a date of fabrication around 1845–50. Stylistically it is a mixture of Biedermeier and neorococo elements.

352   353

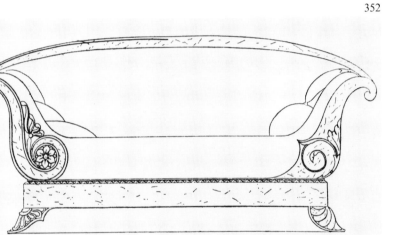
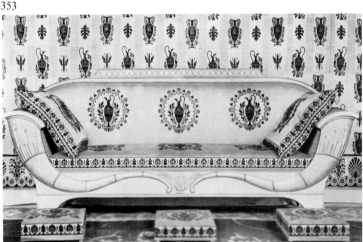

354   355

356

357

358

356 Chair of cherry and ebonized wood. North Germany. Private Collection, Bremen.
The arrangement of the legs—those in front are straight, the rear ones are saber-shaped—is highly typical of Biedermeier chairs. The rather low back with its slightly curved top rail is reminiscent of one of Schadow's designs (see Pl. 334).

357 Biedermeier chair of cherrywood. The fan-shaped back is of ebonized wood. About 1820–25. Museen der Stadt Regensburg.

358 Biedermeier chair of cherrywood. This chair must date from about 1835–40. Schloss Homburg, Hesse.

359 Bentwood chair with cane seat. Michael Thonet, Boppard am Rhein, before 1842. Victoria and Albert Museum, London. Although technically innovative, Thonet was at first unwilling to make his chairs look too different from contemporary ones constructed in the traditional way. This chair can be compared with various others in Biedermeier style.

360 Bentwood chair with cane seat. Model no. 4 by Michael Thonet. Victoria and Albert Museum, London.
When chairs like this were first put on the market, there was a renewed fashion in Europe for chairs with a rounded back in so-called "Louis XV" style. Thonet may have been inspired by these, but if so their influence was only remotely felt, as the outline of Thonet's chairs is highly original. The bentwood chair was so successful that it has never gone out of fashion. "Bistro chairs" currently on the market are direct descendants of Thonet's bentwood chairs.

359   360

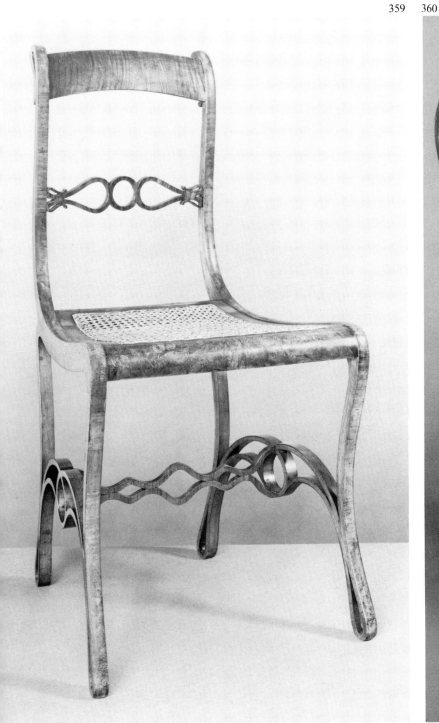

Italian Furniture

At the end of the eighteenth century Italy was an array of different territories without any political unity. Its economic circumstances differed greatly from the late Middle Ages, when the Italians had been the bankers of Europe and had played an important role in international commerce.

Eighteenth-century Italy consisted of a number of medium-sized or petty states. The Milan region, now the economic heart of the nation, had at that time long been under foreign domination. The ducal palace had been remodeled by the architect Piermarini on the arrival in Milan of the Archduke Ferdinand, governor of Lombardy and son of Maria Theresa. During the archduke's rule numerous buildings were constructed in and around Milan. Another archduke, Pierre-Léopold of Lorraine, furnished new apartments in the Pitti Palace, Florence. The work was carried out using funds obtained from the sale to the Holy See of the duchy of Urbino. Prior to this François of Lorraine, heir to the last of the Medici line, had sold the Medici jewelry in order to replenish the Austrian treasury.

In Venice and Genoa commercial life was in decline. Although the Pope still had considerable resources, these had been depleted. Only two Italian states were developing. These were the kingdom of Naples, which had revived after overthrowing a Spanish viceroy, and Piedmont, which was united with Savoy.

There was, therefore, only a limited amount of new building in Italy and few interiors were decorated in the neoclassical style. As we have already seen, many Italian craftsmen, such as architects, marble workers, and painter-decorators, worked abroad. They took their talent and their art elsewhere, and as there was no longer any major artistic center in Italy, French and English influence penetrated the country. The title of a periodical published in 1790 is revealing: *Giornale delle nuove mode di Francia e d'Inghilterra*. English influence was particularly strong in the ports of Venice, Naples and Leghorn, as well as at Florence. French influence extended through Savoy to Piedmont and Genoa, and was also felt in Parma, where the ruler had married one of Louis XV's daughters, as well as in Naples. Neapolitan furniture made at the end of the eighteenth century was closer in style to Louis XVI pieces than to English furniture.

Regional differences in Italian art were more pronounced on account of political divisions. Most Italian scholars have studied the furniture made in their country on a strictly regional basis. In this way similarities, which are as important as divergences, have tended to a be ignored. When we remember that Rome was the international center of eighteenth-century neoclassicism, and that Giovanni Battista Piranesi, Francesco Milizia, the architect Asprucci and the sculptor Antonio Canova all played an important role in the development of this style, then we have some idea of the complexity of artistic life in Italy in the years before the French Revolution.

In general Italian art lagged slightly behind France in stylistic terms. We shall take but one example, that of commodes and other furniture decorated with marquetry in the neoclassical "Maggiolini" style. From about 1785 in Germany Roentgen substituted mahogany and other plain veneers for marquetry. The same stylistic change took place in France. But for about fifteen years after this Giuseppe Maggiolini (1738–1814) and other north Italian craftsmen continued to make marquetry furniture which was closer in style to Louis XVI furniture than to Directory or Empire pieces. The two games tables reproduced in Plate 363 date from 1808. Yet the Italian pieces were very popular both at home and abroad. After supplying the Archduke Ferdinand, Maggiolini sold furniture to Eugène de Beauharnais. Numerous Italian marquetry commodes were exported. They can be found in England as well as in Russia, where several decorate a corridor in the Hermitage Museum, Leningrad.

The arrival of the French in Italy in 1796 was to bring many changes. In general the French army was welcomed, especially at first and in regions which had been under Austrian domination. Napoleon Buonaparte did not sound quite like a foreign name to Italian ears. He was clever enough to surround himself with Italian administrators and artists, the latter profiting from the outset as many important orders were placed. Artistic activity was concentrated in the new courts such as Milan and Venice. There was another court in Lucca, capital of the kingdom of Italy, of which Eugène de Beauharnais was created viceroy. After 1809 Elisa Bacciochi, Napoleon's sister, revivified Florence, while Murat, after becoming king of Naples in 1808, stimulated cultural life in that city. Towards the end of the Empire, Napoleon himself began to furnish the Monte Cavallo Palace (now the Quirinal) in Rome, but never finished the project.

French influence was weakest in Milan, capital of the most important Italian state. This seems to have been because the viceroy preferred to employ Italian artists. Apart from Piermarini, who had been too closely connected with the Austrians, all the other artists carried on working as before under the talented decorator Giocondo Albertolli. The details of Milanese furniture making during the Empire period are still unknown, except in the case of marquetry furniture and bronzes made by the Manfredini concern. Milanese chairs, which have their own special characteristics, deserve to be studied. They frequently have carved decorative supporting pieces forming an arch between the rear legs and the seat rail. Although the armchairs are not as well conceived as French examples, this is not true of chairs and sofas, which are light and elegant despite their size.

Elisa Bacciochi, who thanks to her brother became duchess of Lucca and Princess Piombino, took with her to Italy the architect Bienaimé. He remained in her service until 1814. She also took a Paris furniture maker called Youf, who ran a workshop in Lucca, situated in a former Carmelite convent. It is not surprising, therefore, that the decor and furniture in Elisa's residences is French in style even though she also employed numerous Italians. These included Cacialli, an architect endowed with excellent taste, who has left us several charming interiors. Elisa's furniture is nearly all at the Pitti Palace, Florence, or in Medici palaces outside the city. This furniture, like that of Milan, deserves detailed study. The only two pieces whose origin is known beyond doubt were the work of Italians. Giovanni Socchi devised a desk chair which could be hidden inside the desk or secretaire for which it had been made. Jacopo Ciacchi's label, *fabbricatore di mobili, lungo l'Arno, presso*

361

il Ponte Vecchio, is stuck on an attractive commode in one of the bathrooms in the Pitti Palace. Socchi's desks and Ciacchi's commode are well executed and finely proportioned. They are a credit to their makers and prove that Elisa had talented furniture makers. However, it would be wrong to think that Socchi made all Elisa's furniture, as has been held for far too long. This opinion is no longer tenable. All this Florentine furniture is somewhat uniform in character and goes well together. It also harmonizes with French furniture, some items of which belonged to Elisa.

We have already seen that one of the commodes in the Pitti Palace is mounted with the same bronzes as a Beneman commode now in the Hermitage Museum, Leningrad. Was this also by Beneman? The question must be left open, but this piece, like others there, was certainly made in France. There are, for example, two writing cabinets *(secrétaires en armoire)* which match, even though one is broader than the other. Their construction is identical, and their gilt bronzes the same, with the exception of one mount. On one secretaire the frieze is composed of profile heads, on the other it consists of lyres. The second secretaire, which is thought to have been made in Florence, is in the Villa Poggio at Caiano, near Florence, while the other specimen is in the Royal Palace, Milan, and is described as of "Lombard workmanship." Some of the small gilt bronzes, which are quite distinctive in character, reappear on a secretaire in the same style as the above pieces which is now in the Capodimonte Museum, Naples. Their close relationship seems to be due to their common origin, but what this was is unknown.

Paul Marmottan apparently found the key to the problem when he discovered that furniture to the value of 107,000 francs was bought by the emperor in 1811–12 and sent at his command through Percier and Fontaine to Princess Elisa.[5] This substantial sum, taken together with the date, clearly indicates that we are concerned here with part of the furniture ordered by the emperor in 1811 from many of the makers who were suffering from the economic crisis. The order was so large that there was no question of housing the furniture in the Imperial palaces. Percier and Fontaine must have been instructed to select the pieces. Some were sent to the Imperial furniture depository. Brion's armchairs were still there in 1837.[6] Other items were sent to Elisa and almost certainly to the king of Naples and the viceroy of Italy, as Napoleon's solicitude extended to all members of his family.

Whereas French furniture in Florence has often been confused with the local product which was very similar in many respects, the presence in Naples of numerous pieces imported by Murat, king of Naples, has long been recognized. As in Florence local and imported furniture was mixed together. Neapolitan furniture sometimes directly copied Parisian, although other pieces retained the lightness and elegance characteristic of late eighteenth-century Neapolitan makers. Two small gondola-shaped armchairs of painted white wood now at Caserta are typical. A similar chair can be seen in a portrait by the Comte de Clarac of Queen Caroline Murat at her desk.[7]

When the Bourbons returned, the Duke of Calabria, who preceded the king, publicly expressed his satisfaction with the state of the palaces in Naples. He was almost sorry that Queen Caroline had not had time to complete the refurbishment of the Villa Portici. Nor had work been finished at Caserta and Capodimonte. However, it was continued, according to the original Empire-style scheme, even though the furniture installed already displayed the overornamentation then fashionable throughout Europe. Strangely, some of the chairs are not unlike those designed at the same period for palaces in St. Petersburg by the architect Carlo Rossi, who was of Italian origin. Borsato, a Venetian, designed chairs which were only slightly more restrained, whilst Pelagio Palagi, who had received his artistic education in the Empire period, was to provide a few years later, between 1836 and 1838, a series of chairs for the Royal Palace in Turin which are unique in Europe. They are outlandishly elaborate, and are quite the equal of any High Baroque furniture. The Italians have a natural artistic tendency towards the expression of movement, which means that they have an affinity with the baroque. Many Italian craftsmen of the 1830s made chairs with rounded contours, although none went as far as Palagi. Perhaps the Council Chamber at the Turin palace did not affect contemporaries as strongly as it impresses us. Contemporaries had already grown used to the rather ample style of "Pompadour" and "Renaissance" pieces which are somewhat reminiscent of the "Empire" features found in Pelagio Palagi's furniture.

Before leaving the subject of Italian furniture we should mention two local types. The first is the small chairs made at Chiavari from 1798 when the Marchese Rivarola held a competition for the design of a light but solid chair. During the Second Empire these chairs, which were invariably turned and were of cherry or maple wood, were painted in black and gold. The upper seat rail, which is slightly curved, is rather similar to the "antique style" chairs so fashionable in the late eighteenth and early nineteenth century. Moreover, on the earliest chairs from Chiavari this rail was painted with neoclassical motifs.

The Italians are also famed for their mosaics, created from marble and hardstones. Their work is unrivaled elsewhere and they supplied the whole of Europe with chimneypieces, vases and inlaid tabletops. Many of these were made in the Florentine workshop which had been established by the Medicis.

361 Commode with marquetry of olive and other woods. Lombardy, late eighteenth or early nineteenth century. Sold at Sotheby's, London, July 15, 1983.

362 Gilt wooden furniture. Florence, Empire period. Villa Reale della Petraia, near Florence. The armchair resembles contemporary French examples. The console table, which has a white marble top, is also of a fairly conventional Empire type. However, the sofa is unusual.

361

362

363   Two games tables with marquetry of walnut, olive and other woods. Northern Italy, 1808. Sold at Sotheby's, London, July 15, 1983.
These tables bear the following inscription:
  "Luigi Gallinelli di Citta di Castello fece l'anno 1808." Luigi Gallinelli is known as an organ maker.

363

364

365

364 Secretaire, table of tripod form and worktable of mahogany. Empire period. Villa di Poggio, Caiano, near Florence.
The secretaire is probably of French workmanship. The small mahogany and gilt wood tables seem to be of Italian manufacture. A small tripod table with swan supports, which is of the same construction as the example shown on the left in this illustration, was sold at the Palais Galliera, Paris, by Messrs. Ader, Jean-Louis Picard, Antoine Ader, on December 8, 1969, as Lot no. 142.

365 *Jardinière* of mahogany and gilt wood, gilt bronze mounts. Empire period. Musée Masséna, Nice.
This *jardinière* and its pendant, which were both purchased by Prince Essling around 1900, are of Florentine manufacture. There are comparable pieces in the Pitti Palace.

366 Neapolitan armchair of white- ▷ painted wood with details picked out in gold. Capodimonte Palace, Naples.
Several models of Restoration-period chairs, which are all similar, can be found in Neapolitan palaces.

367 Top of a *guéridon* table, inlaid with marble and hardstones. Florence, Restoration period. Private Collection, France.
The ground is of Belgian black marble; the zigzag design around the border is inlaid in lapis lazuli and Pyrenean red marble. The wreath of naturalistic flowers is tied with a ribbon bow of malachite.

368 Council Chamber, Royal Palace, Turin, with gilt wood furniture by Pelagio Palagi, made in 1836–38.

366

367 △

368

Early Nineteenth-Century Spanish Furniture and Interiors

Charles III of Spain died in 1788. He was intelligent and thrifty and was the best king to rule Spain in a long time. His son's reputation is quite different. He was something of a figure of fun, since his wife was deceiving him with the chief minister. Painted pitilessly by Goya, he was toppled from the throne of Spain by Napoleon. However, Charles IV's reign was important from an artistic point of view as he was fond of fine things and was endowed with taste. Before coming to the throne he built *casitas* (little houses) near the Pardo and Escorial palaces. These are rather like the Petit Trianon at Versailles, Madame du Barry's pavilion at Louveciennes, and Bagatelle, which are all typical of the small buildings that eighteenth-century royalty liked to build in the grounds of their palaces.

After becoming king, Charles IV continued and extended his building programs. He completed the "Prince's House" in the Escorial park, bought a pavilion from the duchess of Alba which he commissioned Dugourc, one of Bélanger's assistants at Bagatelle, to decorate, and built a larger edifice in the park at Aranjuez. This was called the Casita del Labrador. At the same time he redecorated various apartments within the Royal Palace at Madrid and built additons to the Escorial, a palace which had been neglected by the first Bourbon monarchs. In 1788 work began there on a new staircase, built by the architect Juan de Villanueva, who had been responsible for the casita. All this work, which was carried out with considerable refinement, was costly, especially as the king ordered furniture, bronzes, textiles and even carriages from France. As Charles IV emptied the coffers which his economical father had kept well filled, the pace of construction slowed down. It ceased completely in 1808 when there was a political crisis leading to the king's abdication. Some of Charles IV's building and decorating projects remained unfinished until the Spanish monarchy regained power in 1813. Their bright, gay colors give us an intriguing glimpse of a transitional style bridging the gap between Louis XVI and Empire styles. The only equivalent example is in Russia, where Paul I furnished palaces outside St. Petersburg at the same period.

In both cases Italian artists, or those who had been influenced by Italian ideas, were partly responsible for the decorative schemes. However, whereas the story of the refurbishing of Pavlovsk, Gatchina and Peterhof is well known, art historians are still unable to chronicle the story of the Spanish pavilions built by Charles IV. This seems rather paradoxical as the Spanish archives are intact and the documents contain the names of the painters, sculptors and furniture makers who were concerned with the various projects.

The root of the problem appears to reside in the presence in Madrid from April 1800 of the Paris decorator Jean-Démosthène Dugourc. Two recent studies[8] do not in fact allow us to evaluate the importance of Dugourc's role in the refurbishment of these royal residences. Dugourc's name will be mentioned later in connection with textiles, carpets and wall decoration, where his work is better known, but we may give here a short outline of his career which he himself included in his autobiography.[9] As he was not modest by nature, he often gives the impression of exaggerating his own role while omitting details or

circumstances which do not show him to good advantage. Dugourc was born in 1749. He spent fifteen years in Rome in the retinue of Comte de Cany, the French ambassador. He claims to have met Winckelmann and to have returned from Italy imbued with a love of classical antiquity. His career began auspiciously under his brother-in-law, François Bélanger, architect to the Comte d'Artois. Bélanger made Dugourc part of his team and later found him several worthwhile posts. In 1784 Dugourc became designer in the royal furniture depository and *intendant* to the king's brother, Monsieur, in his department of works. His rapid promotion was not entirely undeserved. Dugourc was an able and imaginative designer. His two surviving collections of designs are ample evidence of his skill.[10] Some of the most remarkable drawings are for textiles or wall hangings. Before the Revolution Dugourc was in contact with Camille Pernon, the leading silk manufacturer at Lyons. Señor J. J. Junquera y Mato has shown that some of Dugourc's designs were executed for La Moncloa, which belonged to the Duchess of Alba and was decorated by Dugourc in 1790, and that others were for the prince's casita at the Escorial. Dugourc was evidently working for the Spanish monarchy even earlier, as there are decorative projects for the Escorial and the Pardo, both dated 1786, in the archives of the firm of Tassinari and Châtel.

Dugourc was to lose his job at the Revolution. The royal furniture depository was in fact suppressed in 1797. In his autobiography he says that he founded a wallpaper firm, followed by a firm making playing cards, then a glassworks, as well as being associated with a porcelain factory. The very number of these concerns indicates that none was particularly successful. When Dugourc was invited to Madrid, he therefore immediately accepted. By that time Percier and Fontaine were the most fashionable decorators and Dugourc doubtless felt that at fifty years of age he was unlikely to find a rewarding post in Paris. He explains the circumstances which led to his leaving the French capital. For some years he had been in contact with Godon, a *marchand-mercier* in Madrid who supplied the court. Godon had acted as an intermediary for the king of Spain's purchase of bronzes designed by Dugourc, and probably also for many other items. Señor Junquera considers that various pieces of French furniture in the Spanish royal collections must have been acquired in Paris from sales held during the Revolution and that they were bought through Godon and Dugourc. Godon died in 1799 and his widow suggested to Dugourc that he should go to Spain. This would explain why Dugourc's arrival in Spain is not noted in the archives, since he was not invited by the king. His role was mainly a commercial one but he was a designer by training. It would have been difficult for the king not to take on someone with such impressive references and recognized talent to decorate his buildings. However, Dugourc carried out only a limited number of projects after arriving in 55, 369, 370 Madrid. He designed, and probably supplied, several silk wall hangings woven in Lyons by Pernon. He was commissioned by Charles IV shortly before the end of his reign to decorate two rooms at La Moncloa, which the king had bought from the duchess of Alba. Paintings signed by Dugourc can still be found at La Moncloa. Furniture executed in the royal workshop may have been designed by Dugourc. Five pieces are illustrated here. At this period 369, 371–374 architects and artists usually only provided the maker with a small-scale design, usually executed in watercolor, leaving him a certain amount of freedom to interpret the idea. It is not surprising, therefore, that furniture designed in Spain by Dugourc has certain Spanish characteristics.

It is difficult to discover at this point whether Dugourc played a more important role, although there are several indications that he did not. Soon after 1800 King Charles IV commissioned Percier and Fontaine to decorate the Platinum Room at the Casita del Labrador. The scheme was carried out in Paris and the various parts assembled on site. This shows that Charles IV did not give his unqualified allegiance to Dugourc. The team of craftsmen employed at the Casita del Labrador under the direction of Isidro Gonzales Velásquez consisted of Zacharias Gonzales Velásquez, the architect's brother, who painted the ceiling in the Sculpture Gallery, and their cousin, Salvador Maella, who was also a painter and decorated the ceilings in the principal rooms. This was a family enterprise and collaboration with a foreigner such as Dugourc, who enjoyed a certain notoriety, would have been difficult. Finally, Dugourc himself says relatively little in his autobiography about his role in Spain, and he would doubtless have written more had he been successful. He was still in Spain in 1809. As war put paid to all artistic activity in that country, the date of his return to Paris is of little interest. By 1814 he had returned to France, where he naturally took up his old position in the royal furniture depository.

Despite the presence and influence of Italian and French artists, the *casitas* and apartments built by Charles IV are quite obviously Spanish. The juxtaposition of neoclassical motifs with tapestries or painted ceilings in a more colorful and vigorous style is particularly attractive. These Spanish interiors seem to have a warmth often lacking in Empire interiors elsewhere.

Percier and Fontaine themselves were enthusiastic about the decoration they carried out at the Casita del Labrador: "Everything there has been executed with extreme care. The height of the vault is extended and its richness exaggerated by mirrors placed on the gables; the wood paneling is of mahogany and the ornamental details are in platinum." However, the Platinum Room is not the most successfully decorated room in this little palace.

After the defeat of Napoleon and the restoration of peace, Ferdinand VII (1813–33) carried on his father's projects. He too ordered from France chandeliers, clocks, porcelain and furniture. The Spanish royal workshops also produced a great deal of furniture; indeed they were responsible for the majority of pieces. At this time Spain, like other European countries, was relatively free from outside influences. As in Italy, this freedom was often to mark a spontaneous return to the swirling contours of the baroque style.

375–377

195

369 △

▽ 370

369   Sofa of mahogany inlaid with lemonwood and boxwood; ebony fillets. Casita del Principe, also known as the Casita del Abajo, Escorial Palace.

Dugourc's role in the decoration of this house is documented. One of his drawings preserved in the Tassinari and Châtel Collection, Lyons, is apparently the model for this sofa. It is dated 1788. Legs of square section are rarely found on contemporary French furniture, but do appear in other drawings by Dugourc, for instance in a design for an armchair in the Tassinari and Châtel Collection and in the design reproduced in Plate 370. The marquetry, which was executed in the Spanish royal workshops, gives this sofa a Spanish appearance notwithstanding its Lyons silk upholstery.

370   Design for a wall hanging and for chairs. Watercolor drawing by Dugourc. From the Dugourc Album. Library, Musée des arts décoratifs, Paris.

The hanging is in the second-floor room at the Casita del Abajo which contains the sofa shown in Plate 369. The chairs were never executed, but Dugourc reused the motif of dancing fauns for the wall covering in the ballroom at the Casita del Labrador. As in the case of furniture, the designer merely delivered a sketch for the textile to the craftsmen. This design could not have been reproduced as a woven textile as it is too irregular, so that adaptation by the craftsmen would have been necessary.

371   King Charles IV's bed; mahogany and gilt bronze. Escorial Palace.

The form of this bed is reminiscent of contemporary French beds decorated with Egyptian caryatids (see Pl. 128), but the present example is of superior design. It is known from documents that the bronzes are of French origin and it is therefore likely that they were designed by Dugourc, who may well also have been responsible for the design of the bed itself.

371

372

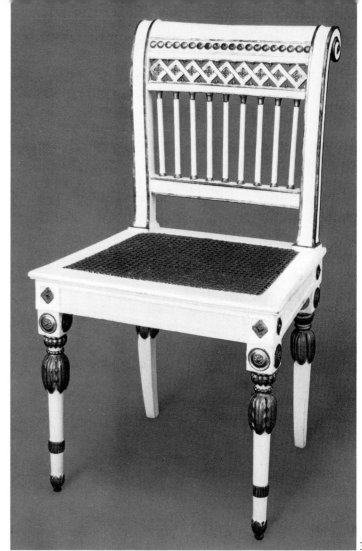

373

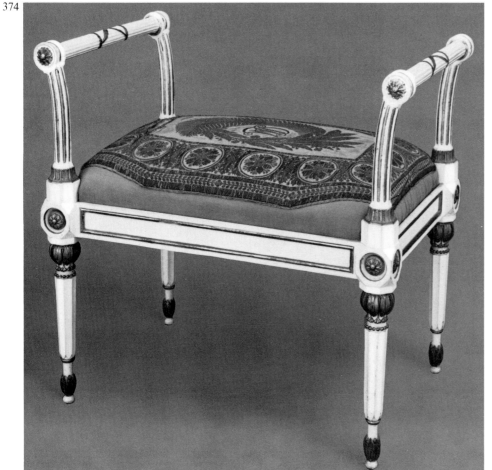

374

372 Chair of white-painted wood with details in gold. Casita del Abajo, Escorial Palace.
This chair has all the stylishness of one made in the Louis XVI period. The small scrolled ornamental device on the cresting is rarely found on chairs of this era, but was to become more common during the Empire period. The coarsely fluted legs are unlike those on French chairs, and are a sure indication that this piece is not of French manufacture. The braid trimming on the edges of the upholstery was undoubtedly designed by Dugourc.

373, 374 Chair and small bench, of painted wood, partly gilt (see also Pl. 55). The queen's drawing room, Casita del Labrador, Aranjuez.
The benches are upholstered with a textile which may have been designed by Dugourc. The chairs have straight backs terminating in a scroll, and are attractive in appearance. Their legs, which are decorated with floral motifs, are unusual, although an armchair reproduced by Krafft and Ransonnette does have similar ones. The height of the scrolled back and the rosettes and lozenges near the junction of the leg and the seat rail are features also found on French chairs.

375

376 △

375, 376 Chair and armchair, of mahogany and gilt wood. La Granja de San Ildefonso.

The rounded, contorted forms found on chairs made during the reign of Ferdinand VII (1813–33) seem rather distantly related to the neoclassical style, of which they are nevertheless a continuation. The same phenomenon can be seen in Italian, Austrian, and occasionally in South German furniture.

377 Boat-shaped bed of mahogany and gilt wood. Royal Palace, Madrid.

The boldness of the scrolled form of this bed is somewhat reminiscent of the undulating lines of the chairs illustrated in Plate 376.

377

199

Furniture in Sweden and Finland

The spread of artistic influences can be closely studied with the aid of examples drawn from Sweden and Finland.

During the reign of Gustavus III (1771–92) Sweden was entirely dominated by French influence, perhaps more so 378–380 than any other country. Pieces of Swedish furniture are so 381–383 close to their French counterparts that they can almost be confused with them. Like French examples, Swedish chairs are marked or signed by their maker and often bear a dated paper label issued by the city of Stockholm which enables us to know precisely in which year the chair was made.

The French Revolution and the assassination of Gustavus III in 1792 brought changes in their wake. However, at the end of the eighteenth century, when French influence was still supreme, there was furniture in Sweden which revealed other influences. As we have seen, many commodes can be compared with similar pieces made in 384 Germany, while chairs with regularly spaced vertical bars on the back are quite unlike any French example. Chairs in this style can, however, be found in Denmark, Russia, 385 Germany and even Italy. The stretchers on the armchair illustrated in Plate 386 might be found on a French provincial or even a Parisian cane chair. Although the form of the chair back can be found in much of Georges Jacob's work, the openwork back splat is derived from English chairs. The 387 dual influence is even more apparent in a chair by Lars Söderholm. Its shield back is close to engravings in Hepplewhite's *Cabinet-Maker and Upholsterer's Guide.*

Sweden's relative isolation during the Napoleonic era meant that its artistic evolution proceeded at a much slower pace. Chairs with a strongly curved back, a feature which had disappeared in France in the early years of the nineteenth century (see p. 12), continued to be made in 391 Sweden up to about 1810, if not later. On the other hand Swedish chairs in the classical style took on more marked 392 national characteristics. New types of sofas were designed to complete suites of furniture for the drawing room. These 393, 395 sofas had no classical antecedents but harmonized well enough with the chairs they accompanied.

The arrival of a new ruler, Bernadotte, in 1810 apparently did not lead to an extension of the influence of French Empire style in Sweden, as had happened in Lucca and Florence under similar circumstances. Armchairs made at this time are more Swedish than Empire in appearance. 394, 396–399 Bernadotte, who inherited the Swedish throne, even though related to the Bonapartes, was not slow to join forces with Napoleon's enemies. After the conclusion of peace, German and English influences again came to the fore in Sweden. Indeed native Swedish furniture seems to have disappeared 400, 401 altogether. A few rare pieces show signs of French influence. 402

During the eighteenth century Finland, which had long been under Swedish domination, became a bone of contention between Sweden and Russia. In 1808 Finland was finally conquered by Alexander I of Russia, who was wise enough to leave the country a large degree of autonomy.

Up to 1808 Finnish furniture cannot be distinguished from Swedish. The finest pieces came from the capital, Stockholm, but stylistically there were no differences between the products of the two countries.

We shall therefore only discuss pieces made after 1808 or rather after 1815, the year in which peace led to a renewal of economic activity all over Europe. Links between Sweden 403 and Finland persisted. The carving on an armchair resembles the decoration on a series of Finnish chairs and the armchair itself may well be Finnish, yet it is very close to an armchair made in the 1820s now in the Nordiska Museet, Stockholm. However, in Finland Swedish influence now took second place to the German Biedermeier style, 404–406 together with a suggestion of English influence, probably transmitted via northern Germany. To complete the picture, Russian influence made itself felt since Finns began to buy furniture in St. Petersburg. Finnish furniture at this 407–413 period therefore exhibits an interesting mixture of styles.

378

379

380

378   Chair of gilt wood upholstered with damask. The green silk was rewoven at Lyons after the original. Private Collection, Finland.
Stamped by Johan Lindgren, a furniture maker working in Stockholm between 1786 and 1800. The chair was part of a suite presented to Count A. F. Munck by King Gustavus III (1771–92).

379   Chair of unpainted wood (formerly painted). Musée national du château de Pau.
Stamped by Georges Jacob (1765–96), it bears the inventory mark of the Tuileries Palace. Simpler than the Swedish chair in Plate 378, Jacob's chair is decorated only with carved rosettes at either end of the seat rail.

380   Chair of carved wood, painted gray. National Museum of Finland, Pukkila estate.
Stamped by Johan Lindgren. Trapezoidal seat backs appeared in France on the eve of the Revolution. Found only on armchairs and cabriole chairs, they became popular in the Directory period (see Pl. 244).

381

382

383

381 Cabriole chair with oval back, of gilt wood. Private Collection, Finland.
Stamped by Erik Holm, master furniture maker in Stockholm between 1774 and 1814 or 1819.

382 Stamp of Erik Holm in chair in Plate 381.

383 Cabriole armchair with oval back. Musée national du château de Pau.
This armchair, which is one of a pair, bears the stamp of Georges Jacob and a label with an inscription which is still legible: *"Comédie française, 2ème loge, Monsieur,"* showing that it was in the king's brother's box at the Comédie française. Jacob's account of these armchairs dated February 20, 1786 is preserved in the Archives Nationales (R5. 522):
"Account on behalf of work undertaken for and supplied to Monsieur [Count of Provence, the King's brother]...Comédie française – Three cabriole armchairs, curved on plan and elevation, molded, with sheathed and fluted legs and rosettes above the legs, at 19 L. 10s ... 58 10s -----"

384 Chair of painted wood, gilt ornaments. Trapezoidal barred back. Sweden or Finland, late eighteenth or early nineteenth century. Private Collection, Finland.

385 Two chairs of unpainted wood, with trapezoidal barred back, seat of oval form, and seat rail decorated with fluting. The rosettes often found above the legs are replaced here by an "antique nail" motif. Northern Italy, late eighteenth century. Sold by Messrs. Couturier and de Nicolay at the Hôtel Drouot, Paris, on May 30, 1980.

386 Armchair of painted wood. Stamped by Melchior Lundberg, master furniture maker in Stockholm. Private Collection, Finland.

387 Chair of painted wood. Stamped by Lars Söderholm, master furniture maker in Stockholm. National Museum of Finland, Helsinki.

384

385

387

386

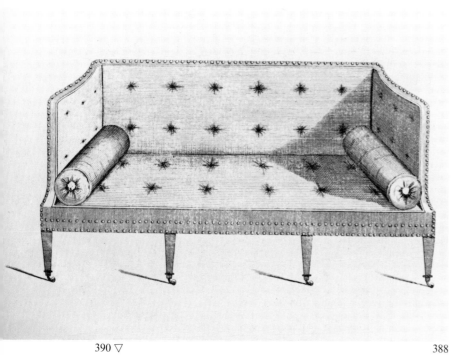

390 ▽   388 389

388 Design for an upholstered sofa. Plate 21 in George Hepplewhite's *Cabinet-Maker and Upholsterer's Guide.* Engraving dated October 1, 1787.

389 Sofa of carved and painted wood. Provincial Finland. Private Collection, Finland.

390 Sofa of carved and painted wood. Sweden, last years of the eighteenth century. Private Collection, Finland.

391 Chair of carved and painted wood. Stamped by Erik Höglander, master furniture maker in Stockholm active between 1777 and about 1800. Private Collection, Finland.

392 Drawing room in the Finnish embassy, Stockholm.
All the furniture is Swedish. The two armchairs at the left are in Louis XVI style, the sofa and the chairs at the right are of slightly later date. The wallpaper consists of two panels from "The History of Psyche," issued in Paris by Joseph Dufour, 1816.

391

392

393

394

395

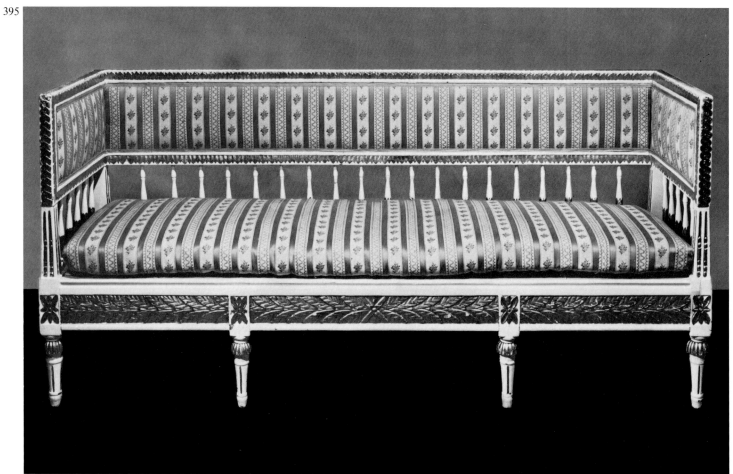

393 Part of a sofa of white-painted wood, gilt. Sweden or Finland, Empire period. Private Collection, Finland.

394 Armchair of carved and painted wood. Sweden, Empire period. Private Collection, Finland.
The back is slightly curved. The openwork frieze along its base is unusual, but other examples exist, notably on chairs by Jacob-Desmalter (Pl. 204). The form of the armrests as well as the extensive use of carving to decorate the chair are reminiscent of Louis XVI furniture.

395 Sofa of white-painted wood, gilt. Sweden or Finland, Empire period. Ehrensvärd Society, Suomenlinna, Helsinki.

396 Chair of carved and painted wood. Sweden, Empire period. Private Collection, Finland.

397 Armchair of carved and painted wood. Sweden, Empire period. Private Collection, Finland.
In form this chair is similar to a desk chair. The carving is not unlike that on the armchair in Plate 394.

396   397

398

400

399

401

398 Armchair of carved and painted wood. Stamped by Melchior Lundberg, father or son. Lundberg junior became a master furniture maker in Stockholm in 1808. Private Collection, Finland.
This armchair is more refined in appearance than the preceding one. The ornamental detail on the front rail is in Empire style but the carved and fluted front legs are similar to those on Louis XVI chairs.

399 Armchair of carved and painted wood. Sweden, Empire period. National Museum of Finland, Helsinki.
The shape is rather original, and is identical with that of certain armchairs from the Stockholm Opera House.

400, 401 Mahogany armchair and chair. Stamped by Melchior Lundberg, master furniture maker in Stockholm between 1808 and 1834. Armfelt Museum, Helsinki.
These chairs, which must date from the 1820s, came from the Åminne estate (Joensuu).

402 Sofa veneered with mahogany; the capitals and bases of the columns supporting the armrests are of gilt bronze. Finnish Embassy, Stockholm.
This Swedish sofa is similar in many respects to French Restoration pieces, but the form of the back is more German.

402

403   Sofa of painted wood. Finland or Sweden, about 1820. Historical Museum, Turku.

404 Chair of unpainted and ebonized wood. Senate Palace, Helsinki.

405 Mahogany chair. Private Collection, Finland.

406 Armchair of unpainted wood, curved armrests. Private Collection, Finland.

The chairs in Plates 404–406, made in the 1820s, are close in style to German ones in Biedermeier style.

407

408

409

410

411

412

413

407 Mahogany chair. Private Collection, Finland.
The arrangement of the legs is characteristic of English Regency chairs, and was adopted in France for a great number of Restoration period chairs.

408 Chair of unpainted wood. Private Collection, Finland.
The carved ornament is reminiscent of the decoration on the chair back shown in Plate 407. The top rail, which is deeper than on the previous example, is rather like that found on Russian chairs.

409 Mahogany chair. Anjala Estate Museum, Finland.
The back is not unlike that found on some late Biedermeier chairs made in Germany. The arrangement of the legs is typical of Russian chairs.

410 Mahogany chair. Private Collection, Finland.
The decoration on the carved chairback is very similar to that on the preceding examples, but all the other characteristics are typical of Russian chairs.

411 Mahogany armchair, upholstered in leather. Private Collection, Finland.
This armchair also closely resembles Russian chairs of the 1830s.

412 Chair of beech, stained to resemble mahogany. National Museum of Finland, Helsinki.
Although this chair is probably contemporary with the preceding examples, it has no Russian characteristics. It has more in common with English Regency, French Restoration and German chairs in Biedermeier style.

413 Chair of stained wood. National Museum of Finland, Helsinki.
This chair has a lower back than the previous ones do and has still more in common with pieces in Biedermeier style. It is similar in design to a drawing of a chair submitted as a masterpiece in 1837 by the furniture maker C. M. Björklöf of Helsinki.

Russian Furniture

Western civilization reached Russia in the time of Peter the Great. This monarch called on foreign scientists, artists and craftsmen in almost every sphere. Foreign artisans and artists were still playing an important role in St. Petersburg, and even in Moscow, a century later. In Moscow a certain P. Spol, who was originally from Metz, ran the leading cabinetmaker's workshop. It is difficult to guess at his real name since "Spol" almost certainly represents the transliteration into Cyrillic of a quite different word in Latin characters. Spol was a gifted wood-carver. Between 1792 and 1798 he executed for Ostankino numerous carved and gilded *torchères,* console tables, perfume burners and other pieces of furniture in a rather heavy Louis XVI idiom which by then was already outdated in Paris. Other Moscow furniture makers had Germanic names, such as Kork, Miller and Pieck.

The same applies to St. Petersburg where Heinrich Gambs (1765–1831) was the leading craftsman. He established a workshop which was to produce the finest furniture in Russia up to the middle of the nineteenth century. Heinrich Gambs was a native of Strasbourg or Baden-Baden. It has often been supposed that he worked for Roentgen at Neuwied, although there is no proof of this. Gambs's furniture certainly exhibits the technical perfection characteristic of Roentgen's work, which it sometimes resembles, but Gambs was probably familiar with Roentgen's furniture in the various imperial palaces in St. Petersburg.

In these palaces there are commodes dating from about 1800 which are exactly like their contemporary German or Swedish counterparts. There are also mahogany chairs with 415 brass inlays which are said to be in the "Jacob" style, although they have nothing to do with real Jacob chairs. The pierced backs, which rise slightly in the center, are more reminiscent of contemporary English chairs, as is the lozenge design, but the general outline of the pieces, which are quite graceful, is rather different from English examples. Most chairs of this type were made by Christian Meyer, who was already working in St. Petersburg by 1782. A few years later the influence of the French Empire style was felt in the 414 Russian capital as elsewhere in Europe. However, Russian 422, 423 furniture in this style has not yet been studied in detail. Better known is the furniture designed by architects, especially by Andrei Voronikhin (1759–1814), who had been brought up in France, and by Carlo Rossi (1775–1849), who was of Italian origin and had been trained in Italy.

Voronikhin refurbished or redecorated numerous rooms at Pavlovsk after the fire of 1803. His furniture is original and even though some pieces are less successful than others this may be the fault of the makers rather than of the designer. For instance the chimeras on the armchairs in the Greek Drawing Room are poorly carved.

Rossi began working in 1816, just at the time when the classical style, freely interpreted, was beginning to diversify. Rossi designed a quantity of furniture for the Winter Palace, 48, 49, 61, 63 the Mikhailovskii Palace and Pavlovsk. It is often completely gilded and ornamented with low relief carving. Like Voronikhin, Rossi was sometimes poorly served by the craftsmen who executed his designs for furniture. The finest pieces were made in the Gambs and Baumann workshops. In numerous other instances the carving and gilding is far inferior in quality to French or Italian workmanship. Rossi's furniture is closest in style to contemporary Italian 416, 417 work but our illustrations show that this artist was open to the most diverse influences. His own taste led him to decorate every available surface almost to excess.

Rossi was far from being the only furniture designer in a period which saw the full flowering of the Empire style in Russia as well as considerable development in the techniques of furniture making. Most craftsmen remained anonymous, but their work is marked by characteristics 418, 419, 42? which are peculiar to Russia. Chairs, for instance, are generally rectangular rather than trapezoidal in plan. The two sides are parallel, the front and rear legs symmetrical and the splat deep. Some examples have horseshoe-shaped 49, 50 seats, like those on chairs and armchairs *en gondole,* but in 420, 425 general chair backs are varied in form and are not joined at their base to the seat rail. Armrests also vary considerably.

Furniture designed by Leo von Klenze for the New Hermitage at St. Petersburg could easily be classified as German, rather than Russian. The Museum building, which was erected according to Klenze's design between 1842 and 1851, is both classical and Germanic in style. It is clearly influenced by Schinkel's late work in Berlin. However Klenze did not forget his early training by, or his work for, Percier. His seat furniture is reminiscent of pieces he designed twenty years earlier at Munich and the chairs are like French examples. The shape of one illustrated is 421 reminiscent of chairs made by P. Bellangé in around 1820[11] for the large drawing room in the Pavillon de Saint-Ouen.

Veneers of light woods were fashionable in Russia as elsewhere in Europe. Poplar, Karelian birch and walnut were used. Stains were sometimes applied to birch and walnut to give darker, greenish or even brown tones resembling the color of mahogany. This wood continued to be widely used for high quality furniture.

Chairs were frequently gilded, but gilt bronze mounts were rarely used except by Gambs. Yet there were gilt bronze workshops in St. Petersburg which were capable of producing huge *torchères,* chandeliers and furniture of solid ormolu. The tripod stand supporting a malachite vase in the 422 Malachite Room in the Hermitage Museum, St. Petersburg, was made in the city. This tripod stand, like the console 423 table, is made of malachite, mahogany, gilded wood and gilt bronze. It is in the strict French Empire style and has no Russian features. Stripped of the malachite vase, the tripod stand could easily be mistaken for a French product.

Far more characteristically Russian is the polished cut-steel furniture with gilt bronze ornaments and silver inlays intended for the luxury market. It was made in Tula in central Russia by craftsmen specializing in small arms. It deserves only a cursory mention as it has more in common with local crafts, which also influence the forms of more strictly classical Russian furniture.

Although, as we have seen, the best craftsmen in the two Russian capitals produced elegant and original furniture, huge numbers of heavy, rustic and naïvely conceived chairs and sofas were also made in Russia.

414   Armchair of painted wood, partly gilt. Hermitage Museum, Leningrad.

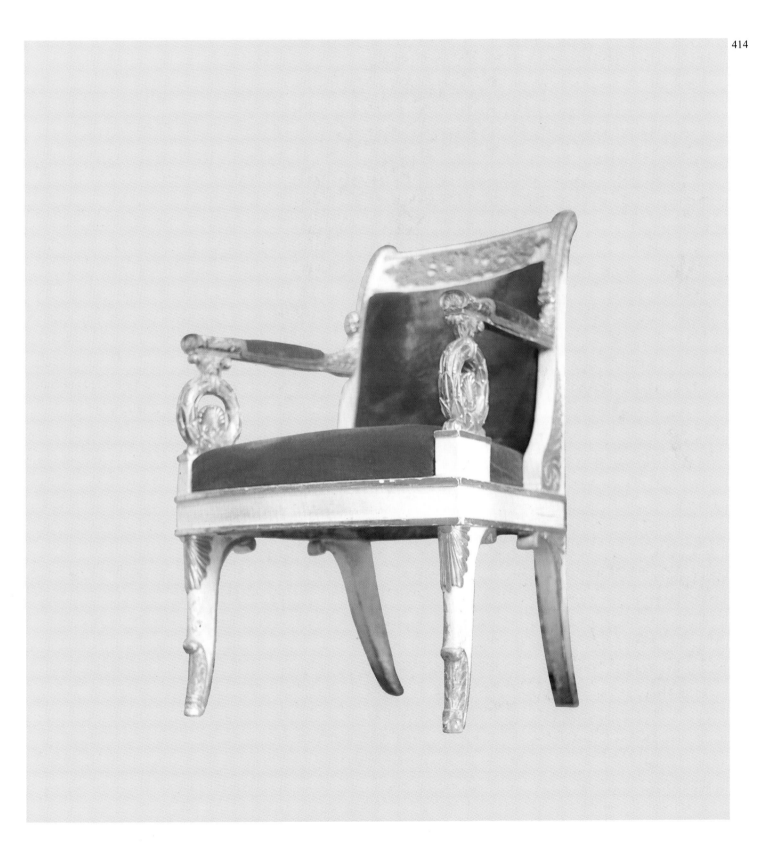

415

416

415 Mahogany armchair, decorated with pewter fillets and pateras; upholstered in leather. Presidential Palace, Helsinki.
There are "Jacob style" chairs at Pavlovsk Palace, near Leningrad, which are the same as the one reproduced here. It was doubtless imported from St. Petersburg. Only the armrests have anything in common with armchairs by Georges Jacob.

416 Sofa. Plate 18 in *Household Furniture and Interior Decoration executed from Designs by Thomas Hope,* London, 1807.

417 Sofa of gilt wood from the White Drawing Room in the Mikhailovskii Palace, St. Petersburg. Russian Museum, Leningrad.
The furniture in the White Drawing Room was made in 1822–23 after designs by Carlo Rossi, who in this instance, seems to have been inspired by the engraving in Hope's book.

418 Mahogany and gilt wood armchair from the Munkkiniemi estate, Helsinki. Private Collection, Finland. The back is the same as that of chairs in Alexander I's study at Tsarskoe Selo. The armrests are similar to those in Plate 414.

419 Mahogany and gilt wood armchair. Presidential Palace, Helsinki.
The Russian emperors were entertained in the present Presidential Palace when they visited Helsinki. All the old furniture there is of Russian origin.

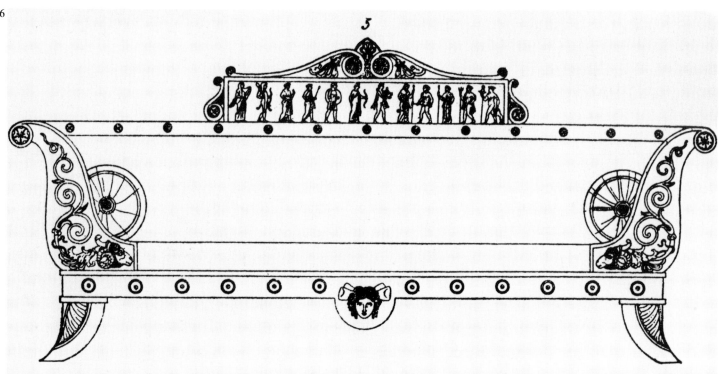

417

418

419

420   Mahogany and gilt wood chair. Hermitage Museum, Leningrad.
The chair *en gondole* has a rounded back, terminating in scrolls, in the same style as the chairs reproduced in Plates 25 and 45–47.

421   Carved mahogany chair, designed by Leo von Klenze (1845–50). Hermitage Museum, Leningrad.

422   Tripod table of gilt bronze and malachite. Hermitage Museum, Leningrad.

423   Console table of mahogany, gilt wood, gilt bronze and malachite. Hermitage Museum, Leningrad.

420   421

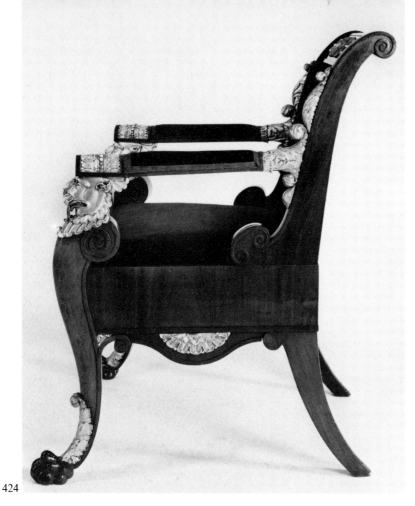

424

424 Ceremonial armchair of mahogany and gilt wood. Helsinki University.
This armchair, which is of Russian origin, is used by the Chancellor of Helsinki University. It must date from after 1830.

425

425 Armchair of burr poplar, upholstered in crimson silk. Armfelt Museum, Helsinki.
The suite to which this armchair belongs comes from the Åminne estate (Joensuu), the residence of Count Armfelt, onetime favorite of Gustavus III, king of Sweden (Pl. 50), who became governor of Finland during the reign of Tsar Alexander I of Russia. The furniture, which postdates the count's death in 1814, is said to have been acquired at St. Petersburg in 1819.

V Gothic, Renaissance, Louis XV and Louis XVI Revival Furniture

There is an element of truth in the view that the Gothic revival was part of the Romantic movement.

The Romantic period saw widespread and deeply felt enthusiasm for Gothic art, which first began to be studied at this time.[1] Until the early nineteenth century it had been little known, and it could almost be said to have been discovered at this point. However, the existence of Gothic taste goes back at least half a century. Père Laugier, one of the most influential architectural writers of the eighteenth century, wrote:

To tell the truth, this architecture is beautiful despite its flaws. Although the most magnificent works are marked by a heaviness of spirit and coarseness of sentiment which shock us, one can only admire its overall boldness, delicate carving and the air of majesty and detachment found in some examples. There is something despairing and inimitable about it.[2]

Laugier was by no means the only one to hold this opinion. Leading French architects tried to recreate the lightness of the great Gothic cathedrals. Among them were Jules Hardouin-Mansart, who was responsible for the dome of the Invalides, and Soufflot, who built the church of St. Geneviève[3]. Soufflot's assistant Brébion wrote: "M. Soufflot's principal objective in building his church was to unite in one of the most beautiful forms the lightness of Gothic buildings with the purity and magnificence of Greek architecture."

Soufflot would not, however, have dared or even wished, to work in the Gothic style. When given the task of restoring the sacristy and treasury of Notre-Dame Cathedral, Paris, he rebuilt them in the neoclassical style. In fact, leaving aside churches which were finished or partly rebuilt in Gothic style so as to maintain their stylistic unity, the only neo-Gothic buildings constructed in France during the eighteenth century were in a fantastic idiom which was similar in character to the Turkish or Chinese pavilions or picturesque ruins found in numerous parks. These buildings were not given any serious consideration.

Towards the end of the eighteenth century, however, "Gothic" decoration began to gain popularity. In 1782 Charles de Wailly designed a classical style château for the Duke of Arenberg which was flanked by two medieval towers.[4] Some architects, such as Jean-Jacques Le Queu, who designed a house based on antique models for the Comte de Bouville at Neuilly, a Gothic gallery in the château at Gaillon, and a Chinese pavilion for Monsieur Bertin at Chatou, already exhibited the eclecticism which was to be so much in vogue thirty years later.

Most neo-Gothic interiors dating from Louis XVI's reign or from the revolutionary years have disappeared without trace. The one illustrated in Plate 426 is a rather rare exception. Its appearance is known thanks to Krafft and Ransonnette,[5] who give valuable details of the materials and colors employed. These differ little from those found in neoclassical interiors of the same date (1801). Mahogany, silver and gilt bronze are used, and sharp color contrasts are evident. Yet the architect, Coffinet, reproduces a well-observed crocketed frieze and Gothic arcading, combining these details with neoclassical features, such as the doors.

The same story could be told about developments in other European countries. Even in Russia, where true Gothic art never existed, some buildings and monuments were constructed in neo-Gothic style towards the end of the eighteenth century. The earliest and most noteworthy are the church and palace built in 1770 by the architect Georg Friedrich Veldten to commemorate the naval battle of Chesmé. It is hard to see why the Empress Catherine II should want to commemorate a naval victory over the Turks with Gothic-style buildings. She was passionately devoted to architecture, and wrote on September 2, 1773 to Falconet: "I should like to have a design for a classical house, its rooms arranged as in antiquity... I am capable of building a Greek or Roman rhapsody in my garden at Tsarskoe Selo... I beg you to assist me in fulfilling this fantasy..."

The construction of Chesmé Palace (the name Chesmé was given to the area at this time) was doubtless due to a "fantasy" of this sort. The palace is on the road from St. Petersburg to Moscow and the court stopped there when traveling between the two capitals. It was never lived in, however, and no other neo-Gothic building of importance was put up in Russia before the end of the eighteenth century.

England, often in the forefront in practical matters, seems to have been the first to have Gothic-style buildings. These were built and decorated by architects anxious to please the proprietors. The earliest and best-known example is Horace Walpole's house, Strawberry Hill, which was begun in 1747. The grandest and most idiosyncratic is Fonthill Abbey, built for William Beckford, a wealthy businessman who owned sugar plantations. Designed by James Wyatt, it was begun in 1796.

427

Even Robert Adam, who is justly recognized as the creator of a type of decoration inspired by classical antiquity, dreamed up Gothic decorative schemes for the duke and duchess of Northumberland at Alnwick on his return from Italy in 1758. Only a few drawings survive as a record of these schemes. They show that Robert Adam was not well versed in the idiom. Like all eighteenth-century architects, he knew a great deal about classical antiquity but little or nothing about medieval architecture, despite the existence of many examples close at hand. In nearly every case the same could be said for other architects who created interiors and objects in the first phase of the medieval revival. All those who espoused the neo-Gothic style did so for sentimental reasons. They may have been influenced by historical or moral factors, or simply have admired the "picturesque" nature of "gothick" ornament but they were never really familiar with Gothic art.

The young Goethe's clear expression of his feelings about Strasbourg Cathedral, which he saw in 1771, is indicative of attitudes towards Gothic architecture at this time:[6] "It rises like the Tree of God with a thousand branches, a million twigs and leaves as innumerable as grains of sand on the seabed, announcing the glory of God its master to everything around..." He admired the fusion of all the numerous details into a harmonious whole, and praised the lightness of this enormous building which thrust upwards into the sky with its lacy structure built for eternity, and added that it was a strong, primitive expression of German genius. Goethe later felt differently and deplored the use of fake medieval elements in German art during the first third of the nineteenth century.

However, the medieval revival had begun and even Goethe could not stop it. In Germany it became an article of faith that Gothic art was German art, as the Germans were descended from the Goths. In the sixteenth century Vasari used "Gothic" as a synonym for barbaric, but the word had gradually taken on its present meaning. The adoption of the neo-Gothic style by German Romantics at the beginning of the nineteenth century is a curious phenomenon which is part of the reaction against French influence in Germany. In their minds Christianity, the Middle Ages and Germanism became inseparably linked. This provides an explanation for the seriousness and conviction of German art.

This high seriousness is less noticeable in French and English art. In France and England the Middle Ages exerted a more poetic and nostalgic influence, through the romances of Queen Hortense and the troubadours in France and through the novels of Sir Walter Scott in England. Scott's works were immediately translated into various European languages and became widely known.

There were no scholarly studies of existing buildings or works of art so that confusion frequently arose. The Middle Ages existed mainly in the imagination of each artist, who lacked factual knowledge. In most cases classicism retained its hold, and many took care not to stray too far from its long-established traditions. The author of the *Report* on the Exhibition of the Products of Industry held in Paris in 1827 wrote in the following terms about a chair designed by Alexandre-Louis Bellangé: "The ebony chair in the Gothic style was particularly remarkable for its fine craftsmanship and sober use of a style which fashion has brought back into favor but which good taste forbids the artist to abuse."

Most "Gothic"-style furniture is related to contemporary Empire, Biedermeier or Restoration pieces. Usually only one or two rooms in a house were furnished in the Gothic style. The most ambitious neo-Gothic furniture, which got furthest away from earlier authentic models, was heavy and ill conceived. Some works almost seem to be caricatures of medievalism. Jacob Petit's pieces, most of those designed by Aimé Chenavard (1798–1838) and some of the work of the architect A. W. N. Pugin (1812–52) falls into this category, although Pugin's furniture became more interesting from 1837 or 1838. Pugin paid more attention to the form of his furniture than to its decoration. In this respect he foreshadowed Viollet-le-Duc, but the Englishman had the advantage of an artistic sensibility. He left works of real merit among the furniture he designed for churches and for the Houses of Parliament.

So far we have discussed only neo-Gothic furniture. Although such pieces are commoner, they cannot be separated from fake Renaissance pieces, and indeed the distinction was often blurred by contemporaries. In the Cluny Museum from Alexandre du Sommerard's time Renaissance and even seventeenth-century furniture was frequently placed beside medieval examples.

The nineteenth century, one should recall, was marked by a great intermingling of styles. A chair called "Renaissance" _{445, 446} at Pau and "Elizabethan" when made in London was in fact inspired by chairs dating from the late seventeenth century.

Furniture in Louis XIV, Louis XV and Louis XVI styles was revived earlier than is often thought. Between 1825 and 1828 King George IV bought several pieces in these styles by the Paris furniture maker A. L. Bellangé. After 1835 furniture in the "Rococo" or "Old French" style became as popular as neo-Gothic and neo-Renaissance pieces.

Examples of these styles are illustrated here in _{428–453} chronological order wherever possible.

426 Gothic decoration in Madame Vanterbergh's reading room, by the architect Coffinet. Published by Krafft and Ransonnette, Plate 100.

The caption reads: A. Mirror. B. Mahogany columns. C. Interlaced ogival arches, frieze, and mahogany cornice. D. Silver decoration on pale blue lacquer ground. E. Gilt bronze decoration, silver animals and vases on black lacquer ground. F. Wooden door decorated in pale blue lacquer. G. Ogival arches of red lacquer. H. Ground of puce lacquer. I. Silver medallions, frames, ornamental motifs and figures on green lacquer ground. K. Silver bas-reliefs on green lacquer ground. L. Gilt bronze mounts.

426

Plate LXIII.

Un Grand Sofa

427

427   "A Large Sofa." Plate LXIII from William Ince and John Mayhew's *The Universal System of Household Furniture*, 1759–63. Not long after the middle of the eighteenth century, fantastic Gothic-style chairs appeared in British furniture pattern books.

428   Chair with arcaded back. Plate 9 in the third edition of Hepplewhite's *Cabinet-Maker and Upholsterer's Guide*, 1794.

429   Chair of painted wood, arcaded back. Schloss Homburg, Hesse.
Chairbacks of this type are found in Germany and also in Russia, in the palaces near Leningrad. Most must date from around 1800.

428

429

430 Bedside table and bed of mahogany in Gothic style. Colored engraving published in La Mésangère's *Meubles et objets de goût*, 1806, no. 232.

431 Chair of unstained and ebonized wood, openwork back decorated with two Gothic-style arcade motifs. Restoration period. Musées royaux d'art et d'histoire, Brussels.

432 Walnut chair in the neo-Gothic idiom, stamped Jacob-Desmalter. Private Collection.
The stamp dates from 1803–13, but the chair seems to have been made after 1815. It is part of a suite of furniture in which most of the chairs bear the mark of a Dijon cabinetmaker. Two or three, which must have served as models for the remainder, bear Jacob-Desmalter's stamp.

433 Tripod table of carved cherrywood. Restoration period. The marble mosaic top is supported on a group of small Gothic-style columns. Musée des arts décoratifs, Paris.

430

431

432

433

434

435

434 Sofa of painted wood. Openwork back and sides decorated with Gothic-style arcading. Seurasaari Open-Air Museum, Helsinki.
The suite of which this sofa is part was made for a pavilion papered with early nineteenth-century French wallpapers.

435 Console table of painted wood in Gothic style. Escorial Palace near Madrid, entrance to Sovereign's private apartments. Made in 1832 by Angel Maeso, cabinetmaker to the court.

436 Mahogany and gilt wood armchair from a drawing room at Eaton Hall, Cheshire. Victoria and Albert Museum, London.

Eaton Hall was rebuilt at great expense in Gothic style by William Porden for the Duke of Westminster, a great London property owner. The first stage of the works lasted from 1803 to 1812, the second from 1823 to 1826. This armchair, which was probably designed by Porden, is likely to have been installed during the latter period. Even the owners soon tired of the somewhat monotonous richness and extravagance of the Gothic idiom at Eaton Hall.

437 Chair of carved oak in neo-Gothic style. Musée national du château de Pau, King Louis-Philippe's study.
The fleurs-de-lys used to ornament the back of this chair suggest that it was made before 1830.

436   437

438 Sideboard in "Jacobean" style, console table in the Gothic style, and chairs. Drawings by A. W. N. Pugin. Victoria and Albert Museum, London.

439 Dining chair of carved oak, upholstered in imitation leather, made for Scarisbrick Hall, Lancashire after drawings by A. W. N. Pugin, about 1837. Victoria and Albert Museum, London.
The design of this chair takes us a long way from the true Gothic idiom and is reminiscent of Jacob-Desmalter's piece (Pl. 432). A chair of the same type can be seen in a gouache by Jean-Claude Rameau, *Sleeping Beauty*, dated 1810 (exhibition catalogue *Le Gothique retrouvé*, no. 353).

440 Oak armchair, designed by A. W. N. Pugin for Oscott Seminary, about 1838. Victoria and Albert Museum, London.
Pugin was inspired by a genuine Gothic chair surviving in the bishop's palace at Wells. The chair he drew is said to be from Glastonbury Abbey.

441 "Lovers' seat" in Gothic style. Watercolor drawing by the architect Lewis Nockalls Cottingham (1787–1847), signed and dated 1842. Victoria and Albert Museum, London.
This was drawn in connection with a plan for the refurbishing of Snelston Hall, which Cottingham built for John Harrison. The damask colors of the upholstery are very vivid.

438

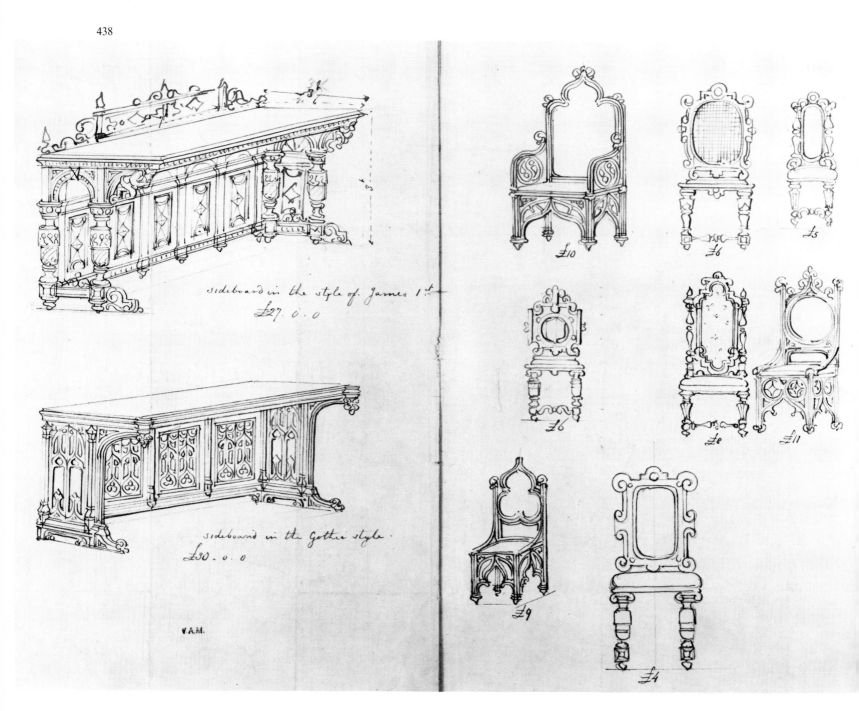

439

440

441

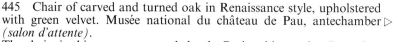

442

442 Two "fourteenth-century tables," engraving from Carl A. Heideloff's *Der Bau- und Möbel-Schreiner oder Ebenist,* Nuremberg, 1837, fasc. 4, Pl. 2.

443 Chair of painted wood, partly gilt, in "Louis XIV" style. Victoria and Albert Museum, London.
Designed by Philip Hardwick and executed in 1834 by W. & C. Wilkinson for Goldsmiths' Hall, London. Philip Hardwick also designed an "antique" dining chair likewise made for Goldsmiths' Hall (Pl. 44).
In England Louis XIV and Louis XV styles were lumped together. In any case this chair bears no resemblance to any French chair in either of these styles, but is more akin to rococo furniture made in Berlin.

444 Oak chair with turned legs, upholstered in blue, gray and white lampas. Musée national du château de Pau, Queen Marie-Amélie's room. The chairs in the queen's room were supplied by the tapestry weaver Laflêche of 94 rue de Cléry, Paris, in 1842. The chairback is typical of numerous chairs made during the Restoration period. Only the wood used and the turned legs reveal that the maker intended to produce "Renaissance"-style furniture.

445 Chair of carved and turned oak in Renaissance style, upholstered with green velvet. Musée national du château de Pau, antechamber ▷ *(salon d'attente).*
The chairs in this room were made by the Paris cabinetmaker Jeanselme and were originally covered with green damask upholstery.

443

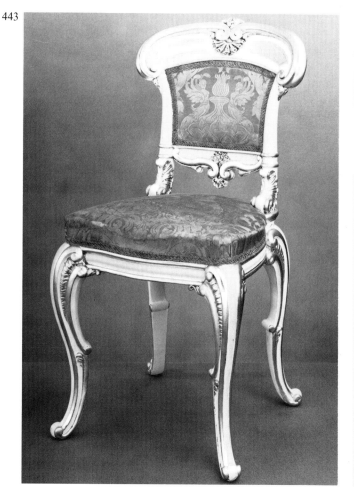

444

446

447

448

446 Chair of carved and turned mahogany in "Elizabethan" style. About 1845. Victoria and Albert Museum, London.
This chair displays numerous similarities to the Pau chairs with which it is exactly contemporary. Although supposedly imitating chairs of the late sixteenth century, it is in fact far closer to English or Dutch chairs made at the end of the seventeenth.

447 Armchair of carved and turned oak, upholstered in crimson damask with a vine-leaf pattern. Musée national du château de Pau, King Louis-Philippe's study.
Stamped Bellangé (Alexandre-Louis Bellangé) this armchair from the king's study has stayed in the same place since 1842. It still has its original silk damask upholstery, ordered from Pernon of Lyons in 1804 by the Imperial furniture depository.

448 Games table in neorococo style. Presidential Palace, Helsinki.

449 Small beech sideboard. Private Collec- ▷
tion, Finland.
The two upper shelves and the twisted columns suggest a date of manufacture between 1840 and 1850.

450

451

452

450 Sofa in neorococo style. Seurasaari Open-Air Museum, Helsinki.
Sofa backs of this shape date from around 1845. They were fashionable for ten or fifteen years.

451 Chair of carved walnut inlaid with a portrait of Queen Victoria on Worcester porcelain. Victoria and Albert Museum, London.
Shown by Henry Eyles of Bath at the 1851 International Exhibition.

452 Armchair of carved and turned oak, upholstered with reps in two shades of green. Musée national du château du Pau.
This armchair is part of a group of chairs delivered in 1852 for the guest rooms at Pau. As they were little used, they are remarkably fresh in appearance. According to the 1855 inventory, the design of the reps is "Renaissance," although it looks almost Art Nouveau.

453 Marquetry table, decorated with gilt bronze and with porcelain plaques bearing the monogram of Queen Victoria and Prince Albert. Signed "E. Kreisser à Paris [18] 52." Victoria and Albert Museum, London.
Until around 1850 furniture in Louis XVI style was much rarer than that in Louis XV style, which was more extravagantly decorated. The Louis XVI pieces were closer to the eighteenth-century originals, although they did not escape the excessive ornamentation characteristic of nineteenth-century furniture.

453

VI Architects, Ornamentalists, Manufacturers and Furniture Makers

Small or medium-sized furniture workshops, such as had existed everywhere in the eighteenth century, did not disappear overnight. They continued to operate, although on a smaller scale, until 1850 and even up to our own time. However, the nineteenth century, like our own, was marked by the establishment of larger enterprises and the complete or partial industrialization of furniture manufacture. Changes had been in the wind since the end of the eighteenth century. David Roentgen's firm was a completely new kind of venture. After taking over from his father in 1772, Roentgen began traveling both in Germany and abroad in search of orders. His first trip to Paris in 1774 led him to change the style of his furniture. In 1780 he succeeded in obtaining the title of master furniture maker (maître-ébéniste) in Paris. He traveled to St. Petersburg in 1783, selling several pieces of furniture there and obtaining important orders which he fulfilled in 1785. He went back to Russia seven times before 1791, when he opened a branch of his business in Berlin. When the French revolutionary armies arrived in Neuwied and effectively stopped production at Roentgen's factory, he had branches in Paris, Berlin, Vienna and Naples.

In 1779, in the early years of his career, Roentgen employed one master furniture maker and 29 journeymen (compagnons) to assist him in the workshop, as well as a painter. He also employed on a regular basis a clockmaker, two bronze founders, a coppersmith, a locksmith and a turner. This amounted to a considerable work force at that time. Its size must have increased as the years went by.

In France the guilds restricted the activity of each workshop to a single speciality. Veneered furniture could not be made in a workshop where joinery was being carried out, and furniture makers were forbidden to cast or found gilt bronze in their workshops. Despite the system there was great disparity in the size of various workshops. A cursory look at the chairs, beds, tables and console tables in the Louvre reveals that the firm run by Georges Jacob was perhaps ten times larger than its chief competitors. As soon as he could, that is after the abolition of the guilds in 1791, Jacob began to make veneered furniture. For a time his firm, which from 1796 was administered by his sons, enjoyed a virtual monopoly of the supply of fine furniture to most of the leading personalities of the day.

In March 1803 the Jacob brothers had no less than sixteen workshops. They were for joinery work in buildings, furniture joinery (two shops), figure carving, ornamental

carving, turning, painting and gilding, veneering, inlaying, polishing, bronze founding, molding, bronze working, gilding on metal, tapestry weaving, and locksmith's work. During the Empire period Jacob-Desmalter, who worked alone after the death of his brother, at times employed as many as three hundred and fifty workers, reduced to one hundred in quieter periods.

In England craftsmen were not subject to the guild system as was the case in Louis XVI's France and elsewhere in Europe where restrictive legislation was still in force. Larger businesses seem to have come into being earlier in England than elsewhere. At the turn of the century there were several large furniture-making concerns. These included Gillows of Lancaster,[1] which had its own London showroom; Marsh and Tatham, who made both furniture and tapestries and usually supplied the architect Henry Holland; George Seddon (1727–1801), who from 1786 employed four hundred workmen (joiners, sculptors, gilders, locksmiths, tapestry weavers, etc.). The Seddon concern, which was associated with the tapestry-making firm Morel, supplied King George IV between 1820 and 1830. The firms mentioned, like Jacob in Paris, were usually able to meet all their clients' furnishing needs.

During the Restoration period Paris makers such as Werner (1791–1849), who in 1818–20 took charge of the furnishing of several rooms at Ellingen for the Prince of Wrede, had businesses similar to the ones found in England. Not long afterwards Werner delivered numerous items of furniture to the Duke of Leuchtenberg (Eugène de Beauharnais) at Munich. In Paris itself it was mainly tapestry makers or department stores such as L'Escalier de cristal, which in the early nineteenth century took over the role of supplying all the furnishings. In the eighteenth century marchands-merciers had fulfilled a similar function.

The next stage was to sell furniture from a catalogue. The Viennese firm of Joseph Danhauser is an early example of this practice, even though the firm did not have a printed catalogue. The client could choose furniture from a large range of numbered designs.[2]

This concern was established in 1807 to make carved wood reliefs imitating bronze or ormolu. From the start it employed one hundred workers. In 1814 Danhauser obtained permission to manufacture all kinds of furniture and still later was allowed to sell curtains, wall hangings, carpets, chandeliers, bronzes and glassware in his shops as well as furniture. There was a tendency in Vienna, as in

London and to a lesser extent in Paris, for firms to set up which could supply a complete range of furnishings.

Joseph Danhauser died suddenly in 1829 and his firm closed down about twelve years later. His furniture was made according to traditional methods. This was not true of furniture made by Michael Thonet, who set up in Vienna in 1842. Thonet was the first to make mass-produced bentwood furniture, which consisted mainly of interchangeable elements. His firm underwent great expansion in the latter half of the century.

The creation of firms such as those mentioned above was bound to lead to changes in furniture design practice. The adoption of neoclassical style in the 1760s initially led to a reinforcement of the role of architects, as well as other artists, who had been in Italy and they studied classical architecture at first hand. They considered themselves, and were considered by their clients, as uniquely qualified to recreate classical furniture. Most prominent eighteenth-century architects beginning with Piranesi, Robert Adam, and Petitot also designed furniture. We have already considered examples of this. These men fathered the new style, and were responsible for its evolution over a considerable period. However, a distinction should be made between countries where furniture making was well organized and prosperous and others where it was not. In the former architects could count on makers to carry out their ideas with little supervision. A recent study[3] has shown, for example, that Robert Adam designed only a relatively small part of the furniture in the houses he decorated. The remainder was supplied by John Linnel or other craftsmen capable of designing as well as making furniture. The role of these craftsmen was particularly important as designers, and even architects, gave makers only a sketch to work from. In surviving drawings of 205–207 classical style chairs these are often shown with highly impractical legs terminating in very pointed feet. The designers rarely seem to have wondered how their chairs would support the weight of the human body. They were content to reproduce classical forms, leaving the chairmaker to modify the design so that it could be successfully executed.

Chairmakers, therefore, often played an important role. This can only be understood by reference to a large number of particular examples. As space does not permit an extended discussion, chairs by the Jacobs will be compared with those made by their chief competitors.

Some chairs made by the Jacob concern (which was headed by Georges Jacob until 1796, was called Jacob Brothers between 1796 and 1803, and was then run by 454–470 Jacob-Desmalter from 1803 until 1825) are characteristic of the firm and their shapes are reused over and over again in slightly different ways. The recurring similarity of proportions, motifs and chair types seems to indicate that in most cases the Jacobs themselves were responsible for their chairs. The same is probably true of other craftsmen,

each of whom displayed his own particular traits. The strangest example is perhaps the series of chairs supplied by Jacob-Desmalter through the tapestry weaver Darrac for the emperor's drawing room at the Grand Trianon. In his tender Darrac states that the designs for the chairs were drawn up by the *Garde-Meuble,* even though they are the usual kind of gilded wood chair made by Jacob. The armrest support and the front leg have been combined to form a double baluster in characteristic fashion. The Imperial furniture depository must have originally supplied a design, but it was doubtless highly schematic, so that Jacob could easily transform it into his usual type of gilt wood armchair. In other instances it is clear that Georges Jacob assimilated and altered for his own purposes a motif which he had not invented. Thus the simulated webbing effect and the palmettes in low relief devised by Hubert Robert reappear 220 in simplified form on the backs of armchairs of Maret. 221 These chairbacks are in turn related to various other carved chairbacks with a palmette motif. 224, 469

A desk chair which is a masterpiece of fantasy and equilibrium has a motif on the chairback which Georges 470 Jacob borrowed from chairs he had made earlier for the Prince of Wales, who ordered them through Daguerre. It seems unlikely that Georges Jacob was the designer of this chairback, as he actually describes the chair as being in English style. It seems to relate to various English eighteenth-century chairs inspired by Chinese originals. Once again Jacob apparently borrowed a motif for a chair which was indeed of his own make.

The question who really created a piece of furniture is a complicated one. At one end of the scale Jacob-Desmalter scrupulously reproduced a design for a commode by Percier. Other furniture makers modified designs supplied by architects or interior decorators so as to make them practical. At the other end of the scale were firms making furniture to their own designs. During the first half of the nineteenth century firms of the last type became more common. Naturally their owners were more concerned with commercial success than artistic excellence.

Around 1840 there were general complaints about the fall in standards of quality of furniture. The designers employed by furniture makers were castigated for their lack of skill. Firms using trained artists were praised and there was concern about professional artistic education which it was proposed to extend to the public. Museums of applied art such as the South Kensington Museum in London sprang up everywhere in response to this suggestion.

Every artist needs models and precedents. The disappearance of a universally accepted style and the consequent freedom of innovation can lead to anarchy or absurdity.

Prince Albert and his contemporaries believed that there was an urgent need to put models whose excellence was recognized at the disposal of artists and craftsmen. But the fruits of their initiatives were disappointing.

454 Armchair of carved and gilt wood. Royal Palace, Brussels. Beneath the now dull gilding and modest upholstery it is hard to recognize that this chair, which is stamped by Jacob-Desmalter, is one of two armchairs from Napoleon I's room at Laeken, refurbished around 1805. The room was hung with crimson silk velvet and had sky blue curtains. The chairs were upholstered in the same velvet and were also embroidered in gold and trimmed with gold braid. The Jacob brothers had already made chairs of this type with armrest supports and front legs of the same flattened baluster form.

455 Armchair of carved and gilt wood. Royal Palace, Brussels. Jacob-Desmalter's stamp and a label inscribed "n° 509 *Grand cabinet de l'Impératrice*" (no. 509, empress's large study), taken together, prove that this armchair was part of the Empire-style furnishings which were installed at Laeken in 1805–06. The front legs, of rectangular section decorated with "flat ornament," are reminiscent of thrones designed by Percier. In most other respects the chair is similar to the preceding piece.

454 455

456

457

458

459

456 Armchair of gilt wood, stamped by Jacob-Desmalter. Musée Masséna, Nice.
According to labels found on some of the matching chairs, the suite of which this armchair was part was intended for "Prince Cambacérès," Imperial High Chancellor and former Second Consul. The silk upholstery was rewoven at Lyons by Tassinari and Châtel after the original which survives on two of the chairs in the suite. Only the details of the carving and the form of the upholstered back, which extends right down to the seat, differentiate this armchair from the one in Plate 454.

457 Armchair of gilt wood upholstered with Beauvais tapestry. Royal Palace, Brussels.
Taken to Brussels in 1832 with the rest of Queen Louise-Marie's furniture, this armchair by Jacob-Desmalter belongs to the same suite as the sofa in Plate 274. Except for the two rosettes on the armrest, this armchair is identical to the one in Plate 454.

458 Chair of painted wood with openwork back, stamped by Jacob-Desmalter. Musée national du château de Fontainebleau.
The perfect balance and fine proportions of this chair are remarkable. Similar chair backs can be seen on earlier pieces by Georges Jacob, such as those made for the dining room at the Hôtel Bourrienne.

459 Lyre-back mahogany chair, stamped by Jacob-Desmalter. Musée du Louvre, Paris.
This chair comes from the Empress Josephine's music room at the Tuileries Palace. The chairs in the dining rooms at Compiègne were based on this model.

460 Chair of painted wood upholstered with Beauvais tapestry, stamped by Jacob-Desmalter. Musée national du château de Versailles, Grand Trianon.
This chair was part of a suite of furniture delivered by the tapestry weaver Darrac to the Trianon for the emperor's family drawing room. The motif of an X within a rectangle surmounted by two scrolls can be found on earlier chairs by the brothers Jacob.

461 Mahogany chair upholstered in leather, openwork X motif on chairback. Stamped by Jacob-Desmalter. Musée national du château de Pau.
The curved back, a form which Jacob-Desmalter used on all his scroll-back chairs, is particularly elegant. The central motif on the chairback is the same as on the preceding one. There are about twenty chairs of this type at Pau. They were formerly in the State Council Chamber.

460 461

462   Chair of gilt wood, upholstered with tapestry. Royal Palace, Brussels.

Taken to Brussels after the wedding of Louis-Philippe's daughter, Louise-Marie, this chair is of the same form as the chairs from the State Council Chamber which are now at Pau. The tapestry upholstery is similar to that on four chairs from Napoleon's Grand Cabinet in the Trianon.

463   Mahogany chair, stamped by Bellangé. Musée national du château de Fontainebleau.

Chairs with a splat in grille form were ordered from various furniture makers in some quantity during the Empire period. They are all fairly similar, despite minor differences of detail even on chairs from the same workshop. The front leg, with its decoration of a small festoon motif on the upper part and its disklike ornament near the foot, is characteristic of Pierre and Louis Bellangé's furniture.

462   463

464 Mahogany chair with pierced back, upholstered in leather, stamped by P. Marcion. Musée national du château de Pau.
The front legs of this chair are like those on numerous chairs by Jacob, but the palmette motif on the splat is peculiar to Marcion.

465 Mahogany chair with pierced back, stamped by P. Marcion. Musée national du château de Pau.
From the same series as the preceding example, this chair does, however, differ in some minor details.

464   465

466 Mahogany chair with openwork back, stamped by P. Marcion. Musée national du château de Pau.
More elegant than the preceding chairs and of different proportions, this chair is very delicately carved. Apart from the front legs, it bears no resemblance to any other chair by Jacob.

467 Stamp of the cabinetmaker Jean-Joseph Chapuis.

468 Cherrywood chair, stamped by Chapuis. Private Collection, Brussels.
The works of two cabinetmakers by the name of Chapuis—the first a Parisian, Claude Chapuis, the second a native of Brussels, Jean-Joseph Chapuis—have not yet been satisfactorily distinguished. The second seems to have been by far the more important. He made furniture for Belgian and Dutch palaces during the French Empire period. His surviving pieces, of which there are a considerable number, have some common features which help to identify them. They are elegant, well proportioned, and entirely French in style. They are often finer and more delicate than pieces by Paris cabinetmakers.
  Eighteen chairs of this model, upholstered with woven horsehair, were in the Grand Marshal's quarters at the Palace of Laeken.

469 Carved mahogany chair, stamped by the Jacob brothers. Musée national du château de Fontainebleau.

470 Desk chair of carved and molded mahogany, cane seat, stamped by Georges Jacob. Musée national du château de Versailles.

Georges Jacob made chairs like these with a circular seat and curved legs over a long period. No other maker succeeded in giving as light an appearance to chair legs of this type. The motifs found on the pierced back are the same as on chairs delivered to the Prince of Wales by Daguerre.

470

VII Lights and Lighting

Air-draft lamps and stearic candles

During the nineteenth century there were several successive revolutions in domestic lighting. The first, which is the only one which concerns us here as it came into being before the beginning of the nineteenth century, and was completed by 1850, was the substitution of oil lamps for candles. These had long been the chief means of lighting in Europe. It is difficult to imagine today just how inconvenient candles were. Wax candles were expensive and were therefore little used. Even tallow candles were not cheap and had to be constantly watched when in use and snuffed so that they did not smoke and smell, which invariably happened when they were extinguished. Candles burnt relatively quickly so that our forebears, who did not care to sleep in total darkness, used simple oil lamps as nightlights. These lamps were similar to ones used in classical antiquity. They were economical and durable but gave only a feeble light. Some 471 enthusiastic admirers of antiquity tried hard to revive the type of lamp used in classical times but their efforts had no practical purpose and the idea never really caught on.

It was a Swiss inventor, Ami Argand, who was responsible for the transformation of oil lamps. He enclosed the flame within a cylindrical chimney giving a through draft. The chimney contained a wick and a duct. The oil descended by gravitational force into a reservoir placed above the flame and oxygen rose inside the chimney into the vacuum formed by the oil duct and the wick. Argand placed another glass chimney around the outside to increase the draft, stabilize the flame and shield it from strong currents of air.

Argand first demonstrated his lamp publicly in 1782 to the States of Languedoc when he was in Montpellier. His invention seems to have caught on immediately as one of his lamps with its transparent reservoir and glass chimney can be seen in David's portrait of the doctor Alphonse Leroy, which was exhibited in the Salon of 1783. The painting is now in the Musée Fabre, Montpellier.

We shall not attempt to disentangle the conflicts between Argand and those who plagiarized his invention in London and Paris. Their maneuvers resulted in Argand failing to benefit from his invention. From 1785 lamps with a through draft became known in Paris as Quinquet lamps, after the pharmacist who manufactured them while Argand was in London. They were known by this name for a long period, even in Russia.

Another of Argand's competitors, Ambroise-Bonaventure Lange, brought out a catalogue in 1790 which gives useful information on the type of lamps being manufactured at that time. Desk lamps, which replaced candles, ranged in price from 16 *livres* for the simplest, "made of tin, unvarnished and mounted on a varnished foot, supplied with chimney, shade and oil reservoir," to 72 *livres* for the most luxurious lamp,

> its reservoir in the form of a vase surmounted by a close fitting, gilt bronze flame-shaped ornament. This vase is varnished to simulate lapis lazuli and decorated with gilded ornament including figures; the wickholder is adjustable, the oil container gilded; the lamp is mounted on a gilt bronze column and is supplied with chimney, shade and oil reservoir.

Most shades were made of sheet metal (*tôle*) but Lange explained that all his lamps could be separated from their foot and incorporated into a chandelier; a gauze shade was then substituted for the tin one. We shall return to this detail later.

Lange's catalogue also included simple lamps, the cheapest of which cost 9 *livres*. It was suitable for "lighting a stairway, an antechamber, a vestibule etc. by fixing on the 472 wall." The catalogue illustrated numerous hanging lamps with two, three or four wicks. The most expensive lamp was 473 described as follows:

> 26. Another lamp with four wicks, its reservoir in the form of an antique lamp. Varnished to imitate precious jewels, supplied with or without decoration in relief of figures, adjustable wickholder, other parts in copper. Suspended from a copper globe, enclosing the stopper for the vase, supplied with chimneys and oil reservoirs. 96 and 102 *livres*. Note that a varnished tin reflector or gauze shade, each costing 3 *livres*, can be supplied for each burner of these hanging lamps.

Argand lamps perhaps remained in use longest as hanging lamps in the more elegant residences. Their elongated central reservoir encircled by lights looked rather like a chandelier in silhouette. A watercolor by Turner of 1818 painted at Farnley Hall, Yorkshire shows a hanging lamp similar to the ones described by Lange. They also appear in a painting of Count Tolstoi and his family, now in the Russian Museum, Leningrad, and in a watercolor by J. S. van den Abele dating from around 1840 but apparently showing the drawing room in the Villa Paolina in Rome as arranged somewhat prior to this date. This watercolor is in the Museo Napoleonico, Rome.

Some lampstands were surmounted by a vase flanked by two lamps. This type, which could also have more than two lamps, was extremely fashionable in England in the years following Napoleon's defeat. A pair of these lamps is in the 68 Victoria and Albert Museum. Three can be seen in Sir John Leicester's picture gallery, depicted as it was in 1819. More surprising is the sight of two Quinquets on the top of a monumental lampstand in the miniaturist Isabey's bed474 room, designed by Percier and Fontaine around 1800. This engraving, published by the architects in 1801, is evidence that already at this early date Quinquet lamps might be used in the main parts of a house. Later they were relegated to a more modest role and were used to illuminate corridors and kitchens. Their place was quickly taken in the main rooms by lamps of a more advanced design. The commonest Quinquet lamps were easily moved from place to place and were about the same height as the candles with holders which they replaced. They had two disadvantages: they were unattractive to look at and their reservoirs cast a shadow.

Several attempts were made to change the position of the reservoir. The solution proposed by a clockmaker named Carcel some time after 1800 was widely adopted towards the end of the Empire period. Instead of reaching the lamp downwards through the force of gravity, the oil was now pumped upwards by a piston powered by clockwork. The reservoir was now under the lamp, which could be in the form of a column or vase and surmounted by a globe shade which diffused an even light. Carcel lamps were taller than the earlier Quinquets and therefore gave out more light. They were more expensive and were seen as works of art on a par with clocks or traditional gilt bronze candelabra. They were in fairly general use from 1815.

69 They can be seen on the table in Queen Hortense's drawing room at Augsburg where the queen lived from 1817. The huge chandelier in the center of the room is a new model, probably containing several wicks covered by a large transparent shade. It seems to be fixed to the ceiling by means of a pulley system allowing it to be raised or lowered at will. This type of hanging lamp was first used in England, but did not become current on the Continent until much later. Queen Hortense seems to have had advanced ideas about lighting. If the Paris drawing room shown in a painting illustrated by Mario Praz[1] is actually hers, then she clearly used the new lamps to light one of her main rooms at the end of the Empire period. The Carcel lamp on the table at the right has an unusual shade in Gothic style. The two other lamps on the chimneypiece at either side of the mirror have ribbed melon-shaped shades covered with gauze. These gauze-covered shades, which, as we have seen, were mentioned by Lange in 1790, are described in contemporary sources.

As the date of the watercolor showing Queen Hortense's drawing room still remains the subject of discussion, it is of interest that a dated watercolor drawing of 1816 by Isabey shows a spherical lamp, placed beside a mirror, with an identical shade.[2]

The earliest surviving Carcel lamps are columnar and are surmounted by a globular glass shade. Shades of opaline or matt glass represent a refinement of the earlier *tôle* (sheet iron) or gauze-covered types. It was not long before all oil lamps, even those in chandeliers, had glass shades. Some early examples can be seen in Sir John Leicester's picture

gallery as it was depicted in 1819. Danhauser's Viennese 68 version dates from around 1820, according to Christian 475 Witt-Dörring.[3] In both instances the shades are glass globes which rest on top of the chimney. Mushroom-shaped globes were used at an early date, particularly in England. Portable oil lamps were in turn provided with globular shades which were small enough to allow the lamp to be placed on the mantelpiece. These were especially popular between 1830 and 1840.

The last development to be introduced was the "regulator" oil lamp invented in 1837 by Franchot. The clockwork mechanism used in the Carcel lamp was replaced by a coiled spring which gradually unwound and pumped the oil upwards with the aid of a piston. These regulator lamps were simpler and cheaper than Carcel ones and just as efficient. They soon became very popular.

It would be a mistake to think that these new models automatically supplanted the old ones. Argand lamps with their gravity feed continued in production over a long period of time. They can be seen in various paintings and engravings up to 1840 in their original or modified form. It should also be remembered that lamps did not take over entirely from more traditional methods of lighting. There are no lamps listed in the inventories of Napoleon's palaces, although chandeliers, and occasionally candelabra and lanterns, do appear. Wall brackets and candleholders are noted with great frequency. Even at the château at Pau, furnished in 1842–43 at the command of Louis-Philippe, hanging oil lamps were used only in passageways and 476 antechambers, although there was a gilt bronze oil lamp at the entrance to the chapel. The main rooms were all lit by 477 candles placed either in chandeliers or wall brackets.

Candles themselves had been improved in 1825 after the discovery of stearic acid by the chemist Chevreul. This acid, which is obtained from animal fats, melts at 70°, has none of the disadvantages of tallow and is much cheaper than wax. Stearic candles were used for domestic lighting from this time onwards and certainly contributed to the survival of the candle.

Chandeliers

Although some Carcel lamps had esthetic appeal, there is no doubt that during our period chandeliers, lanterns, wall brackets, candelabra and tapers, which all used candles, were far more beautiful objects. We shall describe these lighting appliances and outline their development, beginning with chandeliers, which were of considerable importance to our ancestors.

In inventories chandeliers and clocks are invariably the most valuable items. The following prices are given for items provided for Napoleon's Grand Cabinet at Trianon furnished in 1810:

For two armchairs, twenty-four folding stools, two footstools and a gilt wood screen, delivered by the tapestry maker Darrac: 6,784 francs.

For two cabinets *(meubles à hauteur d'appui)* by F. H. G. Jacob-Desmalter in mahogany and gilt bronze with a Napoleon marble top one inch thick: 4,400 francs.

For a regulator clock 2.15 m in height, delivered by the clockmaker Lepaute and described as follows: "a fine large pendulum clock with second hand and striking mechanism with a constant driving force to Lepaute's new specification. Mahogany case decorated with matt gilt bronzes: 4,000 francs.

For an 18-light chandelier (illustrated in Plate 480) supplied by Ladouèpe de Fougerais: 5,200 francs.

Crystal chandeliers had been in fashion since the beginning of the eighteenth century. The earliest were made to show off the glass itself; the drops were cut and beveled and combined with rosettes and pyramidal elements all in glass. The mount was restrained and at times almost invisible. As the century wore on, chandeliers became less elaborate, in line with other decorative objects. Larger cut crystal elements were now drop-shaped, and were surrounded by smaller pieces of glass arranged to form garlands and chains. The glass no longer hid the ormolu but complemented it. The central stem of the chandelier was disguised by an elongated baluster motif or by a spindle-shaped vase whilst the panache was in the shape of a cluster of thin outward-turned metal branches each supporting a crystal pendentive.

The earliest Empire period chandeliers, such as the
478 chandelier in the Grand Trianon reproduced here, preserved this form. Three other contemporary chandeliers from the same palace are of similar form. On one the central vase is painted blue. Another, delivered by Galle in 1805, had "a baluster-form stem, fluted and painted black and a blue-painted base" until 1894.

Colored chandeliers, which were common in Louis XVI's reign, are also found in Russia. A fine series of them survives in palaces outside Leningrad and at Ostankino in the suburbs of Moscow. They date from the early nineteenth century and were made in St. Petersburg. The earliest examples date from the reign of Paul I (1796–1801); the most recent were made at the beginning of the nineteenth century. The chandeliers at Pavlovsk were nearly all
479 made in Johann Zech's workshop. This craftsman had a German name, as had Fischer who was responsible for the chandeliers at Ostankino. Since several of the architects employed at Pavlovsk and Ostankino left designs for chandeliers, it is difficult to know which of them actually made the surviving examples. Fischer's chandeliers are very
481, 482 like Zech's and have plain or colored blown glass elements arranged around a central stem. The glass, blown to resemble vases or rods, was supplied by the Imperial Glassworks in St. Petersburg, which had been making colored glass since 1754. The finely worked gilt bronze framework also contributed to the elegant appearance of these St. Petersburg chandeliers, even when they were very large like the ones at Ostankino.

Most chandeliers we have described have an ormolu body. The English word is directly based on the French "powdered gold" (or moulu), which was warmed before being applied to the bronze. The technique was of French origin and at the beginning of the nineteenth century was still mainly a Parisian speciality. In places where bronze gilding was rarely done, chandeliers were made of iron, tôle (sheet iron), blown glass, gilded wood, and of various components such as plaster and powdered wood glued together. Even papier mâché was used.

Blown glass chandeliers were made in Venice and exported from the seventeenth century. Despite efforts to impose a more up-to-date neoclassical idiom on their traditional shape, the popularity of Venetian chandeliers waned at the beginning of the nineteenth century. They came back into fashion around 1830 when the rococo style was revived. Chandeliers can be found all over Europe but are not always easily datable. A new type of chandelier became popular around 1830 to 1835, when the major glassworks began to make cut and colored crystal. These more elaborate chandeliers remained in fashion for about fifteen years.

The Italians, who were excellent wood-carvers and gilders, made cut crystal chandeliers whose stem passes through a sort of carved and gilded wooden baluster-shaped element to which the supporting arms are fixed. The panache, the acanthus leaves, the arrangement of the drops and the pear shape of these chandeliers are all similar to French models. Other Italian and German chandeliers are in the same style but are more simply constructed and less elaborate in appearance than their French counterparts. The supporting arms and the central stem, which is left visible, are thinner. Perhaps because of their simplicity these chandeliers are 483 often most attractive.

It would be interesting to know the origin of the pyramidal or prismatic crystal glass drops called *mirzas*. They are rather like the *quilles* found in contemporary lace trimming. These drops, which are arranged like fringes around the lower part of the chandelier or around each individual candleholder, are found on numerous chandeliers made after 1815. There are none on the chandeliers in Napoleon's Imperial palaces, but they can be seen on other contemporary French Empire period and foreign chandeliers, especially on Swedish and German ones. 484, 485

Most of the examples we have discussed so far depend for their effect on crystal glass. They were popular during the Empire period, but thereafter "antique" lamps began to replace them. They were based on a Roman lamp with several nozzles which is now in the collections of the Naples Museum.

Thomas Hope, an ardent devotee of classicism, designed lamps which were installed shortly after 1800 in his house in Duchess Street, London. They are among the earliest examples of classical lamps but are known only through his book, *Household Furniture and Interior Decoration executed from Designs by Thomas Hope*.[4] These small-scale engravings do not give any indication whether the lamps burnt oil or, as was more probable, were designed to hold candles. In form they are close to the lamp in the Naples 486 Museum.

This was also the model used by the Russian architect Voronikhin in 1804 for the antique lamps he designed for the Greek Room at Pavlovsk. These are of marble and have candles but retain the form of the oil-burning classical lamp, even down to the indentations between the candleholders. The masks decorating the projections in Voronikhin's lamps are based on another classical amphora-shaped lamp. The Greek Room at Pavlovsk was almost completely destroyed during the last war along with the rest of the palace, but has been painstakingly restored. The lamps were recreated after an original preserved intact in store and now look just as they did in old photographs.

Also in St. Petersburg, the Italian architect Quarenghi decorated the great drawing room in the Smolny Institute, built between 1806 and 1808, with antique-style lamps. There are two different types. The first is a hanging lamp placed between the columns on either side of the room. It is very like Voronikhin's and Hope's lamps. The others are very large and are placed along the central axis of the room. They are hung from chains attached to the ceiling and are shield-shaped, being enclosed within a hexagonal framework which has six smaller lamps at each point. The small lamps are of the same form as the lamps at the sides of the room.

Quarenghi showed more respect towards his classical models, which he knew well, than any other architect. Yet he created an entirely new kind of lamp using elements found on excavated classical lamps.

In France, too, chandeliers were made in imitation of classical hanging lamps. A watercolor signed by A. Garneray and dated 1812 shows the music room at Malmaison, which was furnished during the Consulate period. However, we do not know when the chandeliers were installed. There are at present two others in the library at Malmaison but they do not seem to have been part of Fontaine and Percier's original design, as they are not shown in their perspective drawing of the library.

487 The earliest specimens which can be securely dated therefore seem to be two chandeliers in the library at Fontainebleau, refurbished in 1808. These chandeliers were designed for candles and are only distantly related to their classical original. The palmettes right at the top, the branches which are separate from the central part, and the base all recall contemporary glass chandeliers, even though the Fontainebleau examples are made entirely of gilt bronze. They are richer in appearance and more distinctive than the earliest antique-style lamps. The new chandeliers were henceforth to be at least as popular as glass ones, which at one point seem to have almost been totally superseded. The ormolu version is found throughout Europe, especially in France, England and Russia.

In Russia, where the production of luxury items always remained on a small scale, glass chandeliers actually disappeared entirely from the Imperial palaces. Gilt bronze examples without any glass elements are found in all the rooms in palaces decorated between 1815 and 1825, such as Carlo Rossi's drawing room at Pavlovsk dating from 1816, the Mikhailovskii Palace in St. Petersburg, also designed by Rossi between 1819 and 1823, and Alexander I's study at 488 Tsarskoe Selo, by Vasilii Stasov. In the second decade of the nineteenth century a certain mixture of styles seems to have developed.

Shield-shaped antique-style chandeliers continued to be made but were now more freely treated by designers and architects. The "shield" is sometimes pierced, or executed 488–490 in glass, and may be replaced by a sphere or a vase. An oil reservoir could be placed in the vase, and chandeliers with Argand-type lamps in place of candles soon began to be used. These can still be found in the trade, although they have mostly lost their lamps. Only the absence of candleholders and the rather solid arms indicate that these were originally equipped with lamps.

The well-ordered archives of the Russian Imperial palaces enable us to date precisely many of the chandeliers in the various buildings. It is for this reason that we have discussed these examples in some detail. In France the situation was quite different. The king was obliged to be thrifty and surrounded himself with Napoleon's furniture which he appreciated for its own merits. Royal orders were infrequent during the Restoration period. Paris manufacturers of works of art and furniture remained active, but depended on orders from private clients, who of course did not keep records of their dealings with craftsmen. We are therefore still rather poorly informed about this interesting period.

Paris remained the center of bronze founding and gilding. Chandeliers made there are still common in France and in other countries. As soon as Ferdinand VII, king of Spain, returned to his native land after being confined at Valençay for five years by Napoleon, he sent to France for porcelain and chandeliers for his palaces. In Germany, where France had both former allies and former enemies, the king of Bavaria, Prince Wrede, the duke of Saxe-Coburg and the prince of Thurn and Taxis all ordered chandeliers from Paris. There are French chandeliers in Russia, but they are not easily distinguishable from pieces made locally which are surprisingly close to French work. In some cases this is 492 easily explained but in others the reason is not entirely clear, as the leading Russian architects, in particular Rossi, have left designs for chandeliers. The presence of French bronze makers in St. Petersburg must be the key to the problem. Most of the founders were French. Some of their names, such as Lancry and Chopin, are known, but there were also craftsmen with German-sounding names.

The fashion for gilt bronze chandeliers inspired by antique lamps lasted for more than twenty years. One of these can be seen in Comte de Mornay's room, painted by 76 Delacroix in 1832, but it would be easy to find other examples from 1840 or later.

At this period bronze chandeliers were also made in other forms which were not influenced by classical models. Yet "Gothic" chandeliers often seem far more like their 493 neoclassical counterparts in general appearance than one might imagine. Others again imitated seventeenth-century 494 types.

Like glass chandeliers, which did not disappear overnight, gilt bronze chandeliers without any glass elements tended to increase in size. As the number in any one room grew, they filled up the space available in the galleries and drawing rooms of palaces to the extent that they often destroyed architectural unity. The heaviest and most imposing of all seems to be the central chandelier in the great drawing room at the Ministry of Finance in Paris. It dates from the early years of Napoleon III's reign, but many examples dating from before the middle of the century are apparently almost as large. Leaving aside the monstrous chandeliers in John Nash's Brighton Pavilion dating from 1822, there are examples in the throne room at La Granja de San Ildefonso, the former summer palace of the kings of Spain, and others dating from between 1835 and 1838 in the ballroom at Capodimonte Palace in Naples. There are great 61 chandeliers in several rooms at the Pitti Palace, Florence, 495, 496 and in the Winter Palace, St. Petersburg. Finally there are large bronze chandeliers in the St. George's Hall in part of the Kremlin Palace which was built between 1838 and 1849 by the architect A. Thon.

Carved and gilded wooden chandeliers were made throughout our period in Italy, Russia and even in southern France. Molded papier mâché and wood pulp was used for chandeliers which were similar in appearance to their gilt bronze counterparts. The most interesting examples were made in Vienna around 1810. The largest furniture-making firm in Vienna, J. Danhauser, used a composition consisting of wood shavings, water and glue on an iron framework. The Saxe-Coburg family archives contain details of negotiations leading to the delivery of several chandeliers from Danhauser to Duke Ernest I of Saxe-Coburg in 1816 and 1817. In a letter dated April 22, 1816 the duke complained that these chandeliers were too expensive and that finer bronze ones could be had from Paris for the same price. However, he ordered chandeliers from both Vienna and Paris, several of which have survived. Others which are clearly Viennese can be seen in pictures by Heinrich Krüppel junior in 1832 and in other paintings by Ferdinand Rothbart dating from 1850, which show various rooms in 497, 498 castles owned by the Coburgs. These rather delicate looking chandeliers were popular throughout central Europe. As if to disguise the poor quality of the material used, as well as the workmanship which leaves something to be desired, these chandeliers were made in unusual shapes. One specimen in the collections of the Ethnographical Museum, Leningrad, is in the form of a cupid on a swing, and in another a cupid is standing in a chariot pulled by swans (no. 501 140 in Danhauser's catalogue). An example once in a German collection is in the shape of Medea's chariot supported by a winged lion. Surprisingly enough, these fantastic forms had classical precedents, for a lamp formed of an eagle with outstretched wings was found in the ruins of Pompeii.[5]

Lanterns

Large decorative lanterns—that is, chandeliers with their branches surrounded by mirrors—were highly prized in the eighteenth century. Originally used to illuminate hallways and staircases, these lanterns were soon placed in dining rooms. One reason for this development may have been that, before the invention of dining rooms, people were in the habit of eating in antechambers.

The diary of the dealer Lazare Duvaux, which dates from 1758, reveals that lanterns were being used in drawing rooms. Louis XV bought "a large chased gilt lantern, with six sides and ornamented with tassels," which was placed in the drawing room of his residence at Saint-Hubert. The price of this lantern, 4,850 *livres,* was as high as the cost of a fine chandelier. From the middle of the century the lantern clearly had the royal seal of approval. It could replace a chandelier. Both the drawing and dining rooms at Montgeoffroy castle in Anjou were lit by large lanterns (1775).

During Louis XVI's reign lanterns of cylindrical form were in use, which proves that the technique of making curved mirrors was known then. Lanterns of this type continued to be used until the beginning of the nineteenth 502 century. One of the four fine French lanterns at Pavlovsk is illustrated here. A similar gilt bronze lantern was

delivered on June 9, 1811 to the Petit Trianon by the Lafond firm in the rue de Castiglione.[6] From this time onwards, however, oil lamps usually replaced lanterns with candles. Oil lamps were cheaper and had the same advantage of shielding the flame from drafts by means of a glass shade.

Oil lamps were destined to take over from lanterns, which became rarer and rarer. Exceptionally, they are shown in contemporary illustrations such as one depicting the library at Cassiobury Park, Hertfordshire,[7] seat of the dukes of Essex. In fact, although the room has furnishings dating from around 1820, the six-sided lantern could well date from the eighteenth century. Another type of lantern was fashionable in the 1820s. It was smaller and shaped like a vase or bowl. As it was made of opal glass, clear dark colored glass or even translucent alabaster, it gave only a faint light, despite the fact that it was more like a lamp than a candle lantern. As the sides of this kind of lantern were opaque it is often difficult to decide whether or not it concealed candles, especially as surviving ones have usually been modified at some time or other. These lanterns were normally used in small rooms such as Queen Hortense's 56 boudoir in rue Cerutti in Paris, or the Empress Marie's dressing room and bedroom at Pavlovsk, where a blue opaline glass lantern was used as a night-light. One of these lanterns was in the small library at the Duke of Devonshire's house at Chatsworth[8] as well as in the conservatory at Deepdene, built for Thomas Hope.[9] They can also be seen in larger rooms, as at the Winter Palace in St. Petersburg, where there was one in the Emperor Alexander I's study.[10] A lantern in blue glass was designed by Ricard de Montferrand for the study of Alexander's successor, 503 Nicholas I.

Queen Hortense lived in the rue Cerutti from 1810 to 1814. All the other examples mentioned date from between 1820 and 1825, but more recent lanterns are known as well.

Since most alabaster lanterns were made in Italy, it is logical to believe that this type originated there. Pear-shaped lanterns of transparent glass were made in Italy from the middle of the eighteenth century onward. An example from the palace of Stupinigi, near Turin, is illustrated in Plate 499. Similar glass lanterns are still made in Florence.

Outside Italy, glass lanterns in vase form first appear in the middle of the eighteenth century. They may have been 500, 504–507 based on classical vases or else on the lamp in the Naples Museum, referred to earlier. As our illustrations show, very similar lamps were in use nearly all over Europe at about the same time.

Other Forms of Lighting

Just as chandeliers in the form of oil lamps did not completely replace those still incorporating candles, oil lamps, whether fixed to the wall or portable, did not entirely supplant traditional forms of lighting such as candlesticks, girandoles, candelabra and wall lights.

Candlesticks

Candles are still used today at elegant dinner tables, but this is due largely to nostalgia—or to a failure of the power supply! Unless the candlesticks are old, they are considered valueless and most people would never think of buying expensive modern ones. Yet at the period when they were indispensable, gilt bronze, silver or silvered copper candlesticks were found in every elegant room.

We have already remarked in connection with chandeliers that gilt bronze, or ormolu, was a Parisian speciality. France exported gilt bronze clocks and lights of various kinds all over Europe, while French workmen in various capital cities continued to spread the technique of bronze making.

In countries where ormolu is rarer than silver, such as England, silver candlesticks are far more commonly found. These are the only candlesticks which can be securely dated as they bear hallmarks. Archival research alone enables us to date some gilt bronze pieces. Isolated dates are of only limited importance, since the same models might be kept in production for a dozen years or more. Rather than 508–523 illustrating several dated candlesticks, we have chosen a series which shows the way in which styles evolved.

Candlesticks with two or more branches are often called 524 girandoles. Those with a shade are called desk lamps. In the Paris antique trade they are currently called *bouillotte* lamps, after a card game called *bouillotte,* played around a circular table which had a desk lamp in the center.

Girandoles and candelabra

Girandoles and candelabra both have several branches, but the word girandole is properly applied to the branches themselves.

525 At the beginning of the nineteenth century the word girandole was generally employed instead of candelabrum. Around 1840 only the latter term was in use, so we shall keep to it here. The only real way of distinguishing between the two is by size and weight. The heaviest candelabra, such 526 as those whose body is formed of a bronze figure on a marble base, are often more than three feet high. They are difficult to move and are normally placed in pairs on a mantelpiece, console table, or commode, sometimes on a specially designed socle. The lightest were made of silver, or silvered copper, and were used at table. After the meal they were put on a piece of furniture or on a chimneypiece, as heavier candelabra were. Both types had virtually the same function. It should not be forgotten that candelabra of intermediate sizes were also made. 527–534, ⁵

Lampstands

Large lampstands, or *torchères,* which stood on the floor, 535 were relatively rare in France but more common elsewhere. In Italy and Russia they were of gilded wood and achieved a sculptural quality. They were also extremely rare in England until the advent of oil lamps.

Wall lights

As their name indicates, wall lights are designed to be attached to the wall. As candles give out only a feeble light, they were generally used in groups and were positioned, if possible, all around rooms. Wall lights were sited on either side of mirrors, above tables and around chimneys. They were also used in vestibules, corridors, and on any free wall space.

French wall lights were nearly always made of gilt bronze. In other countries bronze or carved and gilded wood were used. Only a few examples of the wide variety of wall lights 537–539 found in Europe can be reproduced here.

French Empire wall lights, whether luxurious or simple, lost many qualities around 1835 when the "Gothic" and "Renaissance" styles displaced the neoclassical idiom. Like chandeliers, Empire wall lights contrast surprisingly with those made in the same workshop only a few years later.

471 Oil lamp, silver gilt, London, 1806. Victoria and Albert Museum, London.
Closely based on a classical lamp, this example even has a metal flame where the wick would have been on an antique lamp. However, the wick is actually to be found in the center of the vessel.

471

472   Argand lamp, japanned *tôle* and copper. This lamp, which must date from the Empire period, was designed for use as a wall light. Formerly in the E. Forgeron Collection.
From an engraving published in Henry-René d'Allemagne's *L'Histoire du luminaire*, p. 375.

473   Chandelier consisting of four Argand lamps. Varnished and painted tin. The drip pans and glass chimneys are missing. Formerly in the E. Forgeron Collection.
From an engraving published in Henry-René d'Allemagne's *L'Histoire du luminaire*, Pl. 55.

472

473

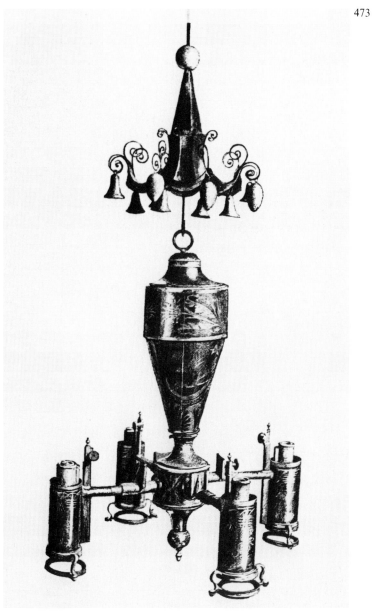

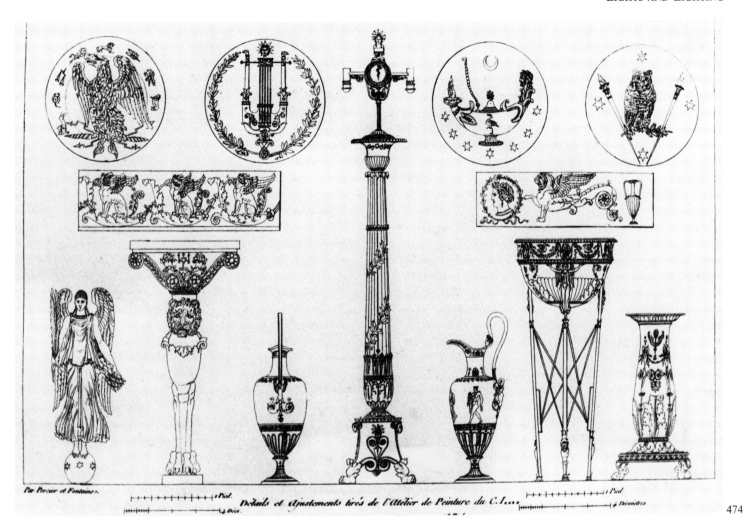

474

475

474 *Center:* Lampstand from Citizen I...'s room. Engraving from Fontaine and Percier's *Recueil de décorations interieures,* 1801 edition.
There is an Argand lamp with two burners at the top of this lampstand, which was almost three meters high. "Citizen I" was none other than the painter Isabey.

475 Chandelier consisting of eight Argand lamps, each with its chimney enclosed within a glass shade. Model no. 7 from Joseph Danhauser's catalogue. Pen and wash drawing. Vienna, about 1820. Österreichisches Museum für angewandte Kunst, Vienna.

476

477

478

476   Three-lamp chandelier. Musée national du château de Pau, Anteroom of the King's Apartment.
This chandelier is described in the Dispersals Ledger of the Royal *Garde-Meuble* in 1843. The entry reads:
A lamp of antique green patina intended for Carcel lights. It incorporates a ball threaded on a stem above plain moldings, to which are attached three scrolled and faceted branches terminating in trays. In addition there are chains formed by linked rods and in the middle scrolls forming double volutes.

477   Chandelier for lamps delivered by Chaumont and Marquis. Musée national du château de Pau, Tower Drawing Room.
In an entry dated 15 June 1842 in the Dispersals Ledger of the Royal *Garde-Meuble* it is described as:
A lamp of cast brass colored with gold-tinted lacquer and chased with neoclassical ornaments. Composed of a cassolette with a plain band and cavetto moldings out of which flames spring, the six branches, which are trumpet-shaped and chased with stylized foliage, are adapted for lamps. The suspension cresting chased with foliate scrolls is crowned by a corolla of thirteen stylized leaves.

478   Twenty-four-light chandelier. Musée national du château de Versailles, Grand Trianon.
Supplied in 1805 by Chaumont, one of the main chandelier makers in Paris, this chandelier remained in the Salon des glaces until 1837.
Several details of the construction are common to numerous chandeliers made at the beginning of the Empire period. These include the panache with its bare curved branches, from which the drops hang down; the strong branches attached to the central column in the form of "classical horns" which support the candleholders; the balustroid element at the upper end of the central column; and the bunch of grapes at its lower end.

479 Chandelier of gilt and chased bronze, crystal glass and rubies. The "feathers" behind the main row of candles are composed of white glass "pearls." St. Petersburg, workshop of Johann Zech, 1797. Italian Room, Pavlovsk Palace, near Leningrad.

This chandelier was originally in the empress's throne room at the Mikhailovskii Palace in St. Petersburg. It was moved to Pavlovsk after Tsar Paul I's death. The Italian Room was decorated by Vincenzo Brenna and was slightly altered by Voronikhin after the fire of 1803.

480 Eighteen-light chandelier supplied on April 24, 1810 by Ladouèpe de Fougerais, owners of the Mont-Cenis glassworks, for the emperor's study, where it remains *in situ*. Musée national du château de Versailles, Grand Trianon.

The general form of this chandelier, which is five years later in date than the last example, shows that the style was already beginning to evolve. The panache consists of a crown of palmlike flowers, a device that was to be widely adopted. The branches supporting the candleholders spring from a circle, itself surmounted by laurel garlands and other gilt bronze ornaments. There were originally six eagles in addition to the six garlands, but the former were suppressed at the time of the Restoration of the monarchy in France. The drops are arranged regularly in long chains, and the chandelier is pear-shaped.

479   480

481

481 Chandelier of crystal glass and gilt bronze. St. Petersburg workshop, late eighteenth or early nineteenth century. Hermitage Museum, Leningrad.

482 Chandelier of crystal and colorless glass and gilt bronze. St. Petersburg workshop, late eighteenth or early nineteenth century. The glass drip pans are apparently of later date.

483 Chandelier from Schloss Homburg, Germany, early nineteenth century.

484 Chandelier of crystal glass and gilt bronze. Swedish. Jenisch-Haus, Hamburg.
Swedish chandeliers made between 1790 and 1820 are among the most elegant and light of their kind from this period. This small chandelier with its pierced openwork central part and long outward curving branches is quite typical of Swedish craftsmanship.

485 Chandelier of crystal glass and gilt bronze, executed after a design by F. K. Schinkel. Jenisch-Haus, Hamburg.
This chandelier, which must date from the 1820s, comes from a castle in Holstein.

486 Hanging lamp with multiple bronze burners. Museo Archeologico Nazionale, Naples.

487 Chandelier in form of an antique lamp. Emperor Napoleon I's library, Musée national du château de Fontainebleau.

488 Gilt bronze chandelier with two rows of lights. Tsarskoe Selo Palace, near Leningrad, Tsar Alexander I's study.
The decoration of the room, which has recently been restored, dates from 1820–25 and was the work of the architect Vasilii Stasov. The clock and candelabra on the mantelpiece were made in Paris.

489 Gilt bronze chandelier purchased at St. Petersburg for the ▷ Senate chamber in Helsinki. Senate House, Helsinki.
The Senate House, designed by the architect C. L. Engel, was built shortly after 1820.

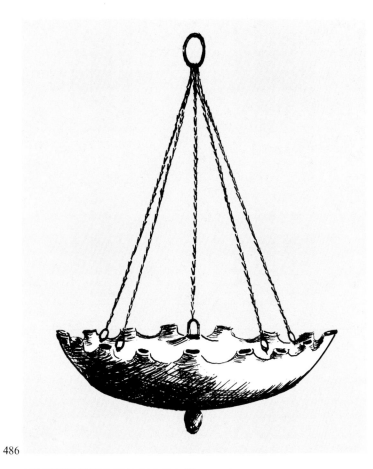

486

487

488

490 Chandelier of colored glass and gilt bronze. Venice. Jenisch-Haus, Hamburg.
The form of this chandelier once again imitates that of classical lamps. It must date from around 1840, as the details are no longer classical in style: the candle arms are in the Louis XV idiom and the grotesque masks from which they spring are in "Renaissance" style.

491 Eight-light chandelier of iron and cast iron painted to resemble bronze, patinated bronze and gilt bronze. Restoration period. Musée national du château de Pau.
A larger version of the same chandelier, which was doubtless made in the same workshop, can be seen in Schloss Ehrenburg, Coburg. It is in the Zweites Holzkabinett, furnished around 1825–30.

492 Design for a chandelier by Auguste de Montferrand.
The French architect Auguste de Montferrand, who was a pupil of Fontaine and Percier and worked in Russia from 1816, designed this chandelier in 1827 for the apartments of the Dowager Empress Maria Feodorovna, Tsar Nicholas I's mother, at the Winter Palace.
A rather similar chandelier, shown in a watercolor reproduced by Mario Praz (op. cit., Pl. 168), was once in one of the Duchess of Berry's drawing rooms at the Tuileries Palace.

493 "Knights Chandelier." Gilt bronze, colored gemstones. Originally designed for the Crusaders' Room at Versailles, these chandeliers were sent to Pau between 1835 and 1840, where they were placed in the Grand Salon and the antechamber. They were executed by the Paris bronze founder Chaumont, one of the leading suppliers to the court during the Empire period. A drawing which is apparently a design for these candelabra survives in the Rouen Museum.

494 Chandelier of varnished copper in seventeenth-century style. Musée national du château de Pau, Officers' Dining Room.

490

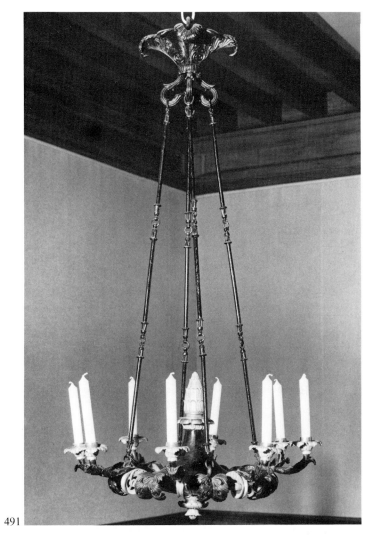

491

492

493

494

495

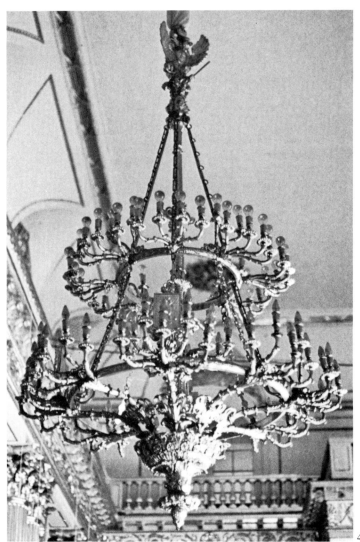

496

497

498

495 Design for a chandelier for the Gold Drawing Room at the Winter Palace, St. Petersburg, by Alexander Briullov, 1838. Tsar Nicholas I did not care for the "rococo flourishes" of this design and rejected it. He demanded another design "in a purely Greek style."

496 Gilt bronze chandelier from the Arms and Armor Room in the Winter Palace, St. Petersburg. Hermitage Museum, Leningrad. This room, which was rebuilt by the architect V. Stasov after the fire of 1837, measures 51 meters by 21. It is lit by thirty-one chandeliers made by A. and P. Schreiber after designs by Stasov. There are three large ones along the long axis of the room, ten medium-size ones such as this example, and eighteen smaller ones between the columns on either side of the room. The room was completed in 1840.

497 Chandelier in serpent form. No. 65 in J. Danhauser's catalogue. Pen and wash drawing. Vienna, 1807–15. Österreichisches Museum für angewandte Kunst, Vienna.

498 Chandelier in basket form. No. 163 in J. Danhauser's catalogue. Pen and wash drawing. Vienna, about 1815–20.

Österreichisches Museum für angewandte Kunst, Vienna. An almost identical chandelier can be seen in a gouache by Heinrich Krüppel jr. dated 1832. It depicts a drawing room in the small castle of Bürglass, Coburg and is now in the Kunstsammlungen der Veste, Coburg.

499 Lantern of blown glass and wrought iron. Stupinigi Palace near Turin, Piedmont, Italy.

500 Lantern of green and colorless glass mounted in gilt bronze. H. 86 cm.
This lantern, together with two others, is still *in situ* on the staircase at Osterley Park near London, a house rebuilt by Robert Adam between 1761 and 1780. A drawing by Adam in the Soane Museum, London, is apparently a sketch for these lanterns, which are mentioned as being on the staircase at Osterley in an inventory of 1782. They were probably executed by Matthew Boulton, the leading bronze founder of the period.
The lantern consists of an oil lamp with several burners on the same principle as classical lamps.

499

500

501

502

501 Chandelier in the form of Medea's (or Diana's?) chariot, made of gilt wood and wood pulp.
Formerly in the D'Allemagne Collection. After an engraving in Henry-René d'Allemagne's *L'Histoire du luminaire*, p. 505.

502 Lantern of gilt bronze. Salle de la Paix, Pavlovsk Palace, near Leningrad.
This lantern and its pendant, both acquired in Paris in 1798, are perhaps the most richly decorated French lanterns of their period. They were originally in the Mikhailovskii Palace, St. Petersburg, but were removed to Pavlovsk after the death of Tsar Paul I. The Salle de la Paix was decorated by the Italian architect Brenna in 1798. The coffered and vaulted ceiling is by the Russian architect Voronikhin and dates from after the fire of 1803. Voronikhin was also responsible for other modifications to the interior.

503 Design for a lantern for Tsar Nicholas I's study at the Winter Palace, St. Petersburg, by Auguste Ricard de Montferrand, shortly before 1830. Central Historical Archives of the USSR.

504 Lantern. Glass, mounted in gilt bronze.
Engraving published in the *Journal des Luxus und der Moden*, 1787.

505 Design for a lantern. Detail of Plate 112 of the third edition of Hepplewhite's *Cabinet-Maker and Upholsterer's Guide*. The third edition appeared in 1794 but this engraving is dated September 1, 1787.

506 Design for a lantern. Engraving from the *Journal des Luxus und der Moden*, 1794, published at Weimar by Justin Bertuch.

503

505 ▽

504

506

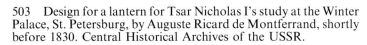

267

507

508

509

510

507   Lantern, Glass and gilt bronze. Musée national du château de Fontainebleau.
This lantern was at Fontainebleau in the Empire period. The central stem supporting the candleholders is missing.

508   Three-light candelabrum (center). Engraving published in the *Cabinet des Modes,* 1785–87.
The engraving is accompanied by the following description:
For a long period fashion has offered nothing new in interior design. Recently changes have been introduced and we feel obliged to inform our readers of some rather beautiful objects now in vogue. Here is a candelabrum of an entirely new form which decorates and adorns any mantelpiece perfectly. It is evidently not highly ornamented, yet remains tasteful.
It is oval, rather than circular like all the candlesticks made hitherto. Its foot, body, branches and candle sockets are all oval.

The central socket is reversed and seems to be suspended in the center; it can be turned over when a third candle is needed. It is taken from Sieur Granchez's well-known shop on the Pont Neuf known as *au Petit Dunkerque au bas du Pont Neuf.*

509–512   Two pairs of candlesticks which can be converted to chandeliers. Silvered copper. End of Louis XVI's reign or Directory period. Musée national du château de Pau.
The elegant simplicity of late eighteenth-century craftsmanship can be seen in both these pairs of candlesticks. The motifs found on the second pair are characteristic of this period and include fan-shaped moldings on the base (already evident in the design taken from the *Cabinet des Modes*), gadrooning on the stem and sawtooth molding on the collar. Chair legs of the same period often exhibit the last two forms of decoration.

511   512

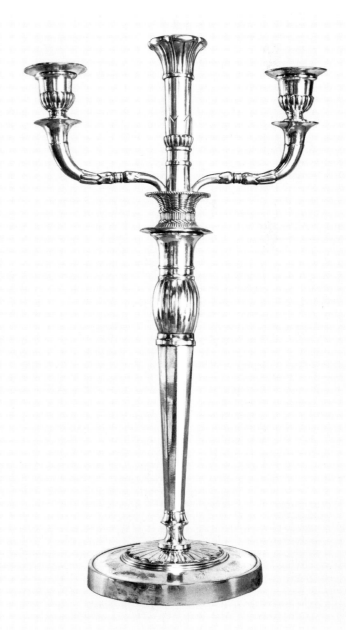

513   Candelabrum. Silvered copper. Musée national du château de Pau.
These candelabra, of which several slightly differing pairs survive, must be slightly later in date than the preceding examples. A pair with identical candle arms is at the Grand Trianon, to which it was supplied by the bronze founder Galle in 1805.

513

514, 515   Two candlesticks of ebonized and gilt wood. Empire period. Musée national du château de Pau.
The first is in the so-called "quiver" form which was current during the Empire period but was first seen during Louis XVI's reign. Most of the decoration was achieved with a roller mill, a mechanical process which was gaining ground at this time.

514

515

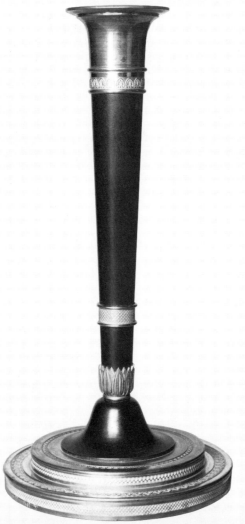

516–518 Three candlesticks of gilt bronze.
The first is at the Residenz, Munich, the two others are at Pau. All three were made in Paris and were decorated mechanically. The use of the roller mill led to an increase in ornamentation. The fleur-de-lys motif on the candlestick in quiver form enables it to be dated to the Restoration period.

516

517

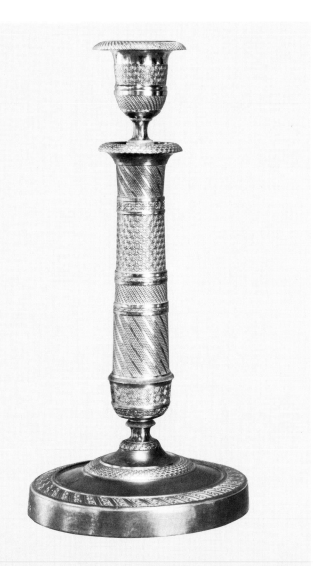

518

519   520

519   Tin candlestick. London, Paul Storr for Rundell, Bridge & Rundell. 1814–15. Victoria and Albert Museum, London.
This candlestick, which once belonged to the duke of Cumberland, is very different from the preceding examples, although it is contemporary with them. Goldsmith's work evolved more rapidly in England than elsewhere. Simplicity and elegant ornament were often replaced in the early years of the nineteenth century by elaborate decoration, which was even applied to pieces in neoclassical style. From 1815 onwards "Greek style" gave way to a kind of neorococo, of which this candlestick is an exemple.

520   Gilt bronze candlestick with snuffer. Empire or Restoration period. Musée national du château de Pau. Only the handle is chiseled by hand. All the other decoration was executed mechanically.

521   Pair of candlesticks, of silver. Stuttgart, Johann ▷ Christian Sick, about 1810–20. Württembergisches Landesmuseum, Stuttgart.
Unlike British craftsmen, German and Austrian goldsmiths continued to use simple forms devised in the eighteenth century for many years thereafter.

522, 523   Candlestick designed to hold an epergne, and twelve-light candelabrum of silver, from the Duke of Wellington's Portuguese Service. Wellington Museum (Apsley House), London.
Presented to Wellington in 1816 by the Portuguese Regency Council, this monumental service took three years to make at the Lisbon Arsenal.
   Highly original in its fluidity, the design of this silver is a tribute to the skill of the painter Antonio de Sequeira, who was chiefly responsible for it, and to the ability of the sculptors and craftsmen who executed it.

521

523

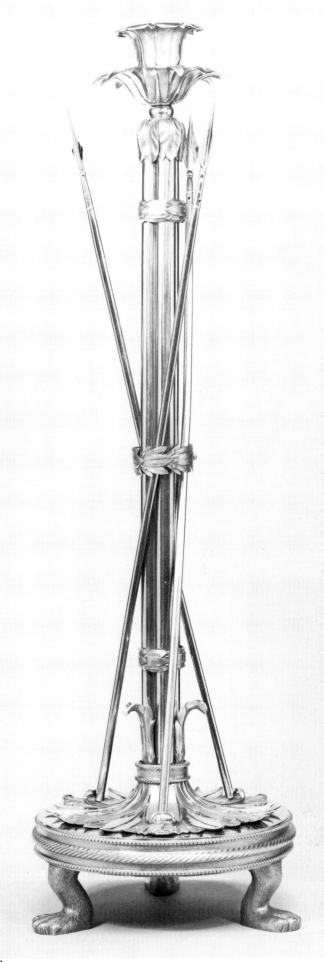

522

CANDÉLABRE ORNÉ DE CRISTAUX.
(D'après le « Journal des Luxus und der Moden » de 1792.)

524 Desk candlestick of gilt bronze. Empire period. Musée national du château de Pau.
The three candleholders and the *tôle* shade can be moved up and down the central rod to regulate their height as desired.
   Desk candlesticks like this were used in the Louis XVI period but were soon replaced by lamps.

525 Girandole candelabrum ornamented with crystal glass. Engraving published in the *Journal des Luxus und der Moden,* 1792.
The central figure still exhibits the suppleness characteristic of the eighteenth century. The influence of Robert Adam and George Hepplewhite can be seen in the scrolls surrounding it. The small cylindrical drops are found on numerous German candelabra.

526 Pair of candelabra of bronze and gilt bronze on marble socle. Musée du Louvre, Paris (formerly in the Schlichting Collection).
Large candelabra with figure sculpture are doubtless the most typical and remarkable form of Empire-period lighting fixtures. The stiffness of the figures endows these candelabra with a monumental character missing from examples made in the reign of Louis XVI.

527 Candelabrum of bronze and gilt bronze. Restoration period. Schloss Ehrenburg, Coburg.
The manufacture of candelabra with figure sculpture continued uninterrupted throughout the Restoration period with little change, so that only minor details enable some pieces to be dated relatively late. This Victory supporting a three-light girandole certainly dates from the Restoration. Duke Ernest of Saxe-Coburg bought furniture and works of art in Paris after 1815.

528 Silver candelabrum. Munich, Anton Weishaupt, 1820. H. 50 cm. Residenz, Munich.
Anton Weishaupt (1774–1832) worked extensively for the Bavarian court in the style of Parisian goldsmiths.

527

528

530

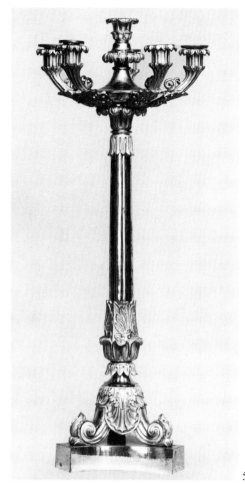

529

531

532

529 Gilt bronze candelabrum. Engraving published in a catalogue by a Paris manufacturer. After 1815.

530 Gilt bronze candelabrum. Paris. H. 65 cm. Residenz, Munich.

531 Candelabrum of matt and burnished gilt bronze. H. 66 cm. Residenz, Munich.
Like the preceding example, this candelabrum was certainly made in Paris, where this type
was in production over many years. Denière and Thomire supplied comparable pieces for
the Grand Trianon in 1837.

532 Gilt bronze candelabrum. H. 54 cm. Residenz, Munich.
This candelabrum is less typical of Paris workmanship than the preceding examples and
may have been made in Munich after designs by Leo von Klenze. It is not unlike Percier's
designs of the malachite and gilt bronze candelabra for the emperor's drawing room at
the Grand Trianon.

533 Three-light candlestick of patinated and gilt bronze. Paris. Schloss Ehrenburg, Coburg.
The form of the paw feet indicates a somewhat late date of manufacture. In 1837 Thomire supplied a pair of baluster candelabra with similar paw feet to the Grand Trianon.

534 Two-light gilt bronze candlestick. Musée national du château de Pau.
Twenty candlesticks of this model were sent to Pau in 1842 and 1845. They are without doubt the work of one of the Paris bronze founders who supplied lighting apparatus to Pau and may have been made by Chaumont or, more probably, Feuchère. In one of the documents recording their arrival at Pau they are described as follows: "Two two-light girandole candlesticks in Renaissance style with circular feet, decorated with cartouches and ornamental foliage, chiseled bronze baluster (stem) and candleholders."

533

534

535 Gilt bronze lampstands signed by Thomire. Musée Masséna, Nice.
These four large lampstands (two shown here) correspond in many respects with the description of those in the Emperor Napoleon's Grand Cabinet at the Tuileries Palace.

536 Three-light candlestick of gilt bronze with monogram of King Ludwig I (1825–48). Residenz, Munich.
This candlestick can be compared with the example in Plate 534 and with the Pau wall lights in "Renaissance" style.

537 Five-light wall bracket of gilt bronze. Probably Paris, Empire period. Residenz, Munich.

538 Four-light wall bracket of gilt bronze. Queen's boudoir, Musée national du château de Pau.
This Renaissance-style wall light was supplied by Feuchère to Pau in 1842.

539 Wall bracket of gilt bronze in Renaissance style. Queen's boudoir, Musée national du château de Pau.
Like the foregoing, this piece by Feuchère was delivered to Pau in 1842.

536

537

538

539

VIII   Bronzes, Pendulum Clocks and Decorative Vases

Bronze furniture mounts

"It is in this article that they [the French] excel us," wrote Sheraton[1] apropos of gilt bronze mounts, "and by which they set off cabinet work; which, without it, would not bear a comparison with ours, neither in design, nor neatness of execution."

Even if the second statement is open to question, the first is certainly true. English furniture with gilt bronze mounts is rare, and such mounts are usually the work of emigre French craftsmen. The same was true at this time (1803) in other European capitals and was hardly to change as long as bronzes remained in fashion, until around 1830 and even beyond. Parisian gilt bronze mounts were superior as they were better designed, of higher quality bronze, better carved and better gilded than any others.

We have already referred to bronzes in connection with lighting and furniture. The three details illustrated in Plates 540–42 demonstrate the technical perfection of gilt 544 bronze furniture mounts. Firedogs, table centers and especially clocks were other important outlets for the bronze industry. Table decoration does not come within the scope of this book, but several bronze centerpieces will be 543, 547 mentioned because they were important in the history of ormolu manufacture.

Clocks

From Louis XVI's reign onwards French clocks conquered Europe. There were excellent clockmakers in France, especially during the Empire and Restoration periods. The technical quality of their products must have helped to make them universally popular, but their appeal rested principally on their cases, which were usually of gilt bronze.

French clocks can be found in every European palace. They were exported throughout our period. In 1803 Thomas Hope brought back at least one from Paris,[2] and the Prince Regent purchased clocks, candelabra and pedestals from Thomire in 1813, during the war against Napoleon.[3] In 1814 and 1815 the allied leaders bought timepieces in Paris during their stay there for the peace negotiations. One of these purchasers was Baron Stein, Napoleon's great enemy, who in 1814 took a fine French clock back to Nassau.[4]

Several examples of some models, such as the one known as the "Oath of the Horatii," survive in various countries.[5] There are three of these clocks in England, two of them in

the collection of Her Majesty the Queen, as well as one in Spain, one in the Residenz, Munich, and one in the Royal 545 Palace, Stockholm. This last was sold by Feuchère but the model was probably made by other craftsmen besides him, as there are differences in construction between the various surviving examples.

Here we are broaching a difficult area as the study of Empire and Restoration clockmaking is still in its infancy. In many cases all we know is the name of the clockmaker who fabricated the movement, signed the dial and delivered the clock to his client. This craftsman was not usually responsible for the bronze mounts, which he purchased from a bronze maker. This is obvious, for instance, from clocks which are clearly of French manufacture but bear the names of clockmakers from Brussels or Liège.[6] 546

Some clocks bear the signature of Feuchère or Ravrio, and a few are signed by Thomire but none of these makers, even Thomire, invariably signed their bronzes. Other bronze makers, such as Galle, hardly ever signed their work.

For this reason, anonymous clocks can usually be classified only according to their quality, which may vary immensely, and is often mediocre. Our forebears had very different views on art from our own, and to them the subject, whether it was of a moralizing or diverting nature, was as important as, if not more important than, the execution of a work of art. They took quite seriously the edifying or heroic miniature scenes found on so many clocks, which we find ridiculous and trivial. These scenes include Belisarius holding out his helmet for alms. Antigone 546 kneeling before Oedipus, and Jason depicted as a helmeted 548, 549 athlete about to claim the Golden Fleece. The less morally elevating scenes are more to our taste, but they seem to be 550–552 confined to clocks of lesser quality. For this reason we tend to favor clocks with bronzes sculpted in figural form. Examples include the Muse Erato, or the female figure 553 symbolizing Reading. These females are well proportioned 554 and are depicted in finely worked flowing garments.

Romantic taste for a sentimentalized Middle Ages could hardly fail to leave its mark on clocks. Just as chairs were made with Gothic-style carving à la cathédrale, so clocks in 555, 556 the form of chapels or oratories appeared. Some are witty, but most were made after 1830 and are of poor quality workmanship.

Not all clocks incorporated figures, and not all were principally made of gilt bronze. Some luxurious specimens were produced at the Sèvres porcelain factory, mainly 557 inspired by Percier's design of a timepiece in the form of a

558 classical altar. Many others were in marble or wood. They included skeleton clocks, fountain clocks and clocks in the form of porticoes. Simple and functional in form, they are often extremely attractive. Several are reproduced here,
559–565 arranged as far as possible in chronological order to demonstrate the way in which their styles evolved.

559 The first, which dates from 1791, was made by Antide Janvier (1751–1835) who was a real mechanical genius and built clocks with sober, clean lines. A comparison with an
566 illustration in Sheraton's work shows that English clocks lagged behind their French counterparts in stylistic terms. Yet this did prevent English craftsmen from inventing fine mechanisms in the early years of the nineteenth century. The reputation of their marine chronometers and traveling clocks is justly deserved, but cases made in England did not reach the standard of the mechanisms. Austria produced the finest work, second only to French pieces. They were
567, 568 simple, but were nevertheless as original as contemporary Austrian furniture.

We have neglected to mention timepieces with marquetry cases, as these became rare at the beginning of the nineteenth century. They were now made exclusively in the provinces, except for regulator clocks. These were large precision clocks, several of them manufactured by Janvier, Lepaute and Bailly. One or two can be found in Napoleon's palaces, but at Trianon, for example, there is only one regulator clock for at least twenty mantel clocks. Clocks could be positioned on console tables or cabinets, where they might be accompanied (or even replaced) by decorative vases, candelabra or pieces of sculpture.

Vases

Vases inspired by classical models were part of neoclassical decorative schemes. Monumental vases which needed a special plinth to support their weight are hardly ever found outside palaces. They are made of marble or of hardstone, and are usually the work of Italian craftsmen, or else were imported from Italy. Semiprecious stones were also carved in Russia, since jasper and other rare minerals were mined
569 in the Urals.

In 1783–84 the Sèvres factory succeeded in making hard-paste porcelain vases which were more than six feet in height. The same material was used for the majority of decorative vases which we shall discuss.
570 Glass vases, which may be of cut crystal or opaline glass, are usually smaller.

At the beginning of the nineteenth century the main porcelain factories were still the ones that had been founded and supported by monarchs during the previous century, such as Sèvres, St. Petersburg, Vienna, Berlin, Nymphenburg, Naples and so on. Their histories will not be given here, as there is an excellent resumé in a recent publication[7] and there are many other reference works on the subject.

Yet it is perhaps worth stressing the uniformity which characterizes the products of these factories. The various
571–585 types of vases made are always the same at each of them: krater vases, amphora vases provided with a foot (unlike their classical prototypes), and trumpet-shaped vases. However, the names by which the models were known, as usual, varied. Krater vases were often called Medici vases. At Sèvres, trumpet-shaped vases were often called "jasmin" 586, 588 vases, and the term Etruscan was applied to various forms. Decorative motifs also tended towards uniformity. They included flowers and flower sprays, which were particularly popular in the Restoration period, scenes with motifs deriving from classical art, portraits and copies of pictures, and landscapes or figures in landscapes. All these were generally placed in cartouches or reserves enclosed within or surrounded by motifs which were also based on classical sources. Abundant gilding and refined sculptural or relief ornament and many other details were common to all the main continental factories.

Common culture and shared taste do not, of course, manifest themselves only in the realm of porcelain, but is exaggerated in this medium. Porcelain is transportable and has always been exported. It was easy to obtain foreign porcelains, and despite competition between the various factories, or because of it, each factory tried to attract artists and craftsmen from rival concerns, sometimes by devious means. Skilled workers therefore tended to migrate from factory to factory. These exchanges of personnel, whether voluntary or involuntary, had been going on since the eighteenth century. A few characteristic examples will be given.

Many pieces made at the Imperial Porcelain Factory at St. Petersburg closely resemble Sèvres porcelains. This is not surprising, as the chief modeler at the St. Petersburg factory between 1779 and 1806 was the Frenchman Antoine-Jacques Rachette. Rachette was also professor of decorative sculpture at the Imperial Academy of Fine Arts, where he trained a number of pupils. Another Frenchman, the porcelain painter G. Adam, worked at the Imperial Porcelain Factory from 1808. In 1815, after the fall of Napoleon, several Frenchmen were taken on at the St. Petersburg factory, including Jacques-François-Joseph Swebach, formerly the leading painter at Sèvres. Swebach was director of the St. Petersburg concern for five years between 1815 and 1820. His return to France three years before his death did not diminish French influence on the products of the St. Petersburg factory. This influence was also felt at many other works, either directly through such men as Louis-Socrate Fouquet, who had been trained at Sèvres and traveled successively to Berlin, Nymphenburg and Saxe-Gotha, where he was painter to the court, or indirectly through foreigners trained in France such as Gustav Friedrich Hetsch. Hetsch was a native of Stuttgart and had worked with Charles Percier. He later became artistic director at the Copenhagen porcelain factory.

The St. Petersburg factory also employed technicians from Berlin. Some Berlin craftsmen worked at Copenhagen, while numerous others looked for inspiration to Viennese porcelains.

All the factories were aware of their rivals' products, even if they only saw the presents made by one prince to another. Alexandre Brongniart, director of the Sèvres factory between 1800 and 1847, made two long trips specially to obtain information about various European centers of porcelain manufacture. He brought back samples which are still in the collections of the Musée national de la céramique at Sèvres. In the same way Gustav Friedrich Hetsch bought models from Sèvres in 1823.

282

All the imperial or royal factories aspired to create pieces of the highest artistic and technical quality. They produced what were undoubtedly the finest porcelains made during the first half of the nineteenth century, but were completely dependent on grants from or purchases by the various courts. When any of the governments concerned decided that their state factory should make a profit, then the quality of its products immediately declined. Meissen survived only by reissuing earlier eighteenth-century models. The Imperial factory in Vienna, whose history had been so brilliant during the Empire period, was to close in 1864.

Finally, several of the leading factories were under the control of the same director or had the same chief modeler for a long period. Alexandre Brongniart was in charge at Sèvres between 1800 and 1847, Count Guriev was director of the St. Petersburg factory from 1801 until 1825, and at Berlin Karl Friedrich Riese was chief modeler between 1789 and 1834. Gustav Friedrich Hetsch, Percier's associate, was chief modeler at Copenhagen from 1821 until 1850 and even later. There were only two artistic directors at Nymphenburg in fifty years. Johann Peter Melchior was a modeler there between 1797 and 1822 and from 1822 until 1848 he was succeeded by the architect Friedrich von Gärtner, who had been trained in France.

All these men favored the neoclassical style that had been fashionable where they had been trained and were unwilling 587 to move with the times. Porcelain in Gothic style, for instance, was not produced in any quantity at Sèvres. The "official" porcelain factories seemed, therefore, like islands of excellence and stability in a changing world during the first half of the nineteenth century.

Besides vases, porcelain figures should also be mentioned, as they were a prestigious part of the output of certain factories, including of course, Sèvres. They were a speciality of the Berlin factory, where they were modeled by Gottfried 590 Schadow, and of Nymphenburg.

Thanks to Brongniart's liberalism, the privately owned 591 Paris factories coexisted with Sèvres. Some produced vases with reliefs which were of an extremely high standard.

If England has not so far been mentioned, this is because porcelain production was very differently organized there. No royal porcelain factory has ever existed in Britain. Porcelain manufacturers operated on a purely commercial basis and were subject to market forces. In order to make a profit, they manufactured only easily salable items, especially dinner and tea services. Vases were usually relatively small and are not in general comparable with most of those illustrated here, which are of course of hard-paste porcelain. This material was little used in England. The bone china formula perfected in the early 1800s was a soft-paste porcelain containing kaolin together with a high proportion of calcined ox bone. It was fired at $1240°$ and could be decorated with a wider range of colors than could withstand the firing temperature of $1410°$ required for hard-paste porcelain.

Early nineteenth-century English porcelain is, therefore, characterized by the variety and brilliance of its decoration, allied to other practical advantages. The introduction of bone china coincided with the imposition of high import duties on oriental porcelain, leaving the way open for a rapid expansion of the china trade in England. Stylistically, English wares were only moderately influenced by continental models, which were perhaps less important in this respect than Far Eastern ones, at least for a time. 592, 593 Chinese and Japanese porcelain had been imported into Britain in quantity during the late eighteenth century. The most striking feature of English porcelain is in fact its rapid development. Each factory tried to outdo its rivals in producing a wide range of models which would attract the customer. Between 1820 and 1825, the neoclassical style, which had yielded some fine porcelain both in England and France, gave way to the rococo revival. Porcelain in this idiom was richly but often rather too flashily decorated.

Unlike English furniture, which was copied on the Continent, English porcelain was not imitated abroad after 1815. The shapes of some teawares which had been in production in England from the beginning of the century finally appeared in French porcelain around 1830–35. The English rococo revival inspired the "Jacob Petit"-style wares in France at this time, but by then the English had turned back to eighteenth-century Sèvres porcelains for 594 inspiration.

Unity of style had completely disappeared by 1840 in porcelain, as in the other decorative arts. Alongside pieces such as those exhibited in 1844 by the retailers "L'Escalier 596 de Cristal," and the "Moorish" vase illustrated in Plate 595, some factories, including Sèvres, made high quality porcelain in a more or less classical idiom. They continued 597 to do so even after 1850.

540

541

542

543

540   Two comports of gilt bronze. Detail of a Sèvres porcelain vase dating from 1787–89 (see Pl. 571). Musée du Louvre, Paris.
The bronzes on this vase are signed by Thomire. The two young women have the inexpressive faces characteristic of Empire figure sculpture, although they are otherwise rather well modeled.

541   Winged lion of bronze and gilt bronze. Detail of tripod table *(guéridon)* in Plate 86 from Saint-Cloud. Victoria and Albert Museum, London.
This lion, which is both highly stylized and tense-looking, is one of the most successful decorative bronzes of the Empire period. There are two companion pieces.

542   The Birth of Venus. Gilt bronze mount. Detail of cupboard in Plate 187. Victoria and Albert Museum, London.
The bronzes on this piece of furniture are probably by Thomire.

543   Table centerpiece of gilt bronze. Restoration period. Musée des arts décoratifs, Paris.
Most bronze founders active during the Empire period, including Thomire who retired in 1823 leaving his business to his sons-in-law, continued working after the Restoration. The bronzes they produced changed little and lost none of their high quality of execution.

544   Firedogs and fender of gilt bronze. Empire period. Royal Palace, Brussels.

544

545

546

545 Gilt bronze clock with marble socle and, above, figures representing The Oath of the Horatii. Residenz, Munich.
According to the 1815 inventory, this clock was in the queen's large drawing room, which was furnished around 1810.

546 Clock on a pillar of marble and gilt bronze. Empire period. Dial signed "Jⁿ Jʰ Hanset à Bruxelles." Royal Collection, Belgium.
The figure represents Belisarius begging for Alms.

547 Three parts of a table centerpiece (comport and two ▷ stands) made for the Duke of Orléans, of gilt bronze partly enameled, cut crystal, precious gemstones. Sold at the Hôtel Drouot, Paris, by Messrs. P. and J.-P. Couturier, and Maître R. de Nicolay, May 30, 1980.
The dessert service to which this table centerpiece belongs was certainly made between the Duke of Orléans' marriage in 1837 and his death in 1842. At this time the neoclassical style was definitely abandoned under the influence of new artists and replaced by other revivalist styles. This table centerpiece is said to be in Renaissance style. It was the work of the sculptor J.-B. Klagman and the bronze founder Guillaume Denière.

548

548 Gilt bronze clock with marble socle. The dial is signed by both Thomire, the bronze founder, and the clockmaker Moinet. Musée du Louvre, Paris.
The figures represent Oedipus and Antigone.

549 Bronze and gilt bronze clock, socle of Alpine green marble. Musée national de la Malmaison.
The sculptural group represents Jason seizing the Golden Fleece, his foot on the dragon which he has just killed.

550 Gilt bronze clock with figure of Diana. Dial marked "P^ie Courtener Strasbourg." Late eighteenth or early nineteenth century. Schloss Ehrenburg, Coburg.

549

550

551 Clock of patinated and gilt bronze set with zircons. Dial marked "Ridel à Paris." Metropolitan Museum, New York.
Around 1800 clocks with Black or Indian figures were as popular as the works of Bernardin de Saint-Pierre and Chateaubriand. The relief scene on the front of the base is totally unrelated to the main figure subject.

552 Gilt bronze clock with a figure of a bacchante. Restoration period. Dial signed "Fˢ Demanet à Bruxelles." Musées royaux d'art et d'histoire, Brussels.

553 Clock with a figure of the Muse Erato, of patinated and gilt bronze, marble socle. Movement by Lepaute. Bayerische Verwaltung der staatlichen Schlösser, Munich.
French clocks with figures were doubtless more popular than other types. A large and attractive clock such as this one might cost as much as a regulator clock. Although Erato was the Muse of Elegiac Poetry, she attended sessions of the Bavarian Council of Ministers! In 1809 King Maximilian Joseph placed this clock in the throne room at his Residence Palace in Munich, where his Council of State met.

551

552

553

554 Gilt bronze clock with a figure representing Reading. On the pillar in low relief "Night Holding Back Time." Royal Collection, Belgium.
Another clock, which could be the pendant to this example as it is of the same form and dimensions and has similar or identical ornament, has a figure of Meditation. It was supplied by the clockmaker Bailly on December 9, 1810 for the Empress Marie-Louise's room at the Grand Trianon, where it remains. It cost 1,400 francs.

555 Clock in Gothic style with figures of a couple courting, of gilt bronze, marble socle, columnar steel fasces. Musée des arts décoratifs, Paris.

556 Clock in the form of a Gothic chapel, of gilt bronze. Musée des arts décoratifs, Paris.

557 Clock of Sèvres porcelain and gilt bronze. Movement by ▷ Lepaute. Musée du Louvre, Paris.
This clock was made in 1821 and cost 2,200 francs. It apparently derives from a model by the architect Percier in the form of a classical altar which dates from 1813. There are four porcelain plaques with a pale blue (bleu agathe) or purple ground on three sides. The main subject, painted by Jean-Baptiste-Ignace Zwinger, depicts Cupid balancing on his bow.

554

555

556

558

559

560

561

562

563

564

558 Astronomical clock of marble and gilt bronze, signed "Decool à Namur." Musées royaux d'art et d'histoire, Brussels. This clock is related to skeleton clocks of the late eighteenth century. It shows the day of the week, the month, the phases of the moon and the time in various parts of the globe.

559 Clock with visible movement by Antide Janvier. Case of mahogany, dial surround of gilt bronze. Musée des arts décoratifs, Paris.
Although dated 1791, this clock anticipates the Empire style.

560 Clock in the form of a classical altar, of mahogany, dial surround of chiseled and gilt bronze. Empire period. Royal Collection, Belgium.
This simple clock with its restrained elegance was the work of an excellent maker. A clock of this type was in the first officers' drawing room at Laeken, which preceded both the great officers' and princes' drawing room but was less luxurious than either.

561 Clock in the form of a portico, of mahogany, ebonized wood and gilt bronze. The dial is inscribed with the name of a Paris clockmaker, partly effaced. Empire period. Musée national du château de Pau.

562 Clock in the form of a portico, of marble and gilt bronze. Dial marked "Lesieur à Paris." Empire period. Schloss Nymphenburg, Bavaria.

563 Clock in the form of a portico, of walnut with boxwood ledge and inlay; dial surround, capitals and column bases of gilt bronze. Paris, Restoration period. Schloss Nymphenburg, Bavaria.

564 Clock in the form of a portico, of ebonized wood and gilt bronze; silvered dial decorated with Gothic arcading. Private Collection, France.
This clock and the preceding one could have been made in the same workshop.

565

566

567

568

565 Clock in the form of a portico, of ebonized wood inlaid with brass and ivory; dial surround, pendulum, capitals and column bases of gilt bronze. French. Musées royaux d'art et d'histoire, Brussels.
The rather unorthodox form of the pedimented upper part, the "barley sugar" columns and the inferior proportions of this clock in comparison with the preceding ones, to which it is related, indicate a slightly later date of manufacture.

566 Two clockcases. Plate 29 in the appendix to Sheraton's *Drawing Book*, engraving dated October 24, 1793.

567 Skeleton clock with weight. Socle and columns of marble, gilt bronze ornaments. Vienna, about 1820. Österreichisches Museum für angewandte Kunst, Vienna.
Austrian clocks of the early nineteenth century are second only to French in interest. Like Viennese furniture, they are both attractive and original.

568 Wall clock, spring mechanism and alarm, cherrywood case, dial signed "Martin Boeck in Wien." Österreichisches Museum für angewandte Kunst, Vienna.
This clock dates from about 1820.

569 Vase of Korgon porphyry. Russia, Kolyvan factory. End of eighteenth century. Hermitage Museum, Leningrad.
The gilt bronze mounts on vases like these were generally made in the workshops at the Imperial Academy of Fine Arts.

570 Vase of red cut crystal; gilt bronze mount. Imperial Glassworks, St. Petersburg. Early nineteenth century. Hermitage Museum, Leningrad.

569   570

571

572

573

574

571 Medici Vase of hard-paste porcelain, blue ground, with gilt bronze mount. Sèvres factory. Musée du Louvre, Paris.
In 1783–84 the Sèvres factory succeeded in making several monumental vases more than six feet high. These were modeled by the sculptor Boizot and mounted by the bronze founder Thomire. Later smaller examples were made, even these being sizable. These too were mounted in gilt bronze. This example, which must date from 1787, is one of the last to have been manufactured, and is also one of the most successful. A detail of one of the bronzes is shown in Plate 540.

572 Medici Vase decorated with cameo portraits of the emperors Tiberius and Galba. Vienna, Imperial porcelain factory. Wellington Museum (Apsley House), London.
This vase is part of a service presented by the emperor of Austria to the Duke of Wellington after Waterloo.

573 Medici Vase, porcelain, Berlin factory. Wellington Museum (Apsley House), London.
This vase is part of a service presented to the Duke of Wellington by the king of Prussia after Waterloo. The scene depicts the battle of Vittoria, fought in June 1813. The shape of the handles is found only on Berlin porcelain.

574 Porcelain vase. Decorated in enamel colors and gold in reserve on a blue ground. Unmarked, 1785–95. Sèvres factory. H. 35.5 cm. Sèvres, Musée national de céramique (on loan from the Musée du Louvre).
The shape of this vase with its molded neck corresponds to "Vase C" of 1780, but the handles have been modified and simplified, giving it a particularly harmonious outline.

575 Medici Vase decorated in enamel colors and gold on a blue ground. Imperial porcelain factory, St. Petersburg, before 1825. H. 69 cm. Russian Museum, Leningrad.

576 Crater Vase. Sèvres porcelain, Restoration period. Pompeian-red ground, painted in reserve with a scene after Carle Vernet signed by P. Soiron. Musée du Louvre, Paris.
This vase is in the form of an ice bucket and retains its cover. However, it seems to be decorative rather than utilitarian. It is mounted on a marble socle which hides the factory marks which would give the date of manufacture.

575   576

577 *Vase fuseau* (one of a pair), blue ground *(bleu agathe)*, painted with classical cameo heads and flower garlands, gilt bronze handles. Sèvres factory. H. 38 cm. Musée national du château de Fontainebleau.

The prototype of these *vases fuseaux* with vertical handles was designed by Asselin in 1804. Two vases of this type were supplied to the Trianon the next year. There are two others with a dark blue *(blue lapis)* ground at Fontainebleau.

578 *Vase fuseau* of soft-paste porcelain, Naples factory. Decorated in matt and burnished gold on a white ground and with a portrait of Queen Caroline signed "[Raffaele] Giovine 1814." H. 41 cm. Residenz, Munich.

Six similar vases decorated with portraits of members of the Neapolitan royal family were presented to the rulers of Bavaria when Joachim and Caroline Murat were attempting to stay on the throne despite Napoleon's defeat. A few years previously Napoleon had sent his sister and brother-in-law a Sèvres *vase fuseau* decorated with his own portrait in coronation robes. This vase, which is now in the Capodimonte Museum, was probably the model used by the artists at the Naples factory.

577

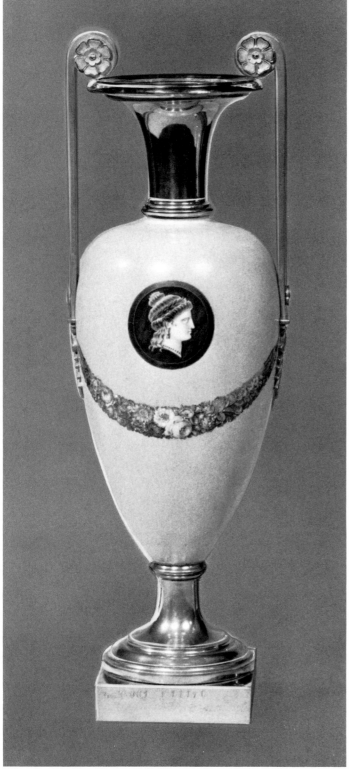

578

579 *Vase fuseau,* gold ground, white porcelain "pearls" on neck and foot, decorated with applied biscuit porcelain flowers on neck and painted with a portrait of Queen Pauline of Württemberg. Ludwigsburg factory, 1824. H. 41 cm. Württembergisches Landesmuseum, Stuttgart.

By the time this *vase fuseau* was manufactured, the decoration incorporating a portrait had become a formula. Although its form is less refined than that of the previous vases and is made even heavier by the applied garland, this vase is redeemed by the skillfully painted portrait.

580 *Vase fuseau,* porcelain. Painted with naturalistic flowers on a white ground. Frédéric-Théodore Faber's factory, established at Ixelles near Brussels in 1818. H. 30 cm. Royal Collection, Belgium.

579

580

581 Two *vases fuseaux,* porcelain. Painted with naturalistic flowers on a blue ground. Neck, lower part and foot gilt and burnished. Brussels, Frédéric-Théodore Faber factory. H. 42 cm. Royal Collection, Belgium.

Faber was principally a decorator. He generally purchased undecorated porcelain from Paris.

582 *Vase fuseau,* porcelain. Painted with naturalistic flowers on ▷ a white ground. Moscow, Alexis Popov factory. H. 45 cm. Russian Museum, Leningrad.

Founded in 1811 in Moscow province, this factory was active until 1875. The style of the flower painting indicates a date around 1835–40. Although this vase is quite similar to the one decorated in Brussels, the flowers are more exuberantly rendered and fill most of the space. There is also a slight clumsiness in the positioning of the gilding on the handles. Both these features are somewhat characteristic of porcelain made at Moscow.

581

Φ-7484
ГРМ

583

584

585

583 Vase with handles, decorated with port scenes on a white ground. Le Nove, Giovanni Baroni factory, before 1825. Victoria and Albert Museum, London.

584 *Vase Percier,* decorated with a classical frieze on a white ground. Sèvres factory, Empire period. Musée national du château de Fontainebleau.
The shape of this vase lies between that of the *vase fuseau* and a classical hydria.

585 Amphora vase. Decorated with a view of the palace in Berlin and with matt and burnished gold. Berlin porcelain factory, about 1840. Residenz, Munich.
Despite its late date of manufacture, the shape and decoration are very similar to that of the *Vase Percier.*

586 Two vases, porcelain. Supplied by the Sèvres Imperial ▷ porcelain factory on July 27, 1805, the vases were described as "Two *vases forme jasmin* with a nankin ground, gray figures and arabesques." H. 22 cm. Musée national du château de Versailles. Their elegant shape and delicate decoration make these vases two of the most successful creations of the Sèvres factory at the beginning of the Empire period.

587 Two vases with gilt decoration in Gothic style on a blue ground. Sèvres factory. Royal Collection, Belgium.
These vases are inscribed on the base *"Souvenir de S. M. le roi Louis-Philippe à M. le comte d'Arschot, Grand Maréchal du palais de S. M. le roi des Belges"* (Souvenir from King Louis-Philippe to Count Arschot, Grand Marshal to the King of Belgium). They were presented to Count Arschot in 1832 at the time of the king of Belgium's wedding.

588

589

590

591

588 Trumpet-shaped vase, decorated in enamel colors and gold on a lilac ground. Berlin factory. Schloss Ehrenburg, Coburg.

589 Bust of the duchess of Angoulême. Sèvres porcelain, about 1818. Musée des arts décoratifs, Paris.

590 Table centerpiece: the Three Graces supporting a basket. Nymphenburg porcelain, modeled by Franz Schwanthaler (1802–48). Residenz, Munich.

591 Detail of a porcelain vase, Nast factory, Paris. Private Collection, Paris.
Jean-Népomucène Nast's factory, established before the Revolution in Paris, had become one of the largest private factories by the Empire period. Aided by the chemist Vauquelin, who invented chrome green, and by gifted sculptors and painters, Nast won a silver medal at the 1806 exhibition. He took out two patents for a special porcelain body for molding, for relief decoration and for mechanical stamping of border decoration. At the following

exhibition, held in 1819, his sons, who had succeeded him in 1817, won a gold medal. Vases of the model illustrated were exhibited in versions 67 cm high. They were remarkable for the quality of the sculpture and relief decoration manufactured according to J.-N. Nast's process.

592 Medici Vase, decorated with naturalistically painted flowers in relief. Flight, Barr and Barr factory, Worcester. Victoria and Albert Museum, London.
The only criticism to be made of this vase is the slightly disproportionate size of the relief flowers. The combination of the white foot and lower part, pale green body, gilt handles and rims and colored flowers with red accents is very successful. This vase must date from about 1830. It seems to have been inspired by eighteenth-century Sèvres vases (see Pl. 593).

593 Medici Vase. Polychrome and gold decoration on a turquoise and white ground. Sèvres, 1855. H. 28 cm. Musée du Louvre, Paris.

592   593

594   Vase and cover in the style of eighteenth-century Sèvres vases. Shown at the Great Exhibition, 1851 by Copeland, Stoke-on-Trent. Victoria and Albert Museum, London.

595   "Moorish" or "Byzantine"-style vase, decorated with relief ornament. Shown at the Industrial Exhibition, 1844, by E. Honoré, Paris. Victoria and Albert Museum, London.
Edouard Honoré, Dagoty's successor, was one of the leading porcelain manufacturers between 1824 and 1850.

596   Porcelain and glass exhibited at the Industrial Exhibition of 1844 by the firm of "Escalier de cristal," Paris.

Engraving published in Jules Burat's *Exposition de l'industrie française, année 1844."*
The "Escalier de cristal" was one of the most elegant stores in Paris. It sold furnishings as well as glass and its mark is found on chairs and other furniture. This engraving shows that in 1844 Jacob Petit was not the only adherent of the rococo style.

597   Jug and basin from the Empress Eugénie's toilet service. Decorated with polychrome sprigs on a white ground. Sèvres, 1853. Musée national du château de Pau.
The toilet set made for Queen Victoria in 1855 at Compiègne included a jug and basin of the same form.

594   595

596

597

307

IX   Curtains, Wall Hangings, Wallpaper and Carpets

Curtains and wall hangings

The nineteenth century has been called the century of the upholsterer. Indeed the contribution of these craftsmen to interior decoration reached its high point at this period. Curtains and wall hangings now became far more common than wood paneling and conventional tapestries. Large upholstered chairs became the ideal of comfort during the reigns of Louis-Philippe and Queen Victoria. Victoria's reign (1837–1901) corresponds almost exactly with the apogee of upholstery. Yet the upholsterers' empire extended well beyond the limits of Britain, taking in all Europe and even North America. The constant expansion of the upholstery trade, which made itself felt in the early 1800s, was already evident at the end of the eighteenth century. Paintings and engravings dating from the reign of Louis XV usually depict only simple curtains hanging from a visible rod.[1] In Louis XVI's reign, as we can see from numerous surviving architectural drawings, windows and alcoves are as a rule draped with textiles, even though these curtains do not always reach down to floor level.

Under Napoleon, the main rooms were usually furnished with velvet or silk drapes, complemented by muslin window curtains. This is clear from High Chancellor Cambacérès's study at the Hôtel d'Elbœuf, which was furnished by the state furniture depository as follows:

Four parts of window curtains in green 15/16, each half width bordered with pale peach and green fringe, height 2.57 m.
Four corded curtain loops, with eight peach and green silk tassels.
Four striped muslin curtains, height 2 m.[2]

Sometimes curtains called *pentes* or pelmets were also used, as in the State Council Chamber at the Tuileries:

Green silk velvet door curtains *(portières)* and *pentes* (pelmets), with gold braid and fine openwork gold fringe, window curtains in green 15/16, with openwork gold fringe; embroidered muslin window curtains.[3]

During the Restoration period curtains of the type just mentioned were the most popular. The top of the curtain was disguised by heavily draped pelmets, while the curtains themselves were asymmetrical. One side might be white, the other green. Around 1820 or 1825 pelmets or curtains were frequently used to cover the whole window area. This fashion, which spread everywhere, was of French origin, as

John Cornforth has shown by drawing attention to a sale catalogue of 1827.[4]

The upholsterer gained status as his role became more important. Jean-Baptiste Boulard was one of the best-known chairmakers during the latter part of the eighteenth century. His son, Michel-Jacques, chose to become an upholsterer. He found favor with the Empress Josephine and was put in charge of furnishing the Great Drawing Room at the Tuileries. The Grand Marshal of the Palace wrote in 1808: "She [the empress] considered that he had excellent taste and chose him in preference to all the others."[5]

At about the same time the administrator of the Imperial furniture depository began to entrust upholsterers with the task of supplying the chairs which they were commissioned to upholster. They were free to obtain these chairs from whichever maker they chose. We have already seen how furnishing stores selling almost everything for interior decoration came into being in England before they spread to France (see p. 194). These businesses sold wall hangings as well as furniture.

Silks

The wide range of textiles now available has almost made us forget the prestige enjoyed for many centuries by fine silks. Silk was introduced into western Europe via Italy, which has remained the leading manufacturer of natural silk. Venice, Genoa, Lucca, Florence, Bologna and Milan were all important silk-weaving centers and maintained active markets. Until the eighteenth century Italian silks for furnishing faced almost no competition from any other European country. This situation no longer obtained by the end of the century, since silk manufacturers in Lyons, whose designs were more modern and more varied, were by that time successfully selling their products abroad. Although the revolutionary period almost killed the Lyons silk industry, it revived and expanded following Napoleon's visit to Lyons in 1802. The First Consul took a personal interest in the development of the industry and gave important commissions via the *Garde-Meuble*. The quantity of silk accumulated in this official depository by the end of the Empire period was so great that it had not been used up by the end of Louis-Philippe's reign. Even under Napoleon III in 1856 the family drawing room at Pau was

559

309

supplied with a wall hanging with borders of crimson cut velvet originally designed for Napoleon I's throne room at Versailles.

These silks are now well known from a complete and precise inventory which has recently been published[6] listing the commissions granted by the official depository and its purchases during the Consulate and Empire periods. Samples of most of the textiles have been traced in the *Garde-Meuble,* and many of them have been rewoven. They can be seen at Versailles, Compiègne, Fontainebleau and Pau, as well as in various other European stately homes and even in the United States. Of the 166 textiles and fringes mentioned in the inventory published in 1980 by J. Coural, sixteen are of unknown provenance, as they were bought through middlemen rather than direct from the makers. All the others—that is, 150 different fabrics—were commissioned from Lyons silk manufacturers. Pernon, and his successor Grand, provided no less than 55 different silks, or more than one third of the total. Their concern must therefore have been the largest and the most reputable, its situation corresponding to that of the furniture-making concern run by the Jacobs. The documents in the Archives Nationales record the exact circumstances of each order from the ruler. However, they only give the name of the manufacturer and the details of his correspondence with the *Garde-Meuble* and contain no information about the artists who were responsible for designing the fabrics. We are, therefore, less well informed about early nineteenth-century textiles than about the Lyons silk industry in the late 1700s, when it was dominated by Philippe de la Salle.

Jean-Démosthène Dugourc (see p. 194) claims in his autobiography to have been "the first to set the fashion for using arabesque and Etruscan motifs which had been popular with architects, in wall hangings and for furniture. Since then all the designs made in Lyons by Pernon... have been invented and overseen by him... ." Dugourc is not always entirely credible, but in this instance there is some evidence to confirm his statement. Among his designs in the *Album* in the Musée des arts décoratifs, Paris, is the design 598, 600 for the fabric listed as no. 1 in the inventory published by J. Coural: a blue and silver brocade with a design of myrtle and ivy wreaths. This fabric was one of the finest made during the Empire period. It was commissioned from Pernon in 1802, that is twelve years after the presumed date of Dugourc's *Album*. This fabric was used in the empress's 55 great drawing room at the Tuileries. By 1802 Dugourc was in Spain, where he created designs for the king and had Pernon weave for him several wall hangings that still survive today. One of these corresponds to another drawing found 369, 370 in Dugourc's *Album*. The drawing is more attractive than the hanging itself, but when one compares the two it is easy to see that the design could not have been realized without adaptation, as it lacked the mechanical regularity of design necessary for the weaving process. On the other hand, the brocade in the empress's great drawing room at the Tuileries, which is enriched by a damask ground, seems superior to the drawing, where the ground is plain. In both instances the role of the maker and his assistants seems to have been almost as important as that of the designer himself.

Pernon died on December 14, 1808. Dugourc never made any claim to have carried on supplying designs to his successor, and any hypothesis on this score would be risky. However there is a puzzling similarity between some of the 602 designs in the *Album* and an embroidered satin textile 601 supplied by the firm of Bissardon, Cousin and Bony. Dugourc's designs seem to have been used by other Lyons silk manufacturers besides Pernon. A closer comparison of these designs with silks that have come down to us would probably yield two or three further instances of this practice.

Most Empire or Restoration period silks, which were much fewer in number in the later era, consisted of alternating motifs of an almost geometric character with plant and floral subjects, including oak and lilac sprays, wreaths of roses, laurel or myrtle, palmettes and palm branches, and scrolls. Vases, helmets, lyres and stars were 603 added to enrich the design, but the style remained homogeneous and all the motifs were given equal importance. A certain variety and contrast are effected by broad borders and braid, often in a color which 605–608 complements that of the hangings.

Only the greats of this world could afford silk wall hangings. They are rarely found in any private residence, however wealthy the owners. Silk was generally used only for window or door curtains in the bedroom and drawing room. Painted calicoes or wallpaper were substituted for silk for the decoration of walls.

Printed calicoes

There is almost no point of contact between the world of silk and that of printed calicoes. The artists, manufacturers, and processes all differ, as does the clientèle. There was a far greater market for printed calicoes, which were produced in enormous quantity. In 1786, 540,000 pieces of calico were manufactured. France was a latecomer to this market, as the printing process was only authorized for use on textiles in 1759. At the beginning foreigners had to be called in to establish factories: Oberkampf, director of the Jouy factory, was German and Petitpierre, one of the leading manufacturers in Nantes, was of Swiss origin. However, in this sphere as in so many others, France made rapid progress and soon became one of the leaders in the field, without, it must be said, eliminating all her competitors, such as England, Germany, Switzerland and Holland, as well as many other nations. Printed calicoes were made everywhere. Techniques varied from place to place and gradually improved. In our period there were three main processes in use. The first of these was color printing using the block method, which derives from the technique of wood engraving. The design was cut in relief on the block, only the raised parts being actually printed. Other blocks each coated with a different color can be used, if correctly aligned, to produce a polychrome effect. The process is a crude and almost primitive one, but it is highly effective. Block-printed calicoes are very decorative but 604, 609–6 their designs are never refined. They are often traditional in character and many give the impression of being older than they actually are.

Copperplate printing on textiles in monochrome is a process closely related to copper engraving. The design is incised onto a copperplate which is inked and then cleaned before being applied to the textile. Designs produced in this way are much finer than the rather stiff effects obtained by using the block method. Human figures, animals, buildings, plants and even landscapes can be correctly reproduced in halftones and subtle shades with almost as much detail as in an engraving on paper.

It is difficult to know who was the first to print small scenes on calico. The introduction of figural scenes seems to have contributed greatly to their success. All sorts of scenes from history, contemporary life, mythology, novels, and popular operas were used. The mass market was certainly more interested in the subject matter than in the quality of these fabrics. Competition between the various factories was fierce and some of them had no hesitation in copying or plagiarizing the most popular fabrics made by their rivals. It is for this reason that subjects such as "The History of Joan of Arc," "A Country Wedding" and various "Hunting Scenes" exist in several versions, some closer to the original than others. Hartmann's design "Hunting and Fishing in the Munster Valley" was copied by Belloncle and Malfeson of Rouen under the title "A Swiss Hunt." Favre and Petitpierre of Nantes, manufacturers of high standing whose reputation for quality almost equaled that of Jouy, were producing calicoes around 1815 which were clearly based on English designs.

The iconography of these printed scenes is drawn from diverse sources, usually from engravings which themselves reproduce paintings. Designers of printed calicoes took their subjects from here, there and everywhere, mixing the styles and periods of their subjects at will. Once a designer had chosen various decorative motifs which were combined and juxtaposed with greater or less skill, he then filled in gaps in the design with any motif that came to hand— such as a ship for example—even if this were quite inappropriate. Working at high speed, these artists were constrained by delivery deadlines. It is quite surprising in the light of these methods, and the purely commercial considerations which prevailed at the beginning of the nineteenth century, that so many charming printed calicoes were produced.

The broad lines of the stylistic evolution of printed calicoes in the years 1780 to 1790 and 1825 to 1835 are not difficult to discern. In the eighteenth century the designs were well spaced, with motifs of differing sizes being separated from one another by fairly large areas left uncolored. Nineteenth-century designs are more dense. From the beginning of the Empire period the space between the motifs tends to lessen and by about 1820 it has almost disappeared, even when the printing is done on a white ground. In almost every case, the ground, which was dyed using different procedures, looks grayish in tone.

The calicoes which have been reproduced in our own day or whose designs have been used for wallpapers are almost always of eighteenth-century date. Without denigrating these early designs, we are of the opinion that the textiles made in the Restoration period are in no way inferior to them. Their dark ground sets off admirably contemporary furniture, adding greatly to its attraction.

For a long period most printed calicoes that were made using the copperplate process had red designs. They were produced using an alumina mordant and a madder dyebath. Violet could be obtained by replacing alumina with

iron pyrolignite. This second color did not come into use in France until about 1815 but was extremely fashionable during the Restoration period. A more complicated technique using sepia, or bister, or dark blue was also employed. Some color-printed calicoes were manufactured using a mixture of techniques. The design itself might be printed from a copperplate and then color highlights added using the block process.

All modern textiles are printed using a continuous or roll cylinder process, which is much faster and more profitable than the block-printing method. It was invented in England in the eighteenth century and adapted at Jouy as well as in Alsace from 1797. It did not displace the copperplate process, as it appears to have suffered from certain limitations for quite a long time. Designs printed by the copperplate method can be up to one meter in length, but the cylinder method can produce designs only 48 centimeters in depth.

During the nineteenth century various other technical improvements were made in textile printing. By around 1850 techniques had been perfected to such an extent that the complexity and variety of effects which could be produced has not been superseded in our own day. The tendency towards realism led to increasing use of "naturalistic" flowers. Some of these calicoes are very fine. The industry seems to have absorbed and digested the Gothic Revival without suffering any ill effect. The same might be said in regard to all the other revivals which so adversely afflicted other applied arts.

Wallpaper

Wallpaper as we know it dates from the eighteenth century. The manufacturing process was perfected in England, where technological progress was particularly marked at that time.

It should be remembered that the raw material, paper, was made in vats. The dimensions of each sheet were relatively small. For a long time these sheets were used individually and were pasted on walls one by one, a laborious and delicate operation. The idea of joining sheets together to make rolls about a dozen meters long, which were then painted or otherwise decorated, originated in England. The roll was laid out on a large table and colored with distemper using long brushes. Stenciled or printed decoration was then applied onto the plain ground.

Towards the middle of the eighteenth century, "English papers," as they were called in France, were highly fashionable there. They had a blue ground and most of them were flocked. Parts of the design were pasted onto the uncolored ground after they had first been dusted with a substance called cropping flock *(tontisse)* made of textile waste. This produced a velvetlike or flocked surface. "English wallpapers" were applied in the same way as today, that is by matching the widths.

The wallpaper manufacturing techniques adopted in France at the end of the eighteenth century are not dissimilar from the methods used to print calicoes. They remained unchanged for about fifty years. Printing was done by the block method, the designs being cut in relief on a fruitwood block. The first patents taken out for copperplate printing using a cylinder date from 1826–27 and were issued to Zuber in France and Dickinson in England. At about the same time paper was first produced in continuous rolls. Various practical difficulties prevented these patents being successfully applied in practice. The first cylindrical printing machine invented by an engineer named Preston did not go into production until 1841.

All the wallpapers discussed here were block-printed. This technique seems a rather primitive one, but refined effects can be achieved. It requires skill and is laborious, but despite this the papers produced in this way are probably better than any produced since.

In the eighteenth century, in spite of Réveillon's[7] efforts, wallpaper, which was a substitute for fabric, was still regarded with mistrust. Napoleon reacted in an eighteenth-century fashion when he flew into a rage because the architect in charge of preparing Fontainebleau for the Papal visit had used wallpaper.

By 1850 this situation had long since changed. Most European palaces had rooms decorated with wallpaper. A recently published work by O. Nouvel[8] shows the surprisingly wide range of printed papers dating from the beginning of the nineteenth century. Some of them had rather predictable designs imitating curtains, friezes and classical bas-reliefs. Others were more original and do not correspond to the generally received idea of Restoration style. Between 1820 and 1830 the two leading French manufacturers were Zuber and a rival concern, Jacquemart and Bénard. Both firms produced unconventional designs, and their products differed in character. Zuber's papers often had iridescent, rather soft-colored grounds which almost completely disguised the neoclassical scrolls used as decorative motifs. Jacquemart's papers, in contrast, had neater and more regular motifs, including an abundance of small stylized flowers, not unlike the type of pattern produced at the beginning of the twentieth century.

In this general work, only a few selected examples of wallpapers will be shown, which cannot do justice to their almost infinite variety.

The most spectacular papers manufactured at the beginning of the nineteenth century were without doubt the panoramic scenes launched by French firms. The earliest, "The Gardens at Bagatelle," was designed by the painter P. A. Mongin before 1800. Mongin was employed by Jean Zuber from 1802. He was responsible for the fine "Swiss Views" of 1804, and later for a complete series of landscapes in color or *en grisaille* (monochrome gray), such as "Arcadia," dating from 1811.

Joseph Dufour, of Mâcon, was one of Zuber's competitors. In 1804 he first issued the wallpaper design called "Savages from the Pacific." He set up in Paris in 1808 and took on an excellent designer and engraver, Xavier Mader, who had trained at Nantes with the firm of Favre, Petitpierre and Company, manufacturers of printed calicoes. One of the most famous of all wallpaper designs, "The History of Psyche," first produced in 1816, was the result of collaboration between Mader and Dufour. Mader was not actually the author of this design, which was the work of Louis Laffitte and Merry-Joseph Blondel. Laffitte was a designer employed by the king and Blondel had won the Prix de Rome in 1793. Mader was responsible for the delicately shaded tones of the background, which are a highly important element of this monochrome gray wallpaper. "The History of Psyche" was exported all over Europe. The scene reproduced can be found *in situ* at Ellingen Castle in Bavaria, and also in the duke of Mecklenburg's palace at Bad Doberan on the Baltic coast. Another scene from "The History of Psyche" decorated the Finnish Embassy in Stockholm.

Mader and Dufour parted in 1823, but this did not prevent Dufour from issuing a new series of wallpapers with designs incorporating illustrations such as the "Incas" wallpaper, first produced in 1826, and "Antenor's Voyages," which dates from 1827.

These wallpapers enjoyed considerable success both in France and abroad. Nancy McClelland has discovered more than 120 examples of panoramic wallpapers from France in the United States. There are also a number in Germany. Only England, where the importation of wallpaper was prohibited from 1779, remained unaffected.

Every large French wallpaper factory produced panoramic designs. Zuber alone made 25 different designs between 1804 and 1850. Some of them have remained in production and are therefore well known, unlike ordinary wallpapers. In the majority of cases only a small sample piece of these once common papers now survives, and so it is difficult to imagine how they would have looked when hung. The numerous surviving interior scenes painted by nineteenth-century artists are therefore a useful guide to the study of wallpaper. They show the popularity of tartan wallpapers, which were produced in quantity, particularly in Germany by Johann Christian Arnold (1758–1842). Striped papers were also in vogue between 1830 and 1840. Paintings also confirm the rarity of wallpaper in Italy, where the tradition of stucco and fresco painting continued.

Carpets

The history of the carpet in Europe is related to the history of Eastern carpets. Leaving aside Spain and Portugal, where carpet making was centered originally in the provinces formerly occupied by the Moors, it seems that countries which imported oriental carpets did not manufacture knotted carpets, or made very few of them. This holds true especially for England. During the sixteenth century "Turkey carpets" had been made there in some quantity, but by the early 1700s the industry had almost completely disappeared, due to competition from the East. Around 1750 two Huguenot immigrants —Parisot, who was based in Fulham, and Passavant of Exeter— tried to revive carpet making with the aid of French craftsmen. They attempted to produce carpets in the style of the Savonnerie but neither of them succeeded.

An Englishman named Moore managed to survive in business slightly longer, thanks to the fashionable architect Robert Adam. Adam commissioned Moore to manufacture carpets in neoclassical style after his own designs. Only Thomas Witty's Axminster factory, which was established at the same time as Moore's concern, had a longer history. It also made neoclassical carpets, as well as those with flower designs and imitations of oriental carpets. The English had become so used to the latter that manufacturers, in order to sell their products, actually had to imitate them. In the long term, however, it was not competition from the Orient which drove the Axminster factory out of business but the mechanization of carpet weaving. Witty's grandson was obliged to close down the factory in 1835.

The most interesting English carpets are undoubtedly those designed by Robert Adam, who in this sphere, as in so many others, anticipated later developments. In general his carpets repeated in a slightly modified form the design of the ceiling of the room for which the carpet was destined. The large central rosette motif invariably used was to become the chief decorative theme of French carpets made during the Directory and Empire periods. Like Axminster carpets, Adam's carpets are often paler and more insipid in tone than contemporary French carpets.

France, which was traditionally a protectionist country, especially since Colbert's day, developed its industries in a way which England did not. The French carpet industry was aided by one favorable circumstance: the general fall from favor in Europe towards the end of the eighteenth century of tapestries for wall hangings. These had been made on a large scale in the Low Countries up to the seventeenth century but then decline set in. Tapestry weavers in Brussels, Tournay and Aubusson now sought to use their skills in other directions and found a new outlet in carpet weaving.

3, 632, 637 Aubusson was entirely successful in this respect. The tapestry-woven carpet produced there is no more than a tapestry for walking on. The wool used is slightly coarser but the weaving technique is exactly the same. The number of carpets made annually at Aubusson during the Empire and Restoration periods is certainly no lower than the number of tapestries woven there in the eighteenth century. Knotted carpets were also made at Aubusson, as the town 630, 631 adapted itself to this new product. A high proportion of Empire carpets in the Savonnerie style were woven at Aubusson. As they are unsigned, they are not easy to distinguish from Belgian products, as similar carpets were woven at Brussels and Tournay, both then under French rule.

The archives of the state furniture depository provide the most reliable source of information about the origin of various carpets in France. They reveal that Napoleon was supplied by two main manufacturers, Sallandrouze and Bellanger. The former was not only a middleman but also manufactured carpets at Aubusson. The latter was apparently only a supplier. Sallandrouze supplied an Aubusson carpet in Savonnerie style for the Salon des Glaces at the Trianon, a tapestry-woven carpet for the empress's bedroom, a fine pile carpet for the emperor's drawing room, and "a superfine pile carpet of Aubusson type and Savonnerie quality" for the emperor's large study. It seems, on the evidence of these documents, that knotted carpets of varying quality were made at Aubusson, and that it is therefore impossible to use the fineness of the weave of a Savonnerie style carpet as a reason for attributing it to Tournay rather than to Aubusson.

Thanks to the factory of Piat and Lefèvre, Tournay was, with Aubusson, the principal manufacturer of Savonnerie-style carpets during the Empire period. It is very probable that this factory was one of the unnamed factories supplying the middleman Bellanger.

True Savonnerie carpets made at the Savonnerie factory itself have not yet been discussed. Following the tradition carried over from the prerevolutionary regime, all carpets made there were destined for the ruler's use. The Savonnerie factory always had a restricted production and it was not possible to furnish all the main rooms in the Imperial residences with Savonneries. However, these carpets were of extremely high quality, and often of considerable size. They remained unchallenged and their designs inspired other carpet manufacturers.

One artist, J. L. de la Hamayde de Saint-Ange, employed as a designer at the official depository, was responsible for every Savonnerie carpet design between 1810 and the end of the Empire period. He was still employed at the factory during the Restoration period. One of his designs for a tricolor carpet dating from 1830 still survives. If we leave aside the few designs for carpets by Jean-Demosthène Dugourc, who once more became a designer in the depository from 1814 until his death in 1826, the Savonnerie style 633–636 can be considered as entirely dependent on Saint-Ange. It is a rich and fairly homogeneous style, with strongly contrasting colors, not always well harmonized. Possibly Saint-Ange was counting on the effect of time to soften these colors.

Many people prefer Aubusson and other privately manu- 628, 632 factured carpets made during the Empire period to the rather solemn designs made by the State-run Savonnerie 630, 631 factory. Despite their uniformity of style, the Aubusson 637 products have simpler, more spontaneous and more varied designs. The freshness of their colors is particularly remarkable.

Steam power was not harnessed to carpet manufacturing until 1851. However, mechanically woven carpets or moquettes are much older than this. They were being made during Colbert's time, that is in the mid-seventeenth century. From the early 1800s the technique of making carpets mechanically developed considerably. A uniform repeating design was even more necessary than for other carpets, as moquette was still woven only in rather small widths, which had to be sewn together to make a carpet.

Machine-made carpets can be found in the less important rooms of French palaces from the Empire period onwards. Carpets from Aubusson, and even from the Savonnerie 637, 638 factory, probably adapted a regular design with a network of compartments in imitation of the motifs found on machine-made carpets.

Carpets with a regular design can be seen in numerous paintings of interiors dating from the first half of the nineteenth century. It is not possible, of course, to tell whether these are moquettes or fine quality carpets.

Very few machine-made carpets from our period have survived. There is one at Pau in the Family Drawing Room, which was furnished around 1856. The design of green and blue squares on a red ground is rather insipid and there is nothing remarkable about this carpet. There is probably little reason to regret the disappearance of these early nineteenth-century moquettes.

Woven, gros point or petit point carpets, on the other 639, 640 hand, are extremely durable and often very fine. A fair number of these were made by society ladies, and doubtless also by some professionals, under the Restoration.

313

598

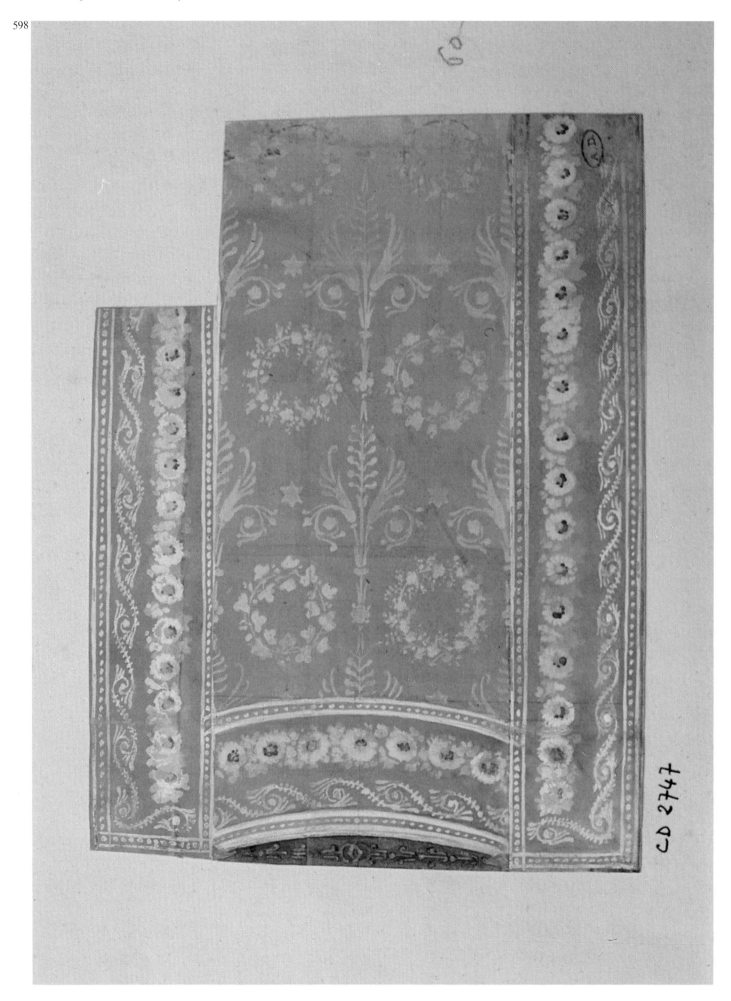

314

599

◁ 598   Watercolor design by Dugourc for a hanging with myrtle wreaths and ivy on a blue ground; border of a marguerite chain and scrolls. Musée des arts décoratifs, Paris.
The hanging executed by Pernon corresponds to this design, but Dugourc's plain ground was replaced by a damask design.

600

599   Two windows draped with curtains separated by a pier glass. Drawing by the tapestry weaver G. M. Egger (1779–1830) of Paris. Restoration period. Musée des arts décoratifs, Paris.
The pelmets are shown draped in alternative ways on the left and right of the drawing, allowing the client a choice of arrangements. The draped curtains at the windows are of two different fabrics, embroidered muslin and (probably) fifteen-sixteen.

600   Fabric designed for the door curtains and draperies matching the wall hanging in Plate 599. Blue *Gros de Tours* (corded silk) with ivy leaves woven in silver thread.

601

602

603

601 White satin embroidered with flowers and birds. Mobilier national, Paris.

Ordered in 1811 from Bissardon, Cousin and Bony of Lyons, this luxurious hanging was destined for the drawing room in the empress's small apartment at Versailles. The makers submitted to the *Garde-Meuble* a watercolor drawing for the fabric which was not approved. The fabric was woven and embroidered after a second drawing. It was supplied at the end of 1812 and the inspector, Sulleau, did not spare his criticism of the design. He principally disliked the arrangement and proportions of the motifs intended for chairbacks and seats. These details are not unimportant since numerous common points can be found between this silk and designs by Dugourc which survive in an album at the Musée des arts décoratifs, Paris. The motifs on Bissardon, Cousin and Bony's satin seem to have been drawn from Dugourc's designs.

602 Design for a fabric by Jean-Démosthène Dugourc. Musée des arts décoratifs, Paris. Album entitled *Mobilier de Madame Elisabeth* ("Madame Elisabeth's Furniture").

603 Lemon and white damask with a design of vases, guelder roses and scrolls. Musée national du château de Compiègne.

Ordered from Camille Pernon and placed in 1809 in the salon de Déjeun at Compiègne, this damask had a border of white foliage on a blue ground.

604 Colored block-printed design on cotton of flowery columns and a spiral motif. Nantes, about 1790. Formerly in the H. d'Allemagne Collection.

605–608 Silk braids, woven or embroidered. Empire period. Maison Brocard Collection, Paris. (Brocard supplied Napoleon I.)

604

605

606

607

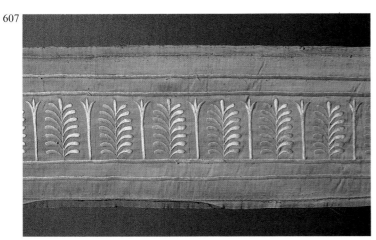

608

609

609 Block-printed cotton with design of flowered branches for Richard Ovey, bearing his mark and a customs seal. England, 1804. Victoria and Albert Museum, London.

610

610 Colored block-printed cotton. Mark of Peel & Co. Church and customs stamp for 1812. The dominant colors are green and red on a white ground with touches of yellow and blue. Victoria and Albert Museum, London. Peel & Co. was founded in 1772 by the Prime Minister Robert Peel's grandfather.

611 Colored block-printed design of ▷ lozenges and flowers. French. Bolbec, Seine-Maritime, about 1798. Formerly in the H. d'Allemagne Collection.

612 Detail of "An Offering to Love," design by J.-B. Huet (1745–1811). Copperplate printed in red on toile de Jouy. Musée des arts décoratifs, Paris. The Oberkampf factory won its reputation by manufacturing classical toile de Jouy of the type shown here.

613 *Le jeu de bague*. Copperplate printed design in red on cotton. Nantes, Favre, Petitpierre et Cie, about 1805. Formerly in the H. d'Allemagne Collection.

613

614

614 "The Return from the Fields." Copperplate printed design on cotton. Mulhouse, Koechlin-Ziegler (?), 1820. Former H. d'Allemagne Collection.

615 "The Life of Joan of Arc." Linen printed at Rouen, about 1820. Formerly in the H. d'Allemagne Collection.
The ground is reticulated. Some firms in Rouen had no hesitation in stealing other makers' designs. This "Life of Joan of Arc" is a pirated design issued in 1817 by Hartmann, of Munster in Alsace, after designs by Charles Chasselat.

615

616 Calico, roller-printed in blue. England, about 1811–15. Victoria and Albert Museum, London.

616

617

617 Rose bushes and lilac. Printed cotton. England, about 1850. Victoria and Albert Museum, London.
Another fabric from the album containing this sample was exhibited in 1852.

618

◁ 618 "Gothic Chapel." Printed calico. England, about 1830. Formerly in the H. d'Allemagne Collection.

619 Wallpaper pattern. Paris, Jacquemart and Bénard, about 1800. Musée des arts décoratifs, Paris.
Flowers and vegetable motifs on a black ground recur frequently on early nineteenth-century wallpapers.

620 Gothic fenestrations. Block-printed design. England, about 1830. Victoria and Albert Museum, London.

621 View through an arch of a steeple and a seascape. Printed cotton. England, about 1835. Victoria and Albert Museum, London.

622 Wallpaper pattern simulating drapery. Early nineteenth century. Musée des arts décoratifs, Paris.
A pattern like this one gives a better idea of how a paper would look on the wall than would a small sample.

620 △ ▽ 621

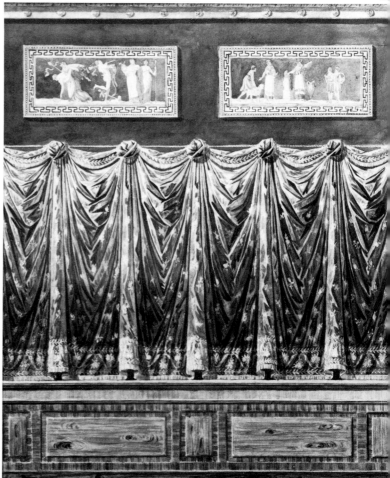

623 Width of wallpaper simulating drapery. Printed in twelve colours, matt ground. Paris, Dufour, about 1815–20. Musée des arts décoratifs, Paris.

624 Fragment of a wallpaper frieze, block-printed in twenty colors, matt ground. Paris, Dufour, about 1812. Musée des arts décoratifs, Paris.

623

624

625   "Psyche Bringing the Elixir of Youth to Venus." Wallpaper
panel with designs of the History of Psyche. Paris, Dufour, 1816.
Schloss Ellingen, Bavaria, formerly at Eichstätt.
The principality of Eichstätt was given to Eugène de Beauharnais
in 1817.

625

626 "The Incas." Panel of a colored panoramic wallpaper. Paris, Dufour and Leroy, 1826. Deutsches Tapeten-museum, Cassel.

626

627

627 "A Dance in the Grotto." Panel of wallpaper with a design of "Antenor's Voyages," issued by Dufour and Leroy in 1827, based on Etienne-François Lantier's novel. Jenisch-Haus, Hamburg. This wallpaper comes from the house of a horse dealer who had business contacts in France.

628   Short pile Aubusson carpet. Empire period.
Historic Columbia Foundation, Columbia, S.C.

629   Two wallpaper patterns by Aimé Chenavard (1798–1838).
Musée des arts décoratifs, Paris.
Aimé Chenavard was one of the best-known ornamentalists in the
early years of Louis-Philippe's reign. These two wallpaper patterns
are in a traditional style, but Chenavard, like most of his
contemporaries, also worked in other styles.

628

Modèle de papier peint..

630 Octagonal Savonnerie carpet. Private Collection.
The batwing motif of the central rosette is of classical origin. It was extremely popular at the end of the eighteenth and beginning of the nineteenth century.

631 Savonnerie carpet. S. Franses Collection, London. ▷

630

631

632   Tapestry-woven Aubusson carpet, chiefly yellow, pink and blue. Private Collection.

633–636   Four designs for carpets by Saint-Ange, desginer to the *Garde-Meuble.* Restoration period. Mobilier national, Paris. Album entitled *Recueil de dessins de tapis, tapisseries, plafonds,* *ornements et meubles composes pour les Manufactures royales de la* ▷ *Savonnerie, des Gobelins, de Beauvais et d'Aubusson par J. L. Delahamayde de Saint-Ange, architect-artiste.* ("Collection of Designs for Carpets, Tapestries, Ceilings, Ornaments and Furniture Drawn Up for the Gobelins, Beauvais and Aubusson [Carpet] Factories by J. L. Delahamayde de Saint-Ange, architect-artist").

632

633   634

635   636

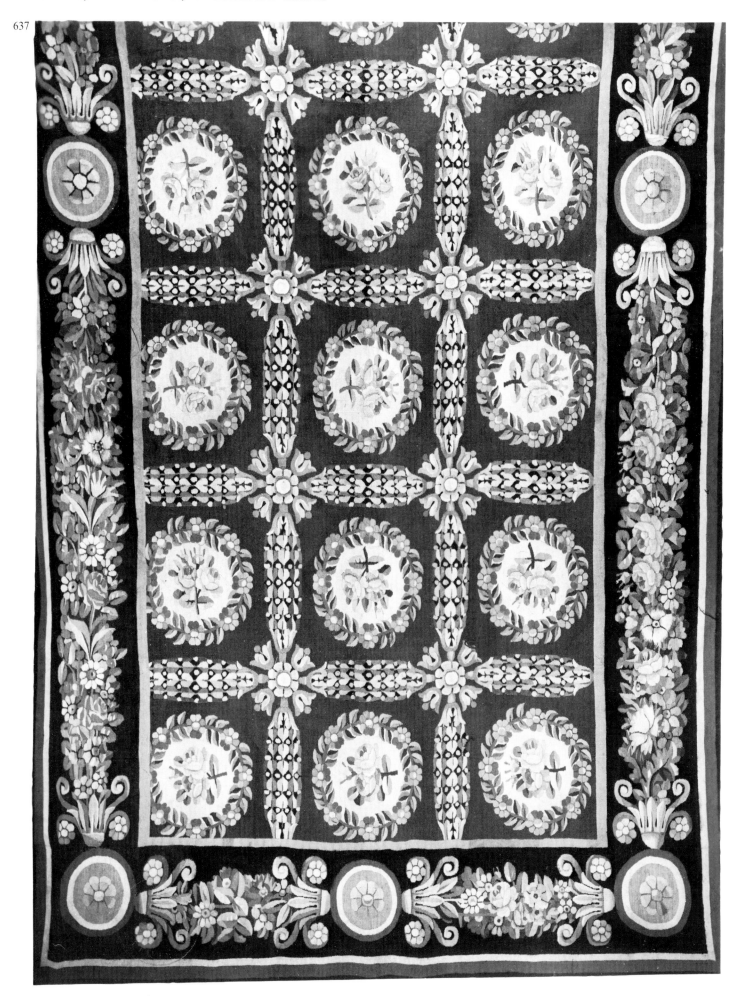

◁ 637   Tapestry-woven Aubusson carpet. Empire and Restoration period.
Design of flowers in medaillons on yellow ground, remainder of ground brown, except border which is black. Private Collection.

638   Design by Saint-Ange for a carpet with regular compartments. Restoration period. Mobilier national, Paris.

638

639 Carpet of petit point embroidery on black ground. English, 1820–30. The flowers are on a black ground; the border is reddish brown. Private Collection.

640 Carpet with a black ground. Louis-Philippe period. Private ▷ Collection.

639

Conclusion

At the beginning of this book, we summarized the ideas put forward by the champions of neoclassicism. We shall conclude by quoting from a work which appeared in the middle of the nineteenth century, entitled *Les Artistes français à l'étranger* ("French Artists Abroad") by Louis Dussieux.[1]

"We have often referred to the detestable influence of the School of David and of the Revolution. Under the pretext of imitating the Antique, all our traditions have been abandoned. For a short time, it seemed as if French taste was to be completely destroyed forever. David's influence on painters, sculptors and architects was harmful enough. His effect on ornamental art was, if anything, even more deplorable and led to the disappearance of all decoration. It is impossible to understand how a country which until this time had produced such charming objects, adding a note of taste and elegance to luxury productions and contributing so many felicitous developments to ornamental art, suddenly, under the influence of fashion and false theory, adopted unreservedly the straight line and the right angle and began to make the ugliest objects ever seen. This situation lasted until the Romantic School won a happy victory in the field of painting and sculpture. Ornamental art was then immediately reborn. Goldsmiths' work, furniture, pottery and interiors immediately began to be decorated. Unfortunately, craftsmen, like architects, now chose decorative themes from past styles according to their own outlook and personal preferences. Some adopted the Renaissance idiom, while others took up the Louis XV style. No one invented a nineteenth-century style."

This author's opinions, expressed in a particularly trenchant fashion, were shared by others. They were formulated without the least hesitation during the reign of Napoleon III, nephew of the monarch who employed David as his official painter. He may have known that the new emperor and his consort preferred Louis XVI and Empire styles. In 1859, Dussieux's work was crowned by the approval of the Académie des inscriptions et belles-lettres, a highly respected body.

It seems clear that neoclassical art was well and truly dead by the middle of the nineteenth century. Its severity and economy were no longer comprehensible and it fell into profound disfavor, from which it did not begin to recover until about 1890 or 1900. Reaction against the overladen decoration of nineteenth-century interiors eventually led to the creation of the so-called "Modern Style" and neoclassicism began its gradual rehabilitation. In the early years of this century, Paul Marmottan started to assemble a collection which was to be the first extensive collection of Empire-period decorative art. In 1902–03 Prince Essling built and furnished his Nice residence in Empire style.

Like many of his contemporaries, Louis Dussieux believed that the nineteenth century had no characteristic style. In the author's opinion, this assertion is unfounded. Gothic Revival, neo-Renaissance, neorococo and "Louis XVI style" all belong to the last century and were interpreted in a totally different spirit from the styles they purported to copy faithfully.

The real originality of the nineteenth century, precursor of our own times, lies in its absence of any unity of style. After the disappearance of neoclassical art, no one style achieved preeminence. The majority of nineteenth-century writers considered this as a regrettable development. However, it can also be viewed as the inevitable evolution of our civilization which is becoming increasingly complex. From now on, tastes and habits will be the product of individual outlook and education rather than of geographical and social factors.

Notes

Chapter I

1 *Essai sur l'architecture*, Paris, 1753. *Observations sur l'architecture*, The Hague, 1765.
2 J. J. Winckelmann, *Geschichte der Kunst des Altertums*, Dresden, 1764. Quoted from the translation by G. Henry Lodge, *The History of Ancient Art among the Greeks*, London, 1850.
3 *Observations sur l'architecture*, p. 1.
4 Charles-Paul Landon, *Annales du Musée et de l'Ecole moderne des Beaux-Arts*, Paris, 1801–08.
5 P. F. L. Fontaine and C. Percier, *Recueil de décorations intérieures*, Paris, 1801–12.
6 G. M. A. Richter, *The Furniture of the Greeks, Etruscans and Romans*, Phaidon Press, London, 1966.
7 The decorative scheme which includes grotesques survived the destruction of the house. It is now in the Victoria and Albert Museum, London.
8 The plans are in the Archives Nationales. The section of the house has been reproduced in Michel Gallet, *Demeures parisiennes de l'époque Louis XVI*, Le Temps, Paris, 1964, Ill. no. 106.
9 The drawing for a chair, seen in profile, has been reproduced by Mme Jarry in *Le Siège français*, Fribourg, Office du Livre, 1973, Dessin no. 56. Le Queu's designs are in the Cabinet des Estampes of the Bibliothèque Nationale.
10 One of the chairs reproduced in the exhibition catalogue *The Age of Neo-classicism* (14th exhibition of the Council of Europe), London, 1972, no. 1642, Ill. no. 144.
11 J. L. David, *Portrait of Madame Trudaine*, 1791 (Louvre Museum, Paris). J. L. David, *Portrait of the Marquise Pastoret*, 1792 (Art Institute of Chicago). J. L. David, *Portrait of a Boy*, 1793 (Private Collection, Paris). L. Gauffier, *Portrait of Count Armfelt*, painted in Florence in 1793. P. L. Debucourt, *The Bouquet*, 1793 (Marmottan Museum, Paris). F. Gérard, *The 10th August 1972*, 1795 (Musée du Louvre, Cabinet des dessins).
12 The guilds were suppressed by the law of March 17, 1791.
13 *Recueil de décorations intérieures*. Published in parts from 1801. Complete editions in 1812 and 1827.
14 *Plans, coupes, élévations des plus belles maisons et des hôtels construits à Paris et dans les environs*, Paris, n.d. (1800 or 1802).
15 Arch. Nat. O² 561.
16 Two armchairs in the library of the château at Lantheuil in Normandy are close to this type. The Jacob family portrait was reproduced by Hector Lefuel, *Georges Jacob*, Paris, 1923, Pl. I.
17 Thomas Sheraton, *The Cabinet-Maker and Upholsterer's Drawing-Book*, part III, p. 440 and Plate 60. This engraving is dated January 16, 1793.
18 If it is not based on a design by Percier, the shape of the back of the chairs found in the Second Vase Room in Hope's residence must have been taken from designs by the Jacob brothers (Ill. no. 22).

Chapter II

1 Stucco, which consists of powdered marble, lime and chalk, dried and polished, has a shiny surface not unlike that of marble and can also imitate the veins found in marble. Like plaster it can be molded and, if necessary, gilded.
2 Dining room, Malmaison; the Salon des Muses at the Beauharnais residence; the drawing room of the counts Gallarati Scotti at Vimerato (Oreno), near Milan; the ballroom of the Royal Palace, Turin.
3 Salon des Saisons in the Beauharnais residence; the doors of the drawing room belonging to Queen Hortense, now in the Marmottan Museum, Paris.
4 For more details on this topic, see Elisabeth Chevallier, "Les peintures découvertes à Herculanum, Pompéi et Stabies vues par les voyageurs du XVIIIᵉ siècle," *Gazette des Beaux-Arts*, December 1977.
5 Watercolor of a certain Anna reproduced in Mario Praz, *L'Ameublement*, Tisné, Paris, 1964, Pl. 190.
6 Watercolor of Garnerey reproduced in Mario Praz, *op. cit*, Ill. no. 167.
7 The pale yellow known as *bois de citron* is a yellow which is close to beige; the color called in French *gris de lin* is a very pale violet shade. Plate no. 129 shows the Emperor's room at Trianon hung with the same fabric some years later and a chair from the music room at the Tuileries (459).
8 H. de Balzac, "The Imaginary Mistress," in *La Grande Bretêche and other Stories*, trans. by Clara Bell, J. M. Dent, London, 1896, pp. 264f.
9 John Harden was the subject of a monograph by Daphne Foskett, *John Harden of Brathay Hall*, 1974.

Chapter III

1 Private collection, Paris. This painting, "A Dining Room Interior", once belonged to the Duchess of Berry. It was engraved by Debucourt in 1821.
2 Former rue Chantereine.
3 Extract from *Livre-journal des fournitures des Frères Jacob pour l'an V et l'an VI* published by H. Lefuel, *F. H. G. Jacob-Desmalter*. Paris, n. d. [1925], p. 49.
4 See Lorenz Seelig, "Wiener Biedermeier in Coburg", *Alte und Moderne Kunst*, 1981, no. 178/179.
5 In England side tables were often provided with several drawers and were called sideboards.
6 We have used the terms found in bills from the suppliers but there is a certain confusion of terminology, especially between the descriptions "quadrille table" and "reversis table," since the games were essentially the same.
7 George Hepplewhite, *The Cabinet-Maker and Upholsterer's Guide*.
8 The engravings published in *The Cabinet-Maker and Upholsterer's Drawing Book* are dated between 1791 and 1794.
9 George Smith, *The Cabinet-Maker and Upholsterer's Guide*.
10 George Smith, *op. cit.*, p. 181.

11 The queen's bed is reminiscent of Louis XIV beds *à la duchesse*. Frederick Cass's bed was also designed to harmonize with its surroundings. The bedhead, which rests against the wall, is surmounted by a baldachin of circular form with hanging curtains. It is neoclassical in style but is interpreted rather heavily. Some of Papworth's designs from the Royal Institute of British Architects have been published by Jill Lever in *Architects' Designs for Furniture*, London, 1982.

12 Krafft and Ransonnette, *op. cit.*

13 Potsdam, Sans Souci. Illustrated by Mario Praz, *op. cit.*, Pl. 8. Sophia of Bavaria, the daughter of Maximilian Joseph and Queen Caroline, was born in 1805. She married the Archduke Francis-Charles of Austria and was the mother of the Emperor Francis Joseph. The Decker watercolors commissioned by her for Laxenburg must date from shortly after her marriage.

14 Some bedside tables were in the form of an altar dedicated to the god of sleep and were inscribed in gold SOMNO. This word soon became a synonym for a bedside table. On May 12, 1837 A. Jacob delivered two tables to the Trianon described as "Deux somnos en frêne à cylindre et tablettes..." (Two *somnos* of cylindrical form made of ash with a spring mechanism, and slide...).

15 It is the property of H. M. The Queen, Windsor Castle.

16 Formerly in the Fabius Frères Collection, Paris. Illustrated by Mario Praz, *op. cit.*, Pl. 357.

17 Paris, Musée des arts décoratifs.

18 *Repository of Arts, Literature, Commerce, Manufactures, Fashions and Politics.*

19 Potsdam, Sans-Souci. Illustrated by Mario Praz, *op. cit.*, Pl. 243.

20 There are examples of desks with drawers of this kind dating from shortly before the Revolution in France.

21 Arch. Nat. O² 531.

22 In 1808 George Smith published *A Collection of Designs for Household Furniture and Interior Decoration*.

23 Paris, Musée du Louvre.

24 Sale, Paris, Galerie Georges Petit, May 11–12, 1931.

25 We shall use the term "saber shape" rather than "Etruscan" or "arched" as it is more expressive.

26 Arch. Nat. R⁵ 522.

27 Montreuil, near Versailles.

28 This album, entitled *Mobilier de Madame Elisabeth, 1790*, is in the library of the Musée des Arts décoratifs, Paris.

29 Reproduced by Hector Lefuel as the frontispiece of his book on Georges Jacob.

30 Lakanal's premises at 20, rue de la Chaussée-d'Antin were built by the architect Henry in about 1797. Krafft and Ransonnette reproduced the house in *Plans, coupes, élévations des plus belles maisons et des hôtels construits à Paris et dans les environs*. It was in the cellar of this house that the carved stone heads of the statues from Notre-Dame Cathedral, Paris, were discovered.

31 Paris, Musée du Louvre.

32 Archives nationales R⁵ 522.

33 There are two unmarked armchairs in the Marmottan Museum, Paris; an armchair by Demay was sold at Versailles by Messrs Chapelle, Perrin, Fromantin on November 16, 1980; two armchairs by Henri Jacob were illustrated by D. Ledoux-Lebard, *Les Ebénistes parisiens, 1795–1970*, Paris, 1965, Pl. XXI, Fig. 46.

34 M. Jarry, *Le Siège français*, Fribourg, 1973, Fig. 286.

35 Cabriole armchairs were easily moved and were smaller and lighter than the traditional *fauteuil à la reine*. Their backs were curved for greater comfort.

36 It appears in armchairs ordered in 1824 for the Coronation of Charles X now at the Préfecture, Châlons-sur-Marne.

37 Quoted by Ralph Fastnedge, *English Furniture Styles, 1500–1830*, London, 1955.

38 *Repository of Arts, Literature, Commerce, Manufactures and Politics*, Vol. XII.

39 Shown in Nash's *Views of the Royal Pavilion* published in 1826. This part of the Pavilion dates from 1822.

40 Arch. Nat. O³ 1984.

41 Here are two examples. On French chairs the wood on the seat rails was always left exposed, whereas on English examples it was usually completely covered with fabric or leather. Some French chairs made just before the Revolution imitated their English counterparts. Georges Jacob's chairs *à l'anglaise* for Montreuil (see p. 114) have "ears of corn in low relief above flowers carved in the upper part of the said backs." This detail is typically English.

42 For example, in 1825 George IV purchased two pieces in Louis XVI style by L. Bellangé.

Chapter IV

1 Pieces made by numerous able furniture makers of German origin living in Paris were completely Parisian in style and entirely related to those made by their French colleagues.

2 See Wolfgang Wiese, *Studien zum Stil des Stuttgarter Ebenisten Johannes Klinkerfuss*, master's thesis, Tübingen University, 1982.

3 *Das Wittelsbacher Album – Interieurs königlicher Wohn- und Festräume 1799–1848*, Munich, 1979, and by the same author, *Die Ausstattung der Residenzen König Max Josephs von Bayern (1799–1825)*; see exhibition catalogue *Wittelsbach und Bayern*, III/1, Krone und Verfassung, Munich, 1980, pp. 371 ff.

4 *Ideen zur äusseren und inneren Verzierung der Gebäude als Anleitung für angehende mechanische Künstler und Handwerker zur Übung im Erfinden und Darstellen*, Vol. I, 1809, Vol. II, 1811.

5 P. Marmottan, *Les Arts en Toscane sous Napoléon. La princesse Elisa*, Paris, 1901, pp. 104, 144.

6 Since then they have been in the Grand Trianon.

7 Museo di San Martino, Naples.

8 See Simone Hartmann's thesis on Jean-Démosthène Dugourc and a doctoral thesis by Señor Juan José Junquera y Mato, *La Decoración y el mobilario de los palacios de Carlos IV*, Madrid, 1979.

9 Published in *Nouvelles Archives de l'art français*, 1st series, V, 1877.

10 One is in the archives of Tassinari and Châtel, successors to Camille Pernon; the other is in the Musée des arts décoratifs, Paris, in an album entitled *Mobilier de Madame Elisabeth et de Monsieur, frère du roy, dessins exécutés par Dugourc, Meunier, Grognard, en 1790* ("Furniture executed by Dugourc, Meunier, Grognard in 1790 for Madame Elisabeth and Monsieur, the king's brother").

11 D. Ledoux-Lebard, *Connaissance des Arts*, no. 153, Nov. 1964.

Chapter V

1 In 1834 Arcisse de Caumont founded the Société française d'archéologie.

2 Abbé Marc-Antoine Laugier, *Essai sur l'architecture*, Paris, 2nd edition, 1755, p. 3.

3 Now the Panthéon, Paris.

4 Much earlier examples of châteaux flanked by two towers are known, but their architecture is baroque or neoclassical. Wailly's drawings for the château at Enghien are preserved in the Archives générales du Royaume, Belgium. Several were published in the exhibition catalogue, *Charles de Wailly*, Caisse nationale des monuments historiques, 1979.

5 *Op. cit.*, Pl. 100.

6 Johann Wolfgang Goethe, *Von deutscher Baukunst*, 1773 (actually 1772).

Chapter VI

1 The archives of the firm, which is still in existence, are an important source of information for British furniture history.

2   2,500 of these drawings are preserved in the Österreichisches Museum für angewandte Kunst, Vienna.
3   Eileen Harris, *The Furniture of Robert Adam*, London, 1965.

Chapter VII

1   Mario Praz, *L'Ameublement*, Paris, 1964, Fig. 163.
2   Mario Praz, *op. cit.*, Fig. 169
3   Christian Witt-Dörring, "Beleuchtungskörper aus der k. u. k. Landes-Fabrik Joseph Danhauser in Wien," *Alte und moderne Kunst*, no. 178/179, 1981.
4   Published in London in 1807.
5   Most of the information on Viennese chandeliers has been taken from two articles published by Lorenz Seelig and Christian Witt-Dörring in *Alte und moderne Kunst*, no. 178/179, 1981.
6   Arch. Nat. O² 555.
7   Engraving illustrated by John Cornforth, *English Interiors, 1790–1848*, London, 1978, Fig. 34.
8   John Cornforth, *op. cit.*, Fig. 11.
9   Mark Girouard, *Life in the English Country House*, New Haven, 1978, Pl. XXIII.
10 Shown in a painting by Lavr Plakhov in the Russian Museum, Leningrad.

Chapter VIII

1   *Cabinet Dictionary*, London, 1803, p. 117.
2   The Egyptian-style clock attributed to Thomas Hope by M. D. Watkin, *Thomas Hope and the Neo-Classical Idea*, London, 1968, Fig. 38, is in fact French. Other examples of the model are known in France. See, for example, Y. Brunhammer, M. de Fayet, *Meubles et ensembles époque Directoire et Empire*, Paris, 1965, Fig. 58.
3   Exhibition catalogue, *The Age of Neo-classicism*, London, 1965, no. 1625.
4   See an article by Philippe Jullian in *Connaissance des Arts*, no. 204, Feb. 1969.
5   See the exhibition catalogues, *The Age of Neo-classicism*, London, 1972, no. 1600 and *Wittelsbach und Bayern*, Munich, 1980, Vol. III/2, no. 1202.

6   Besides the pieces published here, there are several other clocks at Pavlovsk signed by a clockmaker from Liège called L. J. Laguesse. One clock is of porcelain and gilt bronze.
7   A. Faÿ-Hallé and B. Mundt, *Nineteenth-Century European Porcelain*, Fribourg, London, New York, 1983.

Chapter IX

1   See a miniature by Blarengberghe of 1757 depicting the Duc de Choiseul's cabinet on the cover of a gold box, now in the Louvre, and a painting by François Boucher, *Le Petit Déjeuner*, also in the Louvre.
2   Arch. Nat. O² 701. 15/16 was a plain-colored silk fabric.
3   Inventory, Tuileries Palace, 1809, 2nd register, Arch. Nat. O² 680.
4   John Cornforth, *English Interiors, 1790–1848*, London, 1978, p. 85. The sale catalogue relates to the furniture at Attingham Park, Shropshire. The dining-room curtains are described as follows: "The splendid suite of four pair of fine drab cloth French rod window curtains, handsomely bordered with four inch Purple Velvet, and two rows of rich Gold-colour Silk Lace, Elegant deep Cloth and Velvet Drapery, continued over the piers, and tastefully displayed in Festoons, bordered en suite, and trimmed with Gold-colour Silk, and Worsted Parisian Fringe, supported by thick twisted Ropes, and large Turkish Tassels."
5   Archives Nationales O² 6. Letter from Duroc to Baure from Bayonne, dated July 18, 1808.
6   *Inventaire des collections publiques françaises, Paris, Mobilier national. Soieries Empire*, compiled by J. Coural, Paris, 1980.
7   Jean-Baptiste Réveillon (1725–1811), who was a clever businessman with a strongly developed commercial sense, established the first large wallpaper factory in Paris. He employed some excellent artists to design his papers. His "arabesque" wallpapers are among the most attractive ever made. His factory was pillaged by the mob in 1789.
8   Odile Nouvel, *Papiers peints français, 1800–1850*, Fribourg, 1981.

Conclusion

1   Quoted from the 3rd ed., Lecoffre, Paris, 1876, p. 143.

Bibliography

Neoclassical Art and Imitation of Antiquity

The Age of Neo-classicism, Royal Academy, Victoria and Albert Museum, London, 1972, 1037 pp., 160 Pls. (Catalogue of the 14th exhibition organized by the Council of Europe)

CHEVALLIER, Elisabeth, "Les peintures découvertes à Herculanum, Pompéi et Stabies vues par les voyageurs du XVIIIe siècle," in *Gazette des Beaux-Arts*, December 1977, pp. 177–88

ERIKSON, Svend, *Early Neo-classicism in France*, Faber and Faber, London, 1974, 432 pp., 499 ills.

HAUTECŒUR, Louis, *Rome et la renaissance de l'Antiquité à la fin du XVIIIe siècle. Essai sur les origines du style Empire*, Fontemoing, Paris, 1912

HONOUR, Hugh, *Neo-classicism*, Penguin Books, Harmondsworth, 1968, 221 pp., 109 ills.

LAUGIER S. J., Marc-Antoine, *Essai sur l'architecture*, Paris, 1753

–, *Observations sur l'architecture*, The Hague, 1765

PARISET, François-Georges, *L'Art néo-classique*, Presses Universitaires de France, Paris, 1974, 184 pp., 16 Pls.

RICHTER, Gisela M. A., *The Furniture of the Greeks, Etruscans and Romans*, Phaidon Press, London, 1966

WINCKELMANN, Johann Joachim, *Geschichte der Kunst des Altertums*, Dresden, 1764.

Furniture and Decoration

General Works

Le "Gothique" retrouvé, avant Viollet-le-Duc, Caisse nationale des monuments historiques, Paris, 1979, 168 pp., amply illustrated. (Catalogue of exhibition held at the Hôtel de Sully, Paris, in 1979–80.)

GRANDJEAN, Serge, *Empire Furniture, 1800 to 1825*, Faber and Faber, London, 1966, 120 pp., 96 Pls.

HAVARD, Henry, *Dictionnaire de l'ameublement et de la décoration, depuis le XIIIe siècle jusqu'à nos jours*, Quantin, Paris, n.d. [1887–90], 4 vols., XVI + 2752 pp., 256 Pls., 3650 Figs.

HONOUR, Hugh, *Cabinet Makers and Furniture Designers*, Weidenfeld and Nicolson, 1960, 320 pp., amply illustrated

PRAZ, Mario, *L'Ameublement. Psychologie et évolution de la décoration intérieure*, Tisné, Paris, 1964, 396 pp., 400 Figs. and Pls.

I Quaderni dell'antiquariato. Collana di arti decorative diretta da Alvar Gonzáles-Palacios, Fabbri, Milan

–, Mina GREGORI, Renato RUOTOLO, and Luisa BANDERA GREGORI, *Il mobile italiano dal Rinascimento agli anni trenta*, 1981, 80 pp., amply illustrated

–, Christian BAULEZ, and Denise LEDOUX-LEBARD, *Il mobile francese dal Luigi XVI all'Art Déco*, 1981, 77 pp., amply illustrated

–, Hans HUTH, Georg HIMMELHEBER, and Anne BERENDSEN, *Il mobile: Paesi Germanici, Paesi Bassi*, 1982, 79 pp., amply illustrated

–, Juan José JUNQUERA, Peter THORNTON, and Tamara TALBOT RICE, *Il mobile: Spagna, Portogallo, Paesi Scandinavi, Russia*, 1982, 79 pp., amply illustrated

Style, meubles, décors, du Moyen Age à nos jours. Ouvrage publié sous la direction de Pierre Verlet, 2 vols., Larousse, Paris, 1972

Germany and Austria

GREBER, Josef Maria, *Abraham und David Roentgen; Möbel für Europa*, vol. 1, Josef Keller, Starnberg, 1980, 288 pp., amply illustrated, vol. 2, 739 ills.

HIMMELHEBER, Georg, *Die Kunst des deutschen Möbels*. Vol. 3, *Klassizismus, Historismus, Jugendstil*, C. H. Beck, Munich, 1973, X + 417 pp., 28 in-text ills. and 1161 ills. + 12 Pls. (vol. 3 of H. Kreisel, *Die Kunst des deutschen Möbels*.)

HUTH, Hans, *Roentgen Furniture. Abraham and David Roentgen, European Cabinet-Makers*, Sotheby Parke Bernet, London and New York, 1974, 108 pp., 273 ills.

Journal des Luxus und der Moden, ed. by F. J. Bertuch, later by G. M. Kraus, Weimar, 1786–1826

KREISEL, Heinrich: see HIMMELHEBER, Georg

Krone und Verfassung. König Max I. Joseph und der neue Staat, vol. III/2 of exhibition catalogue *Wittelsbach und Bayern*, Völkerkunde Museum, Munich, 1980. (See especially the notes compiled by Hans Ottomeyer and Rainer Rückert.)

KÜSTER, Christian L., *Jenisch-Haus: Museum grossbürgerlicher Wohnkultur*, Schnell und Steiner, Munich, 1982, 15 pp., 14 ills. (*Schnell Kunstführer*, no. 1322)

OTTOMEYER, Hans, *Die Ausstattung der Residenzen König Max Josephs von Bayern (1799–1825)*, in the catalogue of the exhibition *Wittelsbach und Bayern*, III/1, *Krone und Verfassung*, Völkerkunde Museum, Munich, 1980, pp. 371–94

—, *Das Wittelsbacher Album – Interieurs königlicher Wohn- und Festräume, 1799–1848*, Munich, 1979

PEIN, Georg, *Ideen zur äusseren und inneren Verzierung der Gebäude als Anleitung für angehende mechanische Künstler und Handwerker zur Übung im Erfinden und Darstellen*, vol. 1, Vienna, 1809, vol. 2, 1811

SEELIG, Lorenz, "Wiener Biedermeier in Coburg," in *Alte und moderne Kunst*, no. 178/179, 1981, pp. 2–10

Vienna in the Age of Schubert: the Biedermeier Interior, 1815–1848, Victoria and Albert Museum and Elron Press, 1979, 111 pp., 77 ills. (Articles by Gerhart Egger, Gerbert Frodl, Erika Hellich, Walter Koschatzky, Wilhelm Mrazek, Waltraud Neuwirth, Angela Volker, Franz Windisch-Graetz, and Christian Witt-Dörring.)

WIESE, Wolfgang, *Studien zum Stil des Stuttgarter Ebenisten Johannes Klinkerfuss*, Master's thesis, University of Tübingen, 1982

Spain

FEDUCHI, Luis M., *Collecciónes reales de España. El Mueble,* Patrimonio Nacional, Madrid, 1965, 571 pp., 458 ills.

JUNQUERA, Juan José, *La decoración y el mobiliario de los palacios de Carlos IV,* doctoral dissertation, Madrid, 1979, 395 pp., 76 Pls.

—, "Aranjuez, muebles en el Museo del Traje," in *Reales Sitios,* no. 30, 1971, pp. 33–41

JUNQUERA, Paulina, "El arte en la Casa del Labrador," in *Reales Sitios,* no. 15, 1968, pp. 37–49

RUIZ ALCON, Maria Teresa, "Arañas de la Real fabrica de La Granja," in *Reales Sitios,* no. 27, 1971

—, "Obres de arte en la residencia del Palacio Real de El Pardo," in *Reales Sitios,* no. 76, 1983

France and Belgium

BIVER, Marie-Louise, *Pierre Fontaine, premier architecte de l'Empereur,* Ed. d'Art et d'Histoire, Paris, 1964, 234 pp., 54 ills.

COURAL, Jean, "Napoléon, roi du Garde-Meuble," in *L'Œil,* May 1969

DUSSIEUX, Louis, *Les Artistes français à l'étranger,* 3rd ed., Lecoffre, Paris and Lyons, 1876

GALLET, Michel, *Demeures parisiennes: L'époque Louis XVI,* Le Temps, Paris, 1964

GONZÁLEZ-PALACIOS, Alvar, *Dal Direttorio all'Impero Fabbri,* Milan, 1964

GRANDJEAN, Serge, *Inventaire après décès de l'impératrice Joséphine à Malmaison,* Réunion des musées nationaux, Paris, 1964, 294 pp., 24 Pls.

—, "Napoleonic tables from Sèvres," in *The Connoisseur,* May 1959, pp. 147–53

HARTMANN, Simone, "Jean Dugourc, ornemaniste, précurseur de l'Empire," in *L'Estampille,* no. 98, June 1978, pp. 30–36

HAUTECŒUR, Louis, *Histoire de l'architecture classique en France,* vols. IV, V, VI, Picard, Paris, 1953–57

HUBERT, Gérard, *Malmaison,* Réunion des musées nationaux, Paris, 1980, 86 pp. 94 ills.

JANNEAU, Guillaume, *Le Style Directoire, mobilier et décoration,* Ch. Moreau, Paris, n. d. [1938], 62 pp., 48 Pls.

—, *L'Empire,* Vincent, Fréal and Co., Paris, 1965, 111 pp., VIII Pls., 176 ills.

JARRY, Madeleine, and Pierre DEVINOY, *Le Siège français,* Office du Livre, Fribourg, 1973, 366 pp., 400 ills.

Le Journal des dames et des modes, ed. by Pierre de La Mésangère, Paris, 1797–1838

KRAFFT and RANSONNETTE, *Plans, coupes et élévations des plus belles maisons et des hôtels construits à Paris et dans les environs,* Paris, n. d. [1800 or 1802]

LANDON, Charles-Paul, *Annales du Musée et de l'Ecole moderne des beaux-arts,* Paris, 1801–08

LEDOUX-LEBARD, Denise, *Les Ebénistes parisiens, 1795–1870,* de Nobèle, Paris, 1965

—, *Les Ebénistes du XIXe siècle, 1795–1889,* Ed. de l'Amateur, Paris, 1984, 699 pp., amply illustrated

—, *Le Grand Trianon. Meubles et objets d'art,* Musées nationaux, Paris, 1975 (*Inventaire général du Musée national de Versailles et des Trianons,* vol. I.)

—, "Jean-Baptiste Youf, un ebenista parigino a Lucca," in *Arte illustra,* Nov.–Dec., 1971

LEDOUX-LEBARD, R. and G., "La Décoration et l'ameublement de la chambre de Mme Récamier sous le Consulat," in *Gazette des Beaux-Arts,* Oct. 1952, pp. 175–92, May–June 1955, pp. 299–312

LEFUEL, Hector, *Catalogue du Musée Marmottan,* Paris, 1934, 158 pp., XXIV Pls.

—, *François-Honoré-Georges Jacob-Desmalter, ébéniste de Napoléon et de Louis XVIII,* Morancé, Paris, 1926, 461 pp., 24 Pls.

—, *Georges Jacob, ébéniste du XVIIIe siècle,* Morancé, Paris, 1923, 423 pp., 20 Pls.

LEMONNIER, Patricia, *Weisweiler,* with a preface by Maurice Segoura, Monelle Hayot, Paris, 1983

LÉON, Paul, "Le Journal de Fontaine," in *Archives de l'art français, nouvelle période,* vol. 22, 1959, pp. 364–71

Meubles et objets de goût, supplement to *Journal des dames et des modes* by Pierre de La Mésangère, Paris, 1802–35

MONTAIGLON, Anatole de, "Autobiographie de Dugourc," in *Nouvelles Archives de l'art français,* Ist series, vol. V, 1877, pp. 367–71

MOSSER, Monique, and Daniel RABREAU, *Charles de Wailly, peintre architecte dans l'Europe des lumières,* Caisse nationale des monuments historiques, Paris, 1979, 127 pp., XII Pls., amply illustrated. (Catalogue of the Charles de Wailly Exhibition.)

MOULIN, Jean-Marie, *Musée national du château de Compiègne; appartements historiques,* Réunion des musées nationaux, Paris, 1980, 22 pp., 22 ills. (Petits Guides des grands musées, no. 16.)

OTTOMEYER, Hans, *Das frühe Œuvre Charles Perciers (1782–1800). Zu den Anfängen des Historismus in Frankreich,* doctoral dissertation, University of Munich, D. Gräbner, Altendorf, 1981, 392 pp.

PERCIER, Charles, and Pierre-François-Leonard FONTAINE, *Recueil de décorations intérieures,* Paris, 1801–12

PEROT, Jacques, *Musée national du château de Pau,* Réunion des musées nationaux, Paris, 1984, 16 pp., 20 ills. (Petits Guides des grands musées, no. 96.)

PIETRANGELI, Carlo, *Museo Napoleonico "Primoli." Guida,* 3rd ed., Rome, 1966, 152 pp., 32 Pls.

RAY, Monique, *Madame Récamier,* Musée historique, Lyons, 1977, 88 pp., 16 Pls. (Catalogue of the exhibition on the bicentenary of Madame Récamier.)

SAMOYAULT, Jean-Pierre, *Musée national du château de Fontainebleau; petits appartements,* Réunion des musées nationaux, Paris, 1980, 16 pp., 21 ills. (Petits Guides des grands musées, no. 66.)

SAMOYAULT-VERLET, Colombe, *Musée national du château de Fontainebleau,* Réunion des musées nationaux, Paris, 2nd ed., 1976, 16 pp., 16 ills. (Petits Guides des grands musées, no. 7.)

VAN YPERSELE DE STRIHOU, Anne and Paul, *Laeken, résidence impériale et royale,* Arcade, Brussels, 1970

VERLET, Pierre, *Les Meubles français du XVIIIe siècle,* 2nd ed., Presses Universitaires de France, Paris, 1982

WATSON, Francis J. B., *Louis XVI Furniture,* Alec Tiranti, London, 1960, 162 pp., 242 Pls.

Great Britain

CORNFORTH, John, *English Interiors, 1790–1848,* Barrie and Jenkins, London, 1978, 144 pp., 175 ills.

EDWARDS, Ralph, and Desmond FITZGERALD, *English Chairs,* 3rd ed., Victoria and Albert Museum, London, 1970, 28 pp., 129 Pls.

FASTNEDGE, Ralph, *English Furniture Styles from 1500 to 1830,* Penguin Books, Harmondsworth, 1955, XXII + 321 pp., 101 Figs., 64 Pls.

—, *Sheraton Furniture,* Faber and Faber, London, 1962, 125 pp., 100 Pls.

GIROUARD, Mark, *Life in the English Country House, a Social and Architectural History,* 2nd ed., Penguin Books, London, 1980, V + 344 pp., XXII Pls., 204 ills.

HARRIS, Eileen, *The Furniture of Robert Adam,* Alec Tiranti, London, 1963, 110 pp., 156 Pls.

HARRIS, John, Geoffrey de BELLAIGUE, and Oliver MILLAR, *Buckingham Palace,* Nilson, London, 1968, 320 pp., amply illustrated. (The section on architecture and decoration by John Harris, that on *objets d'art* by G. de Bellaigue.)

HEPPLEWHITE, George, *The Cabinet-Maker and Upholsterer's Guide,* Dover Publications, New York, 1969, 24 pp., 124 Pls. (Reprint of 3rd English edition of 1794, with a preface by Joseph Aronson.)

HOPE, Thomas, *Household Furniture and Interior Decoration executed from Designs by Thomas Hope,* London, 1807, reprinted by Transatlantic Arts, New York, 1970.

JOURDAIN, Margaret, *Regency Furniture, 1795–1820,* Country Life, London, 1934, XV + 112 pp., 173 Pls.

LEVER, Jill, *Architects' Designs for Furniture,* Royal Institute of

British Architects and Trefoil Books, London, 1982, 144 pp., XXII + 132 ills.

MUSGRAVE, Clifford, *Regency Furniture, 1800 to 1830,* Faber and Faber, London, 1961, 157 pp., 100 Pls.

SHERATON, Thomas, *The Cabinet-Maker and Upholsterer's Drawing-Book,* Dover Publications, New York, 1972, 240 pp., 98 Pls. (Reprint of Part III of the English edition of 1793, with some reproductions taken from Part II, the Appendix and the Complement; Preface by Joseph Aronson.)

—, *The Cabinet Dictionary,* London, 1803

—, *The Cabinet-Maker, Upholsterer and General Artist's Encyclopedia,* 1 vol., n. p., 1805

SMITH, George, *A Collection of Designs for Household Furniture and Interior Decoration,* n. p., 1808

—, *The Cabinet-Maker and Upholsterer's Guide,* London, 1826

STROUD, Dorothy, *Henry Holland,* London, 1950

—, *Henry Holland: His Life and Architecture,* London, 1966

SUMMERSON, Sir John, *A New Description of Sir John Soane's Museum,* 4th ed., published by the Trustees, London, 1977, 82 pp., 32 ills.

TOMLIN, Maurice, *Catalogue of Adam Period Furniture,* Victoria and Albert Museum, London, 1972, 207 pp., 210 ills.

WATKIN, David, *Thomas Hope and the Neo-Classical Idea,* John Murray, London, 1968, XXI + 316 pp., 133 ills.

"The Wellington Museum, Apsley House," in *Apollo,* Sept. 1973. (The articles on decorative arts are by Denys Sutton, John Hardy, R. J. Charleston, Charles Oman, and Victor Percival.)

Italy

ALBERICI, Clelia, *Il mobile lombardo,* Görlich, Milan, 1969, 264 pp., 368 ills.

—, *Il mobile veneto,* Electa, Milan, 1980

BACCHESCHI, Edi, *Il mobile neoclassico in Italia,* Görlich, Milan, 1962, 143 pp., 175 ills.

BROSIO, Valentino, *Ambienti italiani dell'Ottocento,* Vallardi, Milan, 1963, 126 pp., amply illustrated

—, *Mobili italiani dell'Ottocento,* Vallardi, Milan, 1964, 158 pp., amply illustrated

GONZÁLEZ-PALACIOS, Alvar, "The Furnishings of the Villa Favorita in Resina," in *Burlington Magazine,* April 1979, pp. 226–43

—, "Note sugli arredi," in *Collezioni della Galleria d'arte moderna di Palazzo Pitti. Ottocento, parte prima: cultura neoclassica e romantica nella Toscana granducale,* Soprintendenza alle Gallerie, Florence, 1972, pp. 230 et seq.

—, *Il Tempio del Gusto. Le arti decorative in Italia fra classicismo e barocco. Roma e il Regno delle Due Sicilie,* vols. 1, 2, Longanesi, Milan, 1984

MARMOTTAN, Paul, *Les Arts en Toscane sous Napoléon. La princesse Elisa,* Champion, Paris, 1901

MORAZZONI, Giuseppe, *Il mobile intarsiato di Giuseppe Maggiolini,* Görlich, Milan, 1955 [?], 62 pp., 736 ills.

RUGA, Pietro, *Invenzioni diverse di mobili utensili sacri e profani raccolte ed incise in 100 tavole,* Vallardi, Milan, 1811

Russia

EFREMOVA, Irina K., and Aleksandr Th. CHERVIAKOV, *Ostankino,* Moskovskii rabochii, Moscow, 1980, 104 pp., amply illustrated

GRABAR, Igor, *Istoriia russkago iskusstva,* vol. III: *Peterburgskaia arkhitektura v XVIII i XIX veke* (History of Russian Art, vol. III, Architecture in St. Petersburg in the eighteenth and nineteenth centuries), Knebel, Moscow, n. d. [1912], 584 pp., amply illustrated

IVANOVA, Elena A., *Russische angewandte Kunst, 18. bis Anfang des 20. Jahrhunderts.* Russian Museum, Avrora, Leningrad, 1977, 171 Pls. (Notes by E. A. Ivanova, S. V. Rakhimova, I. M. Iasinskaia.)

KENNETT, Audrey and Victor, *The Palaces of Leningrad,* Introduction by John Russell, Thames and Hudson, London, 1973, 288 pp., 203 Pls.

KUCHUMOV, Anatolii M., *Ubranstvo russkogo zhilogo interiora XIX veka, po materialam vystavki v Pavlovskom dvortse-muzee* (The decoration of Nineteenth-Century Russian Domestic Interiors, with particular reference to the specimens exhibited at the Pavlovsk Palace Museum), Khudozhnik RSFSR, 1977, 302 pp., 30 reproductions of paintings or of photographs, 147 ills.

—, *Pavlovsk, le palais et le parc,* Avrora, Leningrad, 446 pp., 221 ills. (palace), 120 ills. (park)

—, *Pavlovsk, putevoditel* (Pavlovsk, Guide), Lenizdat, Leningrad, 1980, 159 pp., illustrated

LOVGYNSKAIA, Emiliia I., *Interior v russkoi zhivopisi pervoy poloviny XIX veka* (Views of Interiors in Russian Painting, first half of the Nineteenth Century), Iskusstvo, Moscow, 1978, 119 pp., 106 ills.

MAKAROV, Vladimir K., and Anatolii N. PETROV, *Gatchina,* Iskusstvo, Leningrad, 1974, 102 pp., XX + 85 ills.

PILIAVSKII, V. I., *Ermitazh, istoriia i arkhitektura zdanii* (The Hermitage, History and Architecture), Avrora, Leningrad, 1974. (The chapters on the history of the Winter Palace and of the Hermitage during the first half of the nineteenth century were edited by V. I. Piliavskii, V. M. Glinka and R. D. Diulina.)

RASKIN, Abraham, *Petrodvorets (Petergof),* 2nd ed., Avrora, Leningrad, 1979, 236 Pls.

SOKOLOVA, T., *Ocherki po istorii khudozhestvennoi mebeli* (Sketches of the History of Artistic Furniture), Leningrad, 1966

Lighting and Lamps

ALLEMAGNE, Henry-René d', *Histoire du luminaire, depuis l'époque romaine jusqu'au XIXe siècle,* Paris, 1891, VI + 702 pp., 500 ill., 80 Pls.

HOLEY, J., *Der Kristallkronleuchter, seine Entstehung und Entwicklung,* Stifter Jahrbuch VIII, Lochham near Munich, 1964

JANNEAU, Guillaume, *Le Luminaire, de l'Antiquité au XIXe siècle,* Flammarion, Paris, 1950, 64 pp., 106 ills.

Osvetilnye pribory kontsa XVII – nachala XX veka v Rossii (Lighting in Russia, from the end of the seventeenth to the beginning of the twentieth century), Avrora, Leningrad, 1975, 53 pp., 62 ills. (Catalogue of an exhibition at the Hermitage Museum.)

Bronzes, Clocks and Decorative Vases

BELLAIGUE, Geoffrey de, "Sèvres Artists and their Sources," in *Burlington Magazine,* Oct.–Dec. 1980

BRUNET, Marcelle, and Tamara PRÉAUD, *Sèvres, des origines à nos jours,* Office du Livre, Fribourg, 1978, 392 pp., 566 ills.

FAŸ-HALLÉ, Antoinette, and Barbara MUNDT, *La Porcelaine européenne au XIXe siècle,* Office du Livre, Fribourg, 1983, 302 pp., 485 ills. Trans. by Aileen Dawson, *Porcelain of the Nineteenth Century,* Rizzoli, New York, 1983, 304 pp., 485 ills.

GODDEN, Geoffrey A., *British Porcelain: an Illustrated Guide,* Barrie and Jenkins, London, 1974, 451 pp., 12 Pls., 567 ills.

GRANDJEAN, Serge, *L'Orfèvrerie du XIXe siècle en Europe,* Presses Universitaires de France, Paris, 1962, VIII + 161 pp., 32 Pls.

HAVARD, Henry, *Les Bronzes d'art et d'ameublement,* Paris, 1897, 159 pp., 77 Figs.

KÖLLMANN, Erich, *Berliner Porzellan, 1763–1963,* Klinkhardt und Biermann, vol. 1, Brunswick, 1966, 350 pp., 148 ills., vol. 2, 331 pp., 707 ills.

LIVERANI, Giuseppe, *Il Museo delle porcellane di Doccia,* Richard-Ginori, Doccia, 1967, 267 pp., 59 ills., 175 Pls.

MOTTOLA MOLFINO, Alessandra, *L'Arte della porcellana in Italia. Il Veneto e la Toscana,* Bramante, Busto Arsizio [1976], 215 pp., 501 ills.

NICLAUSSE, Juliette, *Thomire, fondeur-ciseleur (1751–1843)*, Gründ, Paris, 1947, 140 pp., 32 Pls.

PLINVAL DE GUILLEBON, Régine de, *Porcelaine de Paris, 1770–1850*, Office du Livre, Fribourg, 1972, 350 pp., 250 ills. Trans. by Robin R. Charleston, *Paris Porcelain, 1770–1850*, Barrie & Jenkins, London, 1972, 364 pp., 250 ills.

POPOV, V. A., *Russkii farfor. Chastnye zavody* (Russian Porcelain. Private Manufactures), Khudozhnik RSFSR, Leningrad, 1980

VERLET, Pierre, Serge GRANDJEAN, and Marcelle BRUNET, *Sèvres*, Le Prat, 2 vols., Paris, 1953

WALCHA, Otto, *Meissner Porzellan*, VEB Verlag der Kunst, Dresden, 1973, 514 pp., 475 ills.

Curtains, Tapestries, Wallpaper and Carpets

ACKERMANN, Phyllis, *Wall-Paper: Its History, Design and Use*, London, 1923

ALLEMAGNE, Henry-René d', and Henri CLOUZOT, *La Toile imprimée et les indiennes de traite*, vol. I., Gründ, Paris, 1942, 183 pp., 52 Pls., vol. II, 16 pp., 244 Pls.

CLOUZOT, Henri, *Histoire de la manufacture de Jouy et de la toile imprimée en France*, Van Oest, Paris, 1928, vol. I, 205 pp., 10 Pls., vol. II, 2 pp., 87 Pls.

—, *Le Papier peint en France, du XVIIIᵉ au XIXᵉ siècle*, Van Oest, Paris, 1931

CLOUZOT, Henri, and C. FOLLOT, *Histoire du papier peint en France*, Ch. Moreau, Paris, 1935

COURAL, Jean, *Paris, Mobilier national. Soieries Empire*, Réunion des musées nationaux, Paris, 1980 (*Inventaire des collections publiques françaises*, no. 25)

DUMONTHIER, Ernest, *Tapis et tapisseries d'ameublement du Mobilier de la Couronne*, Massin, Paris, 1913, album in-fol.

ENTWISLE, Eric Arthur, *Wall-Papers of the Victorian Era*, F. Lewis, Leigh-on-Sea, 1964

HEINZ, Dora, Yvonne BRUNNHAMMER, and Odile NOUVEL, *Tessuti, tappeti carte da parati*, Fabbri, Milan, 1981, 79 pp., amply illustrated. (*I Quaderni dell' antiquariato. Collana di arti decorative diretta da Alvar González-Palacios.*)

JARRY, Madeleine, *The Carpets of Aubusson*, trans. by C. Magdalino, F. Lewis, Leigh-on-Sea, 1969, 67 pp.

—, *The Carpets of the Manufacture de la Savonnerie*, trans. by C. Magdalino, F. Lewis, Leigh-on-Sea, 1966, 47 pp., 96 ills.

McCLELLAND, Nancy, *Historic Wall-Papers*, Philadelphia, 1924

—, "Papiers peints français dans les demeures américaines," in *Renaissance de l'art français*, no. 5, May 1928

NOUVEL, Odile, *Papiers peints français, 1800–1850*, Office du Livre, Fribourg, 1981, 132 pp., 600 ills. Trans. by Margaret Timmers, *Wallpapers of France, 1800–1850*, with an introduction by Jean-Pierre Seguin, Rizzoli, New York, 1981, 130 pp.

OLLIGS, H., *Tapeten, ihre Geschichte bis zur Gegenwart*, Brunswick and Cologne, 1970

OMAN, Charles, *Catalogue of Wall-Papers in the Victoria and Albert Museum*, Victoria and Albert Museum, London, 1929

O'NEILL, Mary, "Originals of Pictorial Designs for French Printed Textiles," in *Burlington Magazine*, Dec. 1981, pp. 722–36

TATTERSALL, Creassey Edward Cecil, *A History of British Carpets, from the Introduction of the Craft until the Present Day*, F. Lewis, Benfleet, 1934, 182 pp., 116 Pls.

TEYNAC, Françoise, Pierre NOLOT, and Jean-Denis VIVIEN, *Le Monde du papier peint*, Berger-Levrault, Paris, 1981, 249 pp., amply illustrated

Toiles de Nantes des XVIIIᵉ et XIXᵉ siècles, n.p., n.d., 159 pp., amply illustrated (Catalogue of an exhibition at the Musée de l'impression sur étoffes, Mulhouse, and the Musée des arts décoratifs, Nantes, and at the Musée des arts décoratifs, Paris, from 8 February to 8 April 1978.)

VERLET, Pierre, *The Savonnerie; its History; the Waddesdon Collection*, Office du Livre, Fribourg, for the National Trust, 1982, 535 pp., 224 ills.

Index

The numbers in italics refer to the Plates

Photo credits

The author and the publishers wish to thank all those who have supplied photographs for this book. 167 photos were taken by the author, but are not listed. The numbers refer to the plates.

A. C. L., Brussels 83, 84, 134, 168, 191, 211, 246, 260, 261, 263, 268, 269, 273, 274, 288, 289, 290, 431, 454, 455, 457, 462, 467, 468, 544, 546, 552, 554, 558, 560, 565, 580, 581, 587
Ader, Picard, Tajan, Paris 313
Alinari, Florence 66, 152, 362, 364
Badisches Landesmuseum, Karlsruhe 308
Bayerisches Nationalmuseum, Munich 108
Bayerische Verwaltung der staatlichen Schlösser, Gärten und Seen, Schloss Nymphenburg, Munich 47, 74, 94, 106, 189, 213, 217, 236, 258, 314, 321, 323, 324, 325, 329, 331, 339, 340, 342, 343, 345, 353, 516, 527, 528, 530, 531, 532, 533, 536, 537, 545, 550, 553, 562, 563, 578, 585, 588, 590, 625
Bibliothèque nationale, Paris 596
British Museum, London 75
Cauvin, Paris 591
Christies, London 77, 100, 150, 163, 167, 175 (photos: A. C. Cooper, London)
De Antonis, Rome 14
Deutsches Tapetenmuseum, Cassel 626
Etude Laurin, Guilloux, Buffetaud, Tailleur, Paris 28
Giraudon, Paris 69
Robert Harding, London 58, 59, 62, 67, 71, 93, 417, 422, 479
I. G. D. A. Archives, Milan 36
Kunsthistorisches Museum, Vienna 144
Michel de Lorenzo, Nice 237, 365, 456, 535
Maison Brocard, Paris 605, 606, 607, 608
Maison Janson, Paris 628 (photo: Chevojon, Paris); 632 (photo: Catan, Paris); 630, 637, 639, 640
The Metropolitan Museum of Art, New York 551
Musée des arts décoratifs, Paris 37, 53, 54, 70, 156, 305, 543, 555, 556, 559, 600, 619, 623, 624, 629 (photos: Laurent Sully-Jaulmes); 127, 143, 149, 176, 177, 193, 199, 200, 227, 433, 589, 599, 612, 622
Musée du Louvre, Paris 3, 4, 5, 9, 12, 13, 306
Musée national de la Malmaison 119, 249 (photos: Laverton, Rueil-Malmaison)
Musée national du château de Fontainebleau 24, 25, 188, 234, 235, 262, 277, 463, 469 (photos: Esparcieux); 78, 81, 214, 458, 487, 507 (photos: G. Richard); 577, 584 (photos: Roussel)
National Museum of Finland, Helsinki 18, 38, 39, 40, 45, 46, 50, 99, 111, 112, 146, 178, 179, 180, 181, 354, 355, 378, 380, 381, 382, 384, 386, 387, 389, 390, 391, 392, 393, 394, 395, 396, 397, 398, 399, 400, 401, 402, 403, 404, 405, 406, 407, 408, 409, 410, 411, 412, 413, 415, 418, 419, 424, 425, 448, 449, 450, 489
Österreichisches Museum für angewandte Kunst, Vienna 337, 497, 498, 567, 568
Palace of the Princes of Turn and Taxis, Regensburg 95, 338
Patrimonio Nacional, Madrid 55, 369, 371, 372, 373, 374, 375, 376, 377, 435
Pedicini, Naples 1, 11, 60, 366
M.-L. Pérony, Pau 22, 105, 115, 116, 117, 118, 155, 166, 182, 190, 192, 201, 202, 212, 216, 244, 245, 271, 272, 278, 285, 379, 383, 437, 444, 445, 447, 452, 461, 464, 465, 476, 477, 491, 493, 494, 509, 510, 511, 512, 513, 514, 515, 517, 518, 520, 524, 534, 538, 539, 561, 597
Réunion des Musées nationaux, Paris 76, 79, 89, 97, 98, 104, 110, 129, 137, 148, 153, 157, 230, 232, 233, 247, 276, 284, 287, 292, 333, 460, 478, 480, 526, 540, 548, 549, 571, 593, 601, 603
Schlossmuseum, Ludwigsburg 312
Walter Schmidt, Karlsruhe 6, 7, 347, 348
Sotheby's, London 363
Studio Lourmel, Georges Routhier, Paris 8, 27, 29, 30, 56, 85, 87, 135, 173, 183, 198, 255, 256, 299, 385, 459, 547, 557, 574, 576, 586, 604, 611, 613, 614, 615, 618
Verwaltung der staatlichen Schlösser und Gärten, Berlin 349 (photo: Jörg P. Anders)
Victoria and Albert Museum, London 15, 33, 34, 43, 44, 86, 88, 90, 91, 92, 96, 101, 103, 107, 113, 186, 187, 195, 196, 197, 210, 241, 250, 251, 253, 257, 264, 267, 282, 283, 291, 296, 297, 298, 302, 303, 304, 359, 360, 427, 434, 436, 438, 439, 440, 441, 443, 446, 451, 453, 471, 519, 522, 523, 541, 542, 572, 573, 583, 592, 594, 595, 609, 610, 616, 617, 620, 621
Vneshtorgizdat, Moscow 61, 575, 582
Württembergisches Landesmuseum, Stuttgart 311, 521, 579

Author's archives: 19, 20, 204, 220, 222, 223, 224, 226, 238, 248, 280, 293, 295, 370, 470

This book was printed in june 1986
Setting: Hertig+Co. SA, Biel
Printing: Hertig+Co. SA, Biel
Binding: Mayer et Soutter S.A., Renens
Photolithographs (color): Cooperativa lavoratori grafici, Verona
(black and white): Cliché+Litho AG, Zurich
Design and production: Franz Stadelmann

Printed in Switzerland